DISORDERS
OF MOOD

AMERICAN PSYCHOPATHOLOGICAL ASSOCIATION

Officers for 1969–1970

DISORDERS OF MOOD

Edited by JOSEPH ZUBIN, Ph.D.
Biometrics Research, New York State Department
of Mental Hygiene; Department of Psychology,
Columbia University

and FRITZ A. FREYHAN, M.D.
Department of Psychiatry, St. Vincent's Hospital and
Medical Center of New York; New York University
Medical Center

Based on the proceedings of the sixtieth annual meeting of the American Psychopathological Association

The Johns Hopkins Press　　*Baltimore and London*

The Johns Hopkins Press, Baltimore, Maryland 21218
The Johns Hopkins Press Ltd., London
Library of Congress Catalog Card Number 74-185972
International Standard Book Number 0-8018-1297-6

CONTENTS

Part III: Therapy in Mood Disorders

Part IV: Critiques of Current Theories and Research

PREFACE

Nearly two decades ago (1952; published 1954) the APPA devoted a symposium to "Depression." In the foreword to this volume the editors, Hoch and Zubin, acknowledged that we are still far from an understanding of the causes of depression. But they expressed the hope that "the joint attack along psychologic, psychodynamic, physiological, biochemical and developmental lines" would be bound to make progress "at least in shedding light in the obscure interstitial areas between the disciplines."

This anticipation of an interdisciplinary attack as the most promising approach has been borne out by major developments in the genetic, ecological (epidemiological), developmental-learning theory, and neurophysiological approaches to the investigation of mood. The most notable progress, however, has been the emergence of psychopharmacology as a new science. This swiftly developing discipline contributed directly and indirectly to an impressive body of interrelated events. These include amazingly advanced experimental technology and methodological sophistication with far-reaching benefits for investigations in etiology, diagnosis, and treatment of mood disorders.

Of course, we still find ourselves ignorant on major aspects of etiology, epidemiology, precision of classification, and accuracy of therapeutic evaluation. Yet we hope that this volume reflects the promise which the more important methods of research hold for application to investigations of mood and mood disorders. We have not yet made any dent in studying normal mood variations, a new frontier that is ready for exploration. Until we get a Kinsey-type survey of mood patterns as they occur in the average population, we will not be able to differentiate the spectrum from normal to abnormal. What we need perhaps most of all is a progression from crude personality types and limited baseline assessments to a comprehensive anthropology of mood in all of its psychological and biological dimensions.

vii

This volume cannot cover the full range of relevant problems. During the past decade many meetings on affective disorders have been held in different parts of the world; the literature is rich; and intensive studies are in progress. But what this volume aims to achieve by presenting original reports, the reviews and critiques, is to sharpen our awareness for new methods and directions on which success and progress in the 1970's will depend.

The editors wish to thank Karen M. Olson for her contributions to the editing of this volume.

Joseph Zubin, Ph.D.
Fritz A. Freyhan, M.D.

Presidential Address:
THE PSYCHOPATHOLOGIST—
WHAT MAN OF SCIENCE?

FRITZ A. FREYHAN, M.D.*

The pleasure I felt when I began to prepare this address arose not only from the honor which it conferred but also because it offerred an opportunity to link two past events with current trends and problems in psychopathology. The first event goes back to May 2, 1910, at the Willard Hotel in Washington, D.C. This, of course, was the birthdate of the American Psychopathological Association. The other event followed in 1913. Here I refer to the publication of Karl Jaspers' *General Psychopathology* (1) which in the words of L. Binswanger placed psychopathology on the map of science. In 1966 we elected Karl Jaspers honorary member of this association. He died on February 26, 1969. His fundamental contribution to the clarification of psychopathology as science relates to the question of my topic.

I shall consider first how we became an association of psychopathologists. I shall then speak of Jaspers' concept of psychopathology in relation to science. Finally, I shall examine some of the problems and questions which recent developments have brought before us.

Development of the American Psychopathological Association

According to Samuel Hamilton (2) the founders of this association were physicians, mostly neurologists with wide and keen interest in the activities of the mind. At the time of a rapidly growing fascination with psychoanalysis and the idea of the unconscious, several Boston psychopathologists, notably Morton Prince and Stanley Hall, initiated the organization of an association concerned with psychopathology. Morton Prince had for some years entertained a "psychopathic club" in his home. Because of his great interest and

---

*St. Vincent's Hospital and Medical Center of New York and New York University Medical Center.

activity he was elected the first president. He assigned the drafting of a constitution to a committee of which Adolf Meyer was a member. The *Journal* of *Abnormal Psychology* was chosen as the official organ of the Association. To recapture the Zeitgeist, it is interesting to review some of the titles published that year: Ernest Jones' essay on Hamlet, translation of Freud's and Jung's lectures at Worcester, and a paper by Ferenczi on dreams. When in 1911 the American Psychoanalytical Association was formed in Baltimore, all the founders were members of the APPA. The early membership of our Association, James Putnam, Adolf Meyer, August Hoch, Ernest Jones, Smith Ely Jelliffe, William A. White, and L. Eugene Emerson, philosopher and psychologist, reads like an honor roll of American psychiatry. It was Emerson who in later years preserved this Association when its discontinuance was proposed.

I wonder whether historians of American psychiatry have recognized the immensely important role which this Association has played. Because the founders were brilliant men who made scientific distinction a requirement for membership, the Association spearheaded new thoughts, unfolded the broader context of behavioral science, and served as catalyst between the analytical, biological, and psychosocial approaches to psychopathology. Not until the annual meeting in 1915 here in New York's McAlpin Hotel was the constitution adopted. I submit that this statement in the constitution (3) documents with unsurpassed clarity the unwavering commitment of this Association to science:

Article II

The object of this Association shall be to promote the study of the scientific problems of abnormal psychology, which will include: the study of phenomena arising from abnormal mental processes; the study of such organic pathological conditions as are directly connected with abnormal mental processes; and the study of means which may remove or modify the social or individual factors operating in the production of mental diseases. The Association shall also encourage the study of the relationship between psychopathological and social or cultural problems.

Active membership, at first limited to 100 in the United States and Canada, included psychologists, psychiatrists, and those engaged in the study of psychological or psychiatric neurological problems. L. Eugene Emerson, doctor of philosophy, explained why he was less interested in the psychological associations and preferred work with physicians: "On the whole," he was quoted as saying with emphasis, "the psychiatrists are the group that seem to keep their feet best on the ground."

In the early years the annual meetings of the APPA directly preceded or followed those of the Neurological Association. This tradition was first broken at the sixteenth annual meeting which was held jointly with the American Psychiatric Association in June, 1926. This was repeated in 1927 and 1928 and it brought trouble. The new relationship with the APA induced some members, notably Drs. White and Sullivan from Washington, to propose a merger under the constitution of the APA. A section of psychopathology was to be created which could maintain non-medical scientists as affiliates. The council of the APA, however, was not in a position to make any concession regarding the proposed section with non-medical affiliates. If the association survived, it is largely due to the efforts of Dr. Emerson, then Secretary, who mobilized the resistance. Nevertheless, it was a narrow margin of victory as the merger proposal was defeated by a vote of 51 for and 29 against, only two votes short of the constitutionally required two-thirds majority.

What were the scientific interests of the membership who defeated the merger at this 1929 meeting in Atlantic City? The program, which seems so strangely ultra-modern that it might be mistaken for one of Joseph Zubin's program proposals for next year, included: "Research in Schizophrenia" by Sullivan, "Chemical Theory of Temperament Applied to Extroversion and Introversion" by MacDougall, "Problems in Causation" by Tiebaut, "Some of the Psychopathology of Marital Adjustment" by Pratt, "Law, Medicine and Psychopathology" by Emerson, and "Some Psychiatric Aspects of Crowded Living Conditions" by Plant. After the near-tragedy of a merger, this Association returned to its old relation with the Neurological Association in 1930 and regained its strength and independence.

Samuel Hamilton ended his review of the APPA's first decade with these words:

> The genius of this Association has been to give opportunity for small groups of earnest men to talk things over freely. In the early days of the Association outstanding figures in various fields were brought in, men with a tremendous enthusiasm for their work, and those who were young members at the time say it was an inspiration to come and hear. So we must continue to do so. Most of the membership has been and probably will continue to be made up of psychiatrists. The members who come from other disciplines are held in very high esteem and have intimated that they enjoy this professional association.

He further asserted that the Association, as it existed in the later thirties and forties, maintained its purpose, proved useful, and brought a collective mood of happiness to the membership. He concluded: "In the opinion of those who have expressed themselves there are things for the organization to do for a long time to come."

Jaspers and Psychopathology

During the formative years of the American Psychopathological Association, Karl Jaspers made his outstanding contribution to the Heidelberg School and to psychiatry generally. From 1909 to 1915 during his brief period as scientific assistant in the Heidelberg Psychiatric Clinic, he published not only a dozen major studies but also in 1913 his *General Psychopathology*, a work of over 800 pages. He was then barely 30 years of age. Although he left the medical faculty to become professor of philosophy in 1916, he kept sufficiently abreast to undertake seven revisions. In his preface to the last one published in 1959 he stated:

> To bring the book up to date on the basis of the psychiatric research of the last two decades, would have necessitated my living for awhile as an observer in a clinic in order to refresh and extend my own experience. Even if this had been possible, nowadays I would not be able to manage it. The book, however, rouses a steady interest and does not seem to be out of date. Considerable extensions in its material might be necessary particularly as regards researches into the brain and somatic research in general, but the methodological principles remain largely unaffected by the increased material.

In his preface to the third edition he made the point which is the essence of his work:

> In general, the methodological climate of the book remains important. In the midst of all the psychopathological talk, we have to learn to know, what we know, and do not know; to know how and in what sense, and within what limits, we know something, by what means that knowledge was gained and on what it was founded. This is so because knowledge is not a smooth expanse of uniform and equivalent truths, but an ordered structure of quite diverse kinds of validity, importance and essence.

Jaspers defined the boundaries of psychiatry as clinical practice and psychopathology as a science:

> Psychiatrists function primarily as living, comprehending, and acting persons to whom science is only one resource among many; for psychopathologists, however, science is the sole and ultimate aim of their work. Their interest is not the individual human being. Their aim

is to know, recognize, describe, and analyze general principles rather than particular individuals. Their major concern is not the usefulness of science but what the real, distinguishable phenomena are, what roots can be discovered about them, and how they can be tested and demonstrated. Empathy and observation bring complex material, indispensable for study, but psychopathologists want more than this; they want communicable concepts for this material which can then be formulated into laws and principles and demonstrable relationships.

But he also reminds us that "Psychopathology is limited in that there can be no final analysis of human beings as such. Since the more we reduce them to what is typical or normative, the more we realize there is something hidden in every human individual which defies recognition. We have to be content with partial knowledge of an infinite which we cannot ignore."

What about the psychopathologist as scientist? In Jaspers' view he must observe these principles: resist the temptation to create absolute and all-explaining systems which produce prejudices but not science and distinguish between *understanding* and *explaining* psychological material. We can understand meaningful connections by empathy in terms of individual evidence. The self-evidence of a meaningful connection, however, does not provide an explanation in terms of causal laws. Peculiar to the psychopathologist as scientist is the distinction between *rational* and *empathic* understanding.

Jaspers clarifies the position of psychopathology. As science it cannot be identified with natural science. While natural science is a basic methodological component, the humanities are of great importance as well. Science is not fixed but assumes an extraordinary number of different forms. Object and meaning change according to method. The scientific attitude must adopt many methods as long as they qualify in terms of universal scientific criteria. But he warns of the error of converting philosophical ideas into supposedly objective knowledge. Disguised philosophy, he stresses, brings endless confusion into science and in the attitude of the psychiatrist in particular.

Jaspers never subscribed to the notion that the study of psychological phenomena can be as objective as research in natural sciences. By recognizing this very clearly in 1913, he might have foreseen the problems which were to follow when technological advances were believed to resolve the issue of objectivity. Jaspers repudiates the "medical prejudice" which regards quantitative assessment as the one and only scientific method. And he questions the scientific posture which regards the examination of qualitative changes as arbitrary, subjective and unscientific. Jaspers emphasizes time and again that the psychopathologist cannot depend exclusively on what can be perceived through the senses. Psychological events can never be directly perceived but only indirectly through the way in which they are expressed. The psychopathologist depends on the range, receptivity and complexity of his power to see and experience. He therefore cannot function in the manner of an objective recorder. Sympathy, according to Jaspers, is not the same as knowledge, but from it springs that vision of things which provide knowledge of indispensable material. Completely dispassionate observation misses the essence of things. Detachment and sympathy belong together, and if we are to gain scientific knowledge, the interplay of both is needed. To understand Jaspers' use of the terms sympathy and empathy, we must remember that his concept of phenomenology differs entirely from what most people think phenomenology means: a descriptive classification of symptoms and behavior. On the contrary, Jaspers' phenomenology is "the study which describes patients' subjective experiences and everything else that exists or comes to be within the field of their awareness." This stands in contrast to those objective data which one obtains by methods of testing and the observation of a patient's activities, his gestures, or behavioral characteristics. Jaspers uses sympathy and empathy in a methodological sense, referring to the understanding and meaningful elicitation of subjective material for objective assessment. In this framework subjective is what we get to know indirectly through the patient's own verbal communication. We would, therefore, be deficient in scientific procedure if we merely register the content of the patient's statement without recognition of individual meaning, the language within the language. I have come to regard as prophetic Jaspers' warning: "A psychopathology which simply confines itself to what can be directly perceived through the senses becomes inevitably a psychopathology without a psyche."

Indeed it would appear there is much common ground between the objectives of the founders of this association and Jaspers. This common ground is the acknowledgment of the essentially subjective nature of psychopathology. The men who organized this Association were searching for new territories of psychological knowldge; these men transcended the confines of medical thought and envisaged psychopathology as the unifying framework for the scientific approach to the vast domain of abnormal psychology. And Jaspers outlined the system which proceeds on comprehensive principles of methodology, recognizes the limitation of the natural science approach, and clarifies the dualistic nature of the scientific psychopathologist whose knowledge derives from subjective and objective sources alike.

Recent Developments

As we look over the past two decades, we encounter an impressive body of interrelated developments of new science, amazingly advanced technology and rigorously conducted experiments. The essentially subjective nature of psychopathology is contained in the experience of reality, of mood, of self, and of body image. The experiences of religion, of the fantastic, of dreams, or of premonitions are no less uniquely personal than experiencing sexual activity, being obsessed or tortured by anxiety. Even our most advanced methods to record, measure and classify such experiential phenomena also run the risk of an unmeasurable loss of essential ingredients of personal nature. Now from the viewpoint of what Elkes (4) so charmingly called "the brash innocence of a young, emerging, materialist science" this dilemma seems disturbing, temporary, and a call-to-arms for solution through technological advances.

Had the swiftly developing science of psychopharmacology contributed nothing else to psychiatry, it could claim the honor of bringing about a new orientation in clinical psychopathology. The conventional, even sterile, application of nosologic entities to evaulations of therapeutic activities had seriously limited scope and significance of reported information. By implication each diagnostic entity was made to appear specific in terms of etiology and treatment. The literature abounded with therapeutic data relating to the four or five subtypes of schizophrenia, to process or defect schizophrenia, and even to backward schizophrenics. In this last case, institutional geography served as the criterion in favor of lobotomy. What made this selection procedure more bizzare was the fact that the majority of such patients were precisely those whose affective impoverishment should have argued against psychosurgical treatment. We have here an extreme but important example of what happens in the absence of psychopathological differentiations.

Except for brain disorders and symptomatic psychoses we have no valid information to justify specific treatment on the basis of specific etiologies. Methodologically, the idea of therapeutic target objectives of specified symptomatology within nosologic entities seemed to me a logical requirement, since clinical evidence indicated that psychoactive drugs act selectively on dysfunctional areas within global diagnostic territory (5, 6, 7). The fact that most diagnostic entities comprise a wealth of symptom spectra and polarities raises many pathogenetic questions which cannot be avoided by the hypothetical assumption of a common underlying cause. Different systems may be involved in producing catatonic excitement or stupor, autistic withdrawal or paranoid aggressiveness, hysterical extroversion or phobic introversion and retarded or agitated depression. Even the evidence of biochemical abnormalities in schizophrenic disorders does not necessarily clarify such different symptom patterns as catatonic excitement, hebephrenic silliness, and paranoid delusional systems. Moreover, should we expect quantitative correlations distinguishing schizoid and schizophrenic behavior and account for episodic, phasic, or permanent psychotic manifestations? The same holds true for the relation of biogenic amines to psychopathological states associated with mood disorders.

The earliest clinical experience with chlorpromazine and other early neuroleptic drugs indicated specific effects on psychomotility and affective functions. Subsequent observations of differential effects of antidepressant compounds made it mandatory to concentrate on those clinical features which could be regarded as "targets" for therapeutic drug effects. This change from disease-oriented therapeutic criteria to an operational classification of dysfunctions revolutionized the methodology of clinical evaluations. The perhaps sudden but overdue recognition of psychopathological differentiations set the stage for the extensive developments of rating instruments which focus on symptom clusters and syndromes. This in turn brought about changes in the map of disciplinary activities and boundaries nearly as drastic as those of the political map after World War I or II. The struggle for better scientific methods and for objectivity in psychiatry was, and remains, a common concern for clinical and non-clinical scientists. But the road to truly multidisciplinary collaboration was not without obstacles due to changing alliances, polemics on strategy and prejudices about partnership.

For research the conceptualization of dysfunctional targets requires constructs based on intimate knowledge of psychopathological processes in the context of the individual organism, personality structure and life situation. For this reason investigation of drug effects necessarily becomes an endeavor in experimental psychopathology. Drug-induced change of symptoms cannot be identified in an atomistic fashion. Symptom interrelation requires comprehension of broader dysfunctional areas. In the case of new drugs, the identification of target areas is the process of observing and comprehending pharmacogenic changes. This begins with observations that lead to global impressions. Only then does it seem fruitful to design procedures for verification based on objective measurement.

In the early period of our Association and also in Jaspers' concept, a cleavage between clinical and experimental psychopathology was more a distinction of approach and setting than of substance and science. Where outstanding men contributed to psychopathology, their working place was their laboratory. With the patient as principal study object, the clinical psychopathologist observed, explored, discovered, and theorized in hospital wards and offices. Freud's famous consulting room in Vienna with its pillow-covered sofa served as much as a laboratory in the historical perspective of psychopathology as the instrument-equipped work benches in research institutes. But the growth of clinical science left no doubt that the clinician could not function as his own research instrument. In too many quarters of psychiatry, progress was hindered by intellectual complacency, professional insulation, and theoretical inbreeding. Psychiatric training and practice did not keep abreast with major developments in relevant sciences. Speculation on the meaning of psychopathology grew endless in those quarters where longing for unifying theories of human behavior, normal or abnormal, silenced doubt, minimized criticism and defied verification.

Illustrative of the melting pot struggle which came about by the avalanche of psychopharmacological penetration into psychopathology and its allied sciences was the rather dramatic confrontation of experimentalists and clinicians, convened by the National Institute of Mental Health, the National Academy of Sciences, and the American Psychiatric Association in Washington in 1956. The symposium was hopefully called "Psychopharmacology: Problems in Evaluation." When the proceedings were published three years later (8), Robert Felix in his foreward stated: "But perhaps most important of all, in my opinion, the conference served—if the editors and participants will forgive me—as an exchange of ignorance." And he went on to say that this was good because research thrives on ignorance. At the conference, however, ignorance was primarily assigned to the not-so-scientific clinicians. We heard much talk about the vagaries of clinical impressions and the art of medicine. The clinicians' initial investigations of the new psychoactive effects were criticized as being the weakest link in the chain of orderly investigation. The complaint was made that the general level of clinical description of the effects of new drugs gave the basic scientists nothing to shoot at in the way of relevant experiments. While individual clinicians were acknowledged for their reputation of competence, collectively they were regarded as amateurs in the universe of exact experimental science. Joseph Wortis stated it well:

> I think many of the comments made so far seem to reflect the one underlying problem and that is the difficulty that we find when a group of scientists, accustomed to exact methods and laboratory situations, seek to apply their skills and techniques to clinical problems. As a clinician who has dabbled in experimental work, I am aware of the condescension with which exact experimentalists look upon the efforts of clinicians. I would, however, like to remind the experimenters of the sense of urgency that we clinicians have. [He went on to say:] At the present time the situation is such that the gap that divides the exact experimenter from the clinician tempts the clinician to make dogmatic statements without scientific examination, while the experimenter makes exact statements without any clinical relevance.

What one outstanding experimentalist thought of subjective phenomena is brilliantly reflected in his assertion: "I believe that extrapolation from the emotional behavior of animals to that of man may be acceptable if we can establish the identity of the behavioral changes and of the causal conditions regardless of what the emotion 'feels like'."

In the deliberations of my committee on patient selection and control I expressed concern about the creation of statistically comparable groups, which, from the psychopathological point of view, could hardly be matched in large numbers. But the emphasis was clearly on statistical expertise and on this account clinical studies had made a poor showing. Recognizing the justification of the criticism, I commented: "If the present criticism is to be corrected, we must first examine the value of some of the recommended remedies. If it is true that there is a naive method of clinical empiricism, it is equally true that there exists a naive phase in technical objectivism." Summing up at the end of the conference, Kety stated: "There is nothing essentially unscientific about clinical evaluation, and it can be used efficiently in a completely scientific framework." He also disagreed with the notion that psychiatric research was not qualitatively different from research in other fields of medicine, and said:

> It is a commonplace thing that the brain has many more degrees of freedom than does the liver. There are more variables in diseases of the brain and behavior which is mediated by the brain than any possible configuration of variables which can be brought together in any other field. [And wisely he added:] Complexity may slow the progress in a science; it may at times exert a frustrating effect upon the optimist who hopes to introduce rigor and definitiveness perhaps prematurely, but complexity in itself does not separate a field from its kindred discipline.

While the conference marked the beginning of a new era in scientific collaboration and the advance of methodology, many problems were unresolved and some continue to give us trouble today. For the sake of my topic, I will stress only those kinds of problems which may clarify controversial aspects of psychopathological research.

What has bothered me ever since that conference is the lack of dispassionate study of the actual contribution of clinical psychopathology to the discovery of psychoactive drug effects. It we are to make progress, it seems unwise to concentrate on what is obsolete in the clinical approach. We should determine the appropriate clinical method which takes into account the dualistic framework of psychopathology. From this follows the indispensability of a clinical approach which rests on competent observation, description and conceptualization. Grinker (9), looking at psychiatric research in our changing world, said: Unfortunately the achievements of modern technology have made us impatient and we often jump to instant solutions. Thus we have skipped over the slow and tedious work necessary to answer the questions of what, how, and why, by observation, description, and classification." Concerning the question of science, Grinker had this to say: "To put it very simply and perhaps naively, psychiatry as a science is limited by the advances in clinical approaches that have been neglected."

I see some neglect in experimental scientists who avoid understanding and integrating the methods by which clinicians made their discoveries. Specifically, how accurate were the observations of binocular clinicans who identified main and differential effects of neuroleptic, antidepressant and hallucinogenic drugs? Is it not a fact that the clinical identifications of prototype action on psychopathology stood the test of time? It would now be most profitable to do a retrospective study and analysis to ascertain the kind and degree of reliability of the original observations in the light of subsequent empirical evidence based on experimentally controlled investigations. Such a study might prove more valuable for the advance of methodology, in which we are all interested, than the unquestioned perpetuation of precise but inappropriately reductive techniques.

I emphasized the difficulty arising from matching procedures based on what patients have in common at the expense of crucial individual variables by which they differ. That this problem has not been resolved, has recently been stressed by Klett (10). In discussing methodological problems of ongoing, national, collaborative studies in 1969, he stated:

> In a typical study of the relative effectiveness of phenothiazine derivatives in schizophrenia, patients are randomly assigned to treatment groups as they are consecutively admitted to the hospital. They are described on some standard rating device before and after a specific interval of treatment. As most rating scales today yield scores for a number of symptom areas, each patient has a number of scores representing his status before and after treatment. The consequence of this approach is that in the analysis of every symptom area, patients are included who did not manifest the particular symptom before or at any time during treatment. There are some important objections to this. First, the important clinical question is not being answered. If the question is how the drugs compare in reducing hostile belligerent behavior, there is no interest in how well they reduce hostility in non-hostile individuals; this is illogical.

To avoid this problem he referred to the kind of approach implied in the concept of "target symptoms." The analysis of each symptom would then be based upon those patients who manifest the symptom prior to treatment. In his opinion, therefore, it is not unlikely that the limited success in finding differences among drugs might be improved by this procedure.

Let us now take a hard look at the critical issues of objectivity, reliability, and validity. We are today dominated by mounting demands for more statistically controlled studies of every facet of behavior. We are all in agreement that these are the indisputable hallmarks of scientific methodology. But how is this to be accomplished? What are the ultimate procedures? How biased is objectivity? How relevant is reliability? What is right and what is rubbish in the incantations about scientific rigor so frequently advanced by research review boards?

To understand the problems of reliability, one must ascertain whether this implies a relative constancy of pathology which would insure the repeatability of the observation and dependability on precision. Even if pathological manifestations are fairly constant, precision or consistency of measurements may lead to consistently wrong judgements. Consistency assuring repeatability does not vouch for accuracy or validity. The question of test-retest reliability in the clinical evaluation of psychopathology depends substantially on the existence of patients who maintain a fixed behavioral status quo. How does one differentiate true variations and fluctuations of pathology from errors of measurement? Chassen (11), who in my opinion is one of our most sophisticated experts on research problems in psychiatry, states:

> There is further a particular danger implicit in seeking clinical tests or data systems with a high test-retest coefficient of correlation, or reliability. First, whatever may be the purpose of a clinical research project with such a criterion for its documentation, a high test-retest reliability can be insured when the particular charactertistics or symptoms under study are relatively invariant in the individual. If it is indeed the object of a study to investigate, for purposes of therapeutic intervention or some other reason, just such traits or just those patients who are the most stereotypic and predictable in their day-to-day or week-to-week behavior, then the criterion of test-retest reliability would appear appropriate.

Chassen goes on to ask whether disagreement among observers diminishes the importance or usefulness of their data: "If one regards differences between investigators as always representing differences in observations of a true-patient state and as departures from some conceptually calibrated observational norm, this amounts to a neglect of some of the more subtle aspects of psychiatric data."

Reliability is judged in terms of interrater scores derived from rating scales. We need rating devices to achieve an objective approach to evaluation. Yet they also limit the scope and context of information which we know to be significant. The more sophisticated psychopathologist who uses the Inpatient Multidimensional Psychiatric Scale encounters many problems indeed. For example, he has to filter observations into a section designated "Anxious Intrapunitiveness." In the first place, this is not a descriptive but interpretative classification. In the second place, one may not agree that this cluster should include items such as obsessions, fears, and apprehensions as well. By what virtue of scientific rigor can these phenomena be judged to be intra-punitive? The real usefulness of many scales can be compared to radar scopes which spot appearance, movement, and disappearance of inadequately config-urated objects. While a rating scale can provide important information on changes in scores, in terms of this analogy, it does not tell us enough about the nature of what changes.

Lehmann (12) spoke of the "new syndrome explosion" and wondered which of the numerous but different syndromes in the case of depressions we should accept. Although these syndromes have been arrived at by automation of scaled and factor-analyzed clinical data, some seem strangely different, not only from each other, but in relation to the clinical material from which they were derived.

If we fail to bridge the gap between clinically perceived complexity on the one hand and the shorthand code of simplistically scaled items on the other hand, we may end up by substituting behavioral technology for sophis-ticated psychopathology. For the psychopathologist, quantification of be-havior is not enough. This must be accepted as fact; it is not a question of dispute in terms of exact science, philosophy or value systems. We need to understand this in terms of a realistic methodology geared for productive research.

If our common aims for the perfection of scientific rigor are to progress toward becoming reality, then we must expand clarifying dialogues between clinical, experimental, and basic science investigators. At this time of growing research bureaucracy the clinical psychopathologist needs not only a voice but also a vote in judgment and decision on what constitutes creative research.

I have traveled over grounds strewn with rocks and holes when I had the option of giving an erudite talk on a safer topic. But my membership in this Association has convinced me that we are the least parochial and the most cosmopolitan group of scientists concerned with psychopathology. As is evi-dent, there is no plain answer to the question of my topic. But in this respect we are not different from the most exact of sciences. When physicists debated the origin of Einstein's inspiration for his theory of relativity, they logically assumed a connection with the Michelson-Morley experiment which had defied Newtonian physics by showing that the speed of light is constant despite the motion of its source, a result later explained by Einstein's equa-tions. But Einstein disagreed. This is his own explanation of the origin of relativity. "There is no logical way to the discover of these elementary laws. There is only the way of intuition." Intuition, far from being a dubious process, is a vital part of the scientist's intellectual equipment. It is a mental process which precedes conceptualization. For the psychopathologist intui-tion is the link between empathic understanding and rational formulation.

The future of psychopathology appears more promising than at any time in the past. The fact that I could discuss so many methodological problems proves more than anything else how far we have come along. Psychopathology as a science was never in doubt. That the psychopathologist is a man of many persuasions, all of which must converge on a blending of subjective and objective evidence, has been and continues to be my main concern.

References

1. Jaspers, K. *General Psychopathology*. Manchester, England: Manchester University Press, 1963. Published in U.S. by The University of Chicago Press.
2. Hamilton, S. W. Notes on the history of the American Psychopathological Association, 1910–1931. Journal of Nervous and Mental Disease, 1945, 102:30.
3. Constitution of The American Psychopathological Association, Article II.
4. Elkes, J. Behavioral pharmacology in relation to psychiatry. *Psychiatrie Der Gengenwart*. Berlin: Springer-Verlag, 1962.
5. Freyhan, F. A. Psychopharmacology and the controversial clinician. In J. G. Miller (Ed.), *Drugs and Behavior*. New York: Wiley, 1960.
6. Freyhan, F. A. The evolution of compensatory therapy with drugs in modern psychiatric practice. *Neuro-Psychopharmacology*. Amsterdam: 1959.
7. Freyhan, F. A. Clinical aspects of psychotropic drugs. In C. Rupp (Ed.), *Mind As A Tissue*. New York: Harper and Row, Hoeber Medical Division, 1968.
8. Felix, R. Foreword. In J. O. Cole and R. W. Gerard (Eds.), *Psychopharmacology: Problems In Evaluation*. Washington, D.C.: National Academy of Sciences—National Research Council. Publication 583.
9. Grinker, R. R., Sr. Psychiatry and our dangerous world. In G. F. D. Heseltine (Ed.), *Psychiatric Research In Our Changing World*. Amsterdam: Excerpta Medica Foundation, 1969.
10. Klett, J. Ongoing National Collaborative Studies in the U.S.A. by the Veterans' Administration. *Psychopharmacology Bulletin*. N.I.M.H., National Clearinghouse for Mental Health Information, 1969, 5:23.
11. Chassen, J. B. *Research Design in Clinical Psychology and Psychiatry*. New York: Appleton-Century-Crofts, Meredith, 1967.
12. Lehmann, H. E. Empathy and perspective or consensus and automation? Implications of the new deal in psychiatric diagnosis. Compr. Psych., 1967, 8:265.

PART I

ADVANCES IN DIAGNOSIS OF MOOD DISORDERS

1

THE MISLABELING OF DEPRESSED PATIENTS IN NEW YORK STATE HOSPITALS*

United States Team: Barry Gurland, M.B., M.R.C.P., D.P.M., Joseph L. Fleiss, Ph.D., Lawrence Sharpe, M.B., D.P.M., Robert Simon, M.A., James E. Barrett, Jr., M.D.**

United Kingdom Team: John Copeland, M.B., M.R.C.P., D.P.M., John E. Cooper, B.M., M.R.C.P., D.P.M., Robert E. Kendell, M.D., M.R.C.P., D.P.M.***

American psychiatrists tend to diagnose depressive disorders far less readily than do their English colleagues. This contrast is true when psychiatrists making routine diagnoses in New York are compared with those making routine diagnoses in London public mental hospitals (Cooper et al., 1969; Gurland et al., 1969); and even holds true when American and English psychiatrists view the same videotaped interview with a patient (Kendell et al., 1969).

This contrast in the diagnostic predilection of English and American psychiatrists is found for nearly all kinds of patients even when they are grouped according to their psychopathology (Gurland et al., 1970). Indeed, there are several kinds of patients a majority of whom are diagnosed as a depressive disorder by English psychiatrists but as schizophrenic by American psychiatrists. One such kind of patient is characterized by a predominance of depressive symptoms.

On the face of it, a group of patients who show mainly depression might be expected to receive a label of depressive disorder rather than one of schizophrenia. Thus, this paper will present further data on patients with

*The work reported here was supported by NIMH Public Health Service Grant MH 09191, Project for the Cross-National Study of the Diagnosis of the Mental Disorders in the United States and United Kingdom, Joseph Zubin, principal investigator. We gratefully acknowledge the help of Miss Pamela Roberts, A.A., Mrs. Jane Gourlay, M.A., Mrs. Judith Kuriansky, Ed.M., and Jeffrey Klein, B.A., in data collection. We appreciate also the cooperation of the Directors and staff of those state hospitals in New York and area mental hospitals in London at which patients were examined by this project and the assistance of the statistical office of the New York State Department of Mental Hygiene.

**Biometrics Research Unit, New York State Psychiatric Institute.

***Institute of Psychiatry, Maudsley Hospital.

predominant depression in order to examine the appropriateness, usefulness, and consequences of the American style of diagnosis in this group of patients.

Sample Selection and Methods of Study

The data we will present here have been provided mostly by the project called "The Cross-National Study of the Diagnosis of the Mental Disorders," which is under the directorship of Dr. Joseph Zubin. Detailed descriptions of the study methods, sample selection, and main findings have been reported elsewhere (Cooper et al., 1969; Gurland et al., 1969; Gurland et al., 1970). Here we will give only a brief description as relevant to the current topic.

The project studied consecutive admissions to state mental hospitals in New York and area mental hospitals in London. The samples of New York and London patients came from three series. The first series, in the age group 35-59, consisted of 145 patients from a single hospital in New York and 145 from a single hospital in London. The second series, in the age group 20-34, consisted of 105 patients from each of the same hospitals. The third series, covering the age range 20-59, consisted of 192 patients drawn, in proportion to their rates of admission, from nine state hospitals in New York, and of 174 patients similarly drawn from nine public mental hospitals in London. Aside from age, the sole criterion for inclusion in the study was that the patient be a current admission to the hospital (not a transfer or a return from leave).

Each patient was administered a mental state interview by a project psychiatrist within 48 hours of admission. The interview was structured and consisted of approximately 700 items covering a wide range of psychiatric symptoms and behaviors. Probes were provided and ratings defined, but some room was left for clinical judgment in rephrasing probes and assessing responses. The universe of items was provided partly by British (Wing et al., 1967) and partly by American (Spitzer et al., 1964) sources. A structured history interview was also administered. A project diagnosis according to the 8th Edition of the ICD was made. The official hospital diagnoses on all patients were collected after they had been passed through the usual administrative channels. There was no interchange of information between the project and hospital staff at any stage during the course of the study.

In order to characterize the psychopathology of patients, we made use of scores on a number of dimensions of pathology. The items rated as positive in each of various sections of the standard mental state interview were added up so as to give each patient a series of scores for dimensions such as depression, hypomania, and paranoid delusions. Of special importance here is the score on depressive mood. Items contributing to this factor reflect a series of symptoms including the patient's reports of sadness, frequent crying, loss of appetite, and feelings of hopelessness.

The Isolation of a Group of Morbid Depressives

We isolated a group of patients within our series whom we have called "morbid depressives" and who were defined in the following terms. At the time of admission to the hospital, or for the month prior to admission, they reported a sufficient number of symptoms of depression to yield a score above the mean for the combined New York and London samples on this scale, but showed no symptoms which could contradict the diagnosis of an affective disorder according to DSM-II or standard textbooks (Noyes and Kolb, 1963; Arieti, 1966) in the United States.

Patients were therefore only placed in the group of morbid depressives if they showed scores above the mean on the scale of depressive mood and no other symptoms except possibly anxiety, retardation, loss of interest, hypomania, depersonalization, and loss of insight. We excluded patients who were given a project diagnosis of alcoholism, drug addiction, or organic disorder, or who had symptoms which are mentioned in textbooks or in DSM-II as suggesting schizophrenia, such as delusions of control, blunting of affect, incomprehensibility, hallucinations, paranoid delusions, or delusions of grandeur. Despite the extreme strictness of the criteria for selecting the morbid depressives, they proved to constitute between 10 and 20 percent of the consecutive admissions we examined in New York state hospitals.

For purposes of comparison, we isolated a second group of patients who were not depressed and who had symptoms highly suggestive of schizophrenia. Patients included in this group were those who had scores below the mean on the scales of depression and hypomania, but high ratings on the scales measuring blunting of affect, incomprehensibility, or delusions of control. Patients diagnosed by the project as alcoholic, drug-addicted, or organically disordered were also excluded from this group. For convenience, we refer to this group with symptoms suggestive of schizophrenia as "nondepressed psychotics." They constituted about the same proportion of admissions as did the morbid depressives. Table 1 contrasts the criteria for the isolation of the two groups of patients described above.

Results

We compared the morbid depressives and the nondepressed psychotics on variables other than psychopathology in order to highlight additional features which might further indicate whether the former group would be best assigned to the depressive disorders. The examination of one feature, namely a favorable outcome, seemed particularly relevant to this issue.

We measured outcome by the one-year outcome index of Burdock and Hardesty (1961), a function of the number of days that the patient spent out

Table 1

Criteria for two kinds of patients

	Morbid depressives	Nondepressed psychotics
Depressed Mood	+	−
Hypomania	±	−
Project diagnosis of alcoholism, drug addiction, or organic disorder	−	−
Anxiety, retardation, loss of interest, depersonalization, loss of insight	±	±
Hallucinations, paranoid delusions, delusions of grandeur	−	±
Delusions of control, blunting of affect, incomprehensibility	−	+*

+ = scores must be above the mean
− = scores must be below the mean
± = scores can be either above or
      below the mean

*At least one of the three scores must be above the mean.

of hospital during the year after his admission, and of the number of releases and readmissions during the course of that year. For convenience, we considered only what we arbitrarily defined as good or poor outcome. The frequency distribution of scores on the outcome index showed a dip at an index of 0.75, and we therefore took this figure as the boundary between good and bad outcome. A patient with good outcome was one with an outcome index exceeding 0.75, that is, one who was discharged within three months after admission and was not readmitted during the course of one year. The necessary data were obtained from the statistical office of the New York State Department of Mental Hygiene at Albany, and also by a direct search of the patients' case notes. Table 2 shows that the majority of the morbid depressives had a good early outcome in contrast to the nondepressed psychotics, where the majority had a poor early outcome."*

*Each separate chi square value incorporates Yates' correction for continuity. The pooled chi square value, also with one degree of freedom, is determined using Cochran's procedure (1954).

Table 2

Psychopathology by Early Outcome
in Three Series of New York Patients

Series	Morbid Depressives		Non-depressed Psychotics		Chi Square
	N	% Good	N	% Good	
•1	24	75.0%	24	33.3%	6.81**
2	12	66.7%	19	21.1%	4.67*
3	21	66.7%	15	26.7%	4.11*

Pooled Chi Square = 15.52***

* = p < .05   ** = p < .01   *** = p < .001

The morbid depressives were thus distinguished by the predominance of depression in their clinical picture, the absence of clinical signs conflicting with the diagnosis of a depressive disorder, and a favorable early outcome in a majority of cases. We might therefore have expected that at least a majority of the morbid depressive group would be given a diagnosis of depressive disorder by the hospital clinicians if we included under this rubric a wide range of depressive disorders, namely manic-depressive psychosis, depressed type; reactive-depressive psychosis; involutional melancholia; and depressive neurosis. As is shown in Table 3 this was, in fact, the case for the morbid depressives in the London hospitals. However, the striking paradox is that in the majority of cases the morbid depressives were called schizophrenic by the New York hospitals, although there was no tendency for the morbid depressives to be put in any one specific subcategory of schizophrenia by the New York hospital psychiatrists.

Table 3

Hospital Diagnoses Given to Morbid
Depressives in New York and London

Hospital Diagnosis	Series 1		Series 2		Series 3	
	New York	London	New York	London	New York	London
Depression	37.5%	73.1%	0%	47.2%	19.0%	58.1%
Schizophrenia	50.0%	15.4%	66.7%	13.9%	71.5%	14.0%
Other	12.5%	11.5%	33.3%	38.9%	9.5%	27.9%
N	24	52	12	36	21	43
Chi Square	10.85**		15.00***		21.14***	

** = p < .01   *** = p < .001

In accounting for this paradox, we first considered whether the New York hospital psychiatrists were overlooking the depressive symptoms displayed by these patients. This did not appear to be the case. There is ample evidence that the New York psychiatrists behaved toward the majority of morbid depressives as if they were depressed, and toward the majority of nonde-pressed psychotics as if they were not depressed.

In the first place, as shown by Table 4, the hospital staff gave a diagnosis of a depressive disorder significantly more often to the morbidly depressed patients than to the nondepressed psychotics. In two out of the three series, the morbid depressives were diagnosed as depression more frequently than were the nondepressed psychotics. In series 2, none of the patients in these two contrasted groups was diagnosed as depression.

Table 4

Psychopathology By Hospital Diagnosis of
Depression in Three Series of New York Patients

Series	Morbid Depressives		Non-depressed Psychotics		Chi Square
	N	% Depression	N	% Depression	
1	24	37.5%	24	4.2%	6.17*
2	12	0%	19	0%	—
3	21	19.0%	15	0%	1.57

Pooled Chi Square = 7.63**

* = p < .05   ** = p < .01

Furthermore, as shown by Table 5, the hospital psychiatrists prescribed antidepressive therapy (either in the form of drugs or EST) within a month of the patient's admission significantly more often to the patients with morbid depression than to the nondepressed psychotics regardless of the label they placed on them.

Even in series 2, where none of these patients was diagnosed as a depres-sive disorder by the hospital psychiatrists, slightly more of the morbid depres-sives were treated early for depression than were the nondepressed psy-chotics. (The total frequencies in this table, and in others in which treatment is considered, are not equal to the numbers given in other tables because there were some patients for whom treatment data were unavailable.) Even those patients in the morbid depressive category who were not diagnosed as having a depressive disorder by the hospital staff were nonetheless more likely to

Table 5

Psychopathology By Early Treatment
of Depression in Three Series of New York Patients

Series	Morbid Depressives		Non-depressed Psychotics		Chi Square
	N	% Treated Early	N	% Treated Early	
1	24	33.3%	23	4.3%	4.65*
2	11	36.4%	17	11.8%	1.16
3	21	57.1%	15	0%	10.40**

Pooled Chi Square = 14.95***

* = p < .05   ** = p < .01   *** = p < .001

receive early antidepressive therapy than the nondepressed psychotics (see Table 6).

The group of patients in New York State hospitals called morbid depressives thus have depression as their cardinal symptom, have no symptoms that militate against a diagnosis of depressive disorder, and tend, more often than a group of patients called nondepressed psychotics, to be given antidepressive therapy, to be called a depressive disorder by the hospital psychiatrists, and to have a favorable early outcome. Nonetheless, a labeling paradox is found in that the majority of the morbid depressives are given a diagnosis of schizophrenia by the hospital doctors.

Table 6

Psychopathology By Early Treatment of Depression
For Patients Not Diagnosed Depressed By the Hospitals
in Three Series of New York Patients

Series	Morbid Depressives		Non-depressed Psychotics		Chi Square
	N	% Treated	N	% Treated	
1	15	20.0%	22	4.5%	0.91
2	11	36.4%	17	11.8%	1.16
3	17	47.1%	15	0%	7.08**

Pooled Chi Square = 8.01**

** = p < .01

The Recent History of the Diagnosis of Depression in the U.S.

A reasonable explanation of the paradox noted above might be that there is a strong bias on the part of American psychiatrists against diagnosing depressive disorders and in favor of diagnosing schizophrenia, and that this bias can be understood in terms of the training and recent traditions of American psychiatry. Eugen Bleuler (1951) taught that in most cases the diagnosis of manic-depressive psychosis can only be made after excluding schizophrenia and since this is a widely held view, the diminishing popularity of the diagnosis of the depressive disorders can perhaps best be understood by considering the expanding concept of schizophrenia.

The domain of schizophrenia mapped out by Kraepelin was enlarged by Eugen Bleuler's psychological definition and the later work of the psychodynamic school. Borderline states were added by Langfeldt, Kasanin and others, and were given names reminiscent of schizophrenia, such as the schizophreniform or acute schizo-affective psychoses. Adolf Meyer emphasized that the schizophrenic reaction could have a good outcome and that therapeutic nihilism was not justified.

Early, subtle, unclear, and disguised states of schizophrenia attracted attention and culminated in the delineation of the pseudoneurotic schizophrenic by Hoch and Polatin (1949). A ten year follow-up of pseudoneurotic schizophrenics revealed that only 10 percent had developed chronic schizophrenia in the long run (Hoch et al., 1962). The concept of schizophrenia in the United States had become very different from that in Europe. Outright abuses of the concept of schizophrenia have also occurred, sometimes making it synonymous with craziness, or failure to respond to psychotherapy. Malzberg (1959) followed the trends in the diagnosis of first admissions to New York state hospitals and showed a steady decrease in the diagnosis of manic-depressive disorders from 1932 to 1950, with a corresponding increase in the diagnosis of schizophrenia over the same years.

Some Consequences of this Trend

The bias introduced for traditional reasons has led to such an overemphasis on schizophrenia that the major psychopathological distinctions between affective disorder and schizophrenia have broken down in American diagnoses. We have reported elsewhere (Gurland et al., 1970) that the association between the patient's psychopathology and the hospital diagnosis he received was far weaker in New York than in London. A circular process has been initiated in which the standards of diagnosis in the United States have become less rational and thus less useful, leading to a disregard of diagnosis.

As evidence of this disregard for diagnosis we show in Table 7 that in the group of morbid depressives the relationship between the hospital's diagnosis

Table 7

Hospital Diagnosis By Early Treatment of
Depression for Morbid Depressives in Two
Series of New York Patients

Series	Depression N	% Treated	Other N	% Treated	Chi Square
1	9	55.6%	15	20.0%	1.81
3	4	100.0%	17	47.1%	1.86

Pooled Chi Square = 3.61

and the administration of antidepressive or EST therapy was weak and not statistically significant. (In this and the next table, the second series is omitted because not a single morbid depressive from that series received a hospital diagnosis of a depressive disorder.)

Even though the hospital psychiatrists paid little attention to their diagnoses in prescribing treatment, we might wonder whether they were influenced in their management of the patient by whatever prognostic implications they attached to their diagnoses. However, Table 8 shows that there was no relationship at all between diagnosis and early outcome within the group of morbid depressives; that is, within this relatively favorable outcome group, the outcome was the same whatever the patient was called.

The New York hospital psychiatrists appear to have turned to a consideration of symptomatology rather than to diagnosis as a guide to their treatment. It is more the patient's psychopathology than his diagnosis which leads to the different treatment given by New York hospital psychiatrists to the morbid depressive group, as opposed to the nondepressed psychotics. Thus, at

Table 8

Hospital Diagnosis By Early Outcome for Morbid
Depressives in Two Series of New York Patients

Series	Depression N	% Good	Other N	% Good	Chi Square
1	9	77.8%	15	73.3%	0.02
3	4	75.0%	17	64.7%	0.09

Pooled Chi Square = 0.09

least for the morbid depressives in New York state hospitals, the diagnosis given to a patient by the hospital psychiatrist is of little consequence to that patient.

However, a tempting speculation presents itself, of great relevance to the welfare of patients. Suppose we assume that as a consequence of bias in diagnosis the depressive disorders have been greatly underestimated in the American hospital populations. Is it not then likely that this would lead to neglect of the needs of depressed patients in the hospital? Our data indicate that this may be so. For instance, we can point to the smaller numbers of morbid depressives who received treatment appropriate for depression in the New York sample than in the London sample (see Table 9).*

Table 9

Treatment of Depression Within a Year
of Admission for Morbid Depressives
From Series 1 in New York and London

	New York		London	
N	% Treated	N		% Treated
24	50.0%	51		84.3%

Chi Square = 8.14**

** = p < .01

Consequences for Research

There are equally important consequences for psychiatric research of the tendency to underdiagnose depressive disorders. Many state hospitals throughout this country bear within their colossal structures a cell in which research workers from such disciplines as psychology, physiology and bio-chemistry are located. Insofar as they wish to base their work on patients within certain diagnostic groups, they are usually dependent on the hospital psychiatrists to provide those diagnoses. The problems arising in research as a result of the heterogeneous behaviors included under the diagnosis of schizo-phrenia are well known. To some extent this is inevitable but the inclusion of

*These data are for the first series only because treatment data from the second and third London series are not yet available. The proportions are for those treated for depression within a year of admission (rather than within a month as in the previous tables) because the data from London were in this form only.

morbid depressives in schizophrenia would appear to be a gratuitous complication.

Furthermore, studies that seek to find objective discriminators of affective disorder and schizophrenia will be hampered by the partial and erroneous inclusion of the former in the latter. Fortunately, those workers concentrating on the affective disorders will *not* be so much troubled by the converse problem, the inclusion in the affective disorders of patients with symptoms highly suggestive of schizophrenia. Only a single one of all the nondepressed psychotics in our three series received a diagnosis of depression. Furthermore, in our previous work we have shown that patients with ambiguous or mixed symptomatology are hardly ever called an affective disorder by the New York hospital staff (Gurland et al., 1970).

Conclusions

We fear that much of this presentation will be regarded as critical in tone. We will therefore close on a positive note. We have shown that there are more patients with a depressive disorder in New York hospitals than is generally recognized from reported statistics. New York hospital psychiatrists have turned to psychopathology rather than diagnosis in treating these patients and show themselves to be sensitive to such patients' depressive symptoms. It seems well within the grasp of the hospital psychiatrists to give a distinctive label embodying the term depression to those patients whose predominant symptom is depression and who present no obvious and reliable features of schizophrenia. Such a label would be more consistent with the treatment the psychiatrist gives than are the diagnoses he now makes, and would also be a more useful predictor of early outcome. There are labels within the international classification of disease, and its American version, DSM-II, which would answer this purpose well.

The appropriate labeling, in one form or another, of patients such as the morbid depressives would seem likely to lead to the recognition of the higher frequency of morbid depressives in state hospitals, to a greater awareness of the need for antidepressive therapy, to more rational planning of hospital services, and to more fruitful collaboration between clinicians and research workers.

References

Arieti, S. (Ed.). American Handbook of Psychiatry. New York: Basic Books, 1966.

Bleuler, E. P. Textbook of Psychiatry. Transl. by A. A. Brill. Dover Pub. Inc., 1951.

Burdock, E. I., and Hardesty, A. S. An outcome index for mental hospital patients. J. Abnorm. Soc. Psychol., 1961, 63, 666–670.

Cochran, W. G. Some methods for strengthening the common X^2 tests. Biometrics, 1954, 10, 417–451.

Cooper, J. E., Kendell, R. E., Gurland, B. J., Sartorius, N., and Farkas, T. Cross-national study of diagnosis of the mental disorders: Some results from the first comparative investigation. Amer. J. Psychiat., 1969 (April supp.), 125, 21-29.

Gurland, B. J., Fleiss, J. L., Cooper, J. E., Kendell, R. E., and Simon, R. Cross-national study of diagnosis of the mental disorders: Some comparisons of diagnostic criteria from the first investigation. Amer. J. Psychiat., 1969 (April supp.), 125, 30-39.

Gurland, B. J., Fleiss, J. L., Cooper, J. E., Sharpe, L., Kendell, R. E., and Roberts, P. Cross-national study of diagnosis of mental disorders: Hospital diagnoses and hospital patients in New York and London. Compr. Psychiat., 1970, 11, 18-25.

Hoch, P. H., and Polatin, P. Pseudoneurotic forms of schizophrenia. Psychiat. Quart., 1949, 23, 248-296.

Hoch, P. H., Cattell, J. P., Strahl, M. O., and Pennes, H. H. The course and outcome of pseudoneurotic schizophrenia. Amer. J. Psychiat., 1962, 119, 106-115.

Kendell, R. E., Gourlay, J., and Cooper, J. E. Videotape studies I: Differences in American and British usage of key diagnostic terms. Presented at Annual APA Meeting, Miami Beach, 1969.

Malzberg, B. Chapter 7. In American Handbook of Psychiatry, ed. S. Arieti. New York: Basic Books, 1959.

Noyes, A. P., and Kolb, L. C. Modern Clinical Psychiatry, 6th Ed. Saunders, 1963.

Spitzer, R. L., Fleiss, J. L., Burdock, E. I., and Hardesty, A. S. The Mental Status Schedule: Rationale, Reliability and Validity. Compr. Psychiat., 1964, 5, 384-395.

Wing, J. K., Birley, J. L. T., Cooper, J. E., Graham, P., and Isaacs, A. D. Reliability of a Procedure for Measuring and Classifying "Present Psychiatric State." Brit. J. Psychiat., 1967, 113, 499-515.

DISCUSSION OF
DR. GURLAND'S PAPER

JEROME D. FRANK

The Johns Hopkins University School of Medicine

This study is characterized by the painstaking, thorough, and lucid presentation and analysis of data that we have come to expect from Dr. Gurland and his colleagues.

Before turning to a discussion of the main finding, I should like to call attention to a subsidiary one which may be of some interest but which the paper did not discuss. This is the relationship of age to diagnosis. In both the United States and the United Kingdom, for patients with the morbid depressive syndrome (i.e., having above the mean number of symptoms of depression and no symptoms which could contradict this diagnosis) patients under 34 are less often diagnosed depressed and more often diagnosed as neither schizophrenic nor depressed. Furthermore, the "other" category is used about three times as often for the younger than the older patients in both countries. Perhaps this reflects the less stable and more confusing manifestations of psychoses in younger people, or perhaps the greater incidence of behavioral problems which might lead to a diagnosis of character disorder. The paper does not give the age breakdown for the largest series, that is, number three. It would be interesting to see whether the same finding holds true for it.

The major finding is indeed startling, and is seen most clearly with the morbid depressive patients who are under 34. In the United States, of 12 such patients, who, it will be remembered, had more than the mean number of signs of depression and no signs incompatible with this diagnosis, not one was diagnosed as depressed and two-thirds were diagnosed as schizophrenic, as compared with 47 percent depressed and 14 percent schizophrenic in the London series. Since other analyses showed that the American psychiatrists were no less sensitive to the symptoms of depression than the British ones, one must concur with the conclusion that American psychiatrists are biased

29

in favor of diagnosing schizophrenia and against diagnosing depression as compared to their London colleagues.

I believe the major reason for this is the difference in the preferred conceptualization of schizophrenia in the United States and Great Britain. In the United States, initially under the leadership of Adolf Meyer, and later, powerfully reinforced by that of Sullivan and Frieda Fromm-Reichmann, we have favored a view of schizophrenia as resulting from faulty habit patterns developed in pathogenic family constellations and therefore best treated by offering patients a new human relationship that might counteract these unfortunate influences. This has implied that psychotherapy is the perferred treatment, and that if the therapy were good enough, the prognosis could be hopeful. On the other hand, English psychiatric thinking, dominated by the Kraeplinian tradition and reinforced by Mayer-Gross, has viewed schizophrenia as an organic disease which, often taking the form of dementia praecox with an ominous prognosis, is not especially amenable to psychotherapy. One must add that psychotherapy, primarily as a result of the psychoanalytic influence, has always enjoyed the highest prestige of all forms of psychiatric treatment in the United States, which is not true in Britain.

The depressed patient is a poor candidate for psychotherapy. He interacts sparsely with others, is dull and unproductive, sees the world in an impoverished and stereotyped way, and really wants to be left alone. Furthermore, on the one hand his illness is self-limited and his improvement can clearly be facilitated by antidepressants and electroshock therapy and, on the other, he is apt to relapse from time to time with or without psychotherapy. The few reports in the literature of psychotherapy with depressed patients stress what a difficult, long, drawn-out, and dubious undertaking it is.

Young schizophrenics, on the other hand, are considered in the United States to be ideal candidates for psychotherapy—at least, psychotherapy with them is always a rewarding and challenging experience for the therapist. They have a rich inner life, are very sensitive to nuances in interpersonal behavior, and the therapeutic relationship is a lively and eventful one with constant shifts and challenges. The literature is full of fascinating accounts of long-term therapy of schizophrenics, which every young psychiatrist hopes to emulate. To be sure, the effects of intensive, long-term psychotherapy on schizophrenics remain problematical, especially in view of the recent studies of May and his colleagues (1). However, let me hasten to add, they do recognize the importance of what they call psychotherapeutic management of such patients—i.e., they do not dismiss the role of psychological factors in exacerbating or reducing schizophrenic manifestations. But, even if the patient does not get better, the therapist has had an interesting time and, in view of the stresses that long-term treatment of schizophrenics puts him under, he can feel that he is earning his fee.

A more troublesome question raised by this study is whether diagnosis is useful with this group of patients. Although diagnosis has several functions, its ultimate purpose is to guide treatment. In the United States the findings of this study are equivocal in this respect. More of the group of morbid depressives diagnosed depressed received antidepressant medication early than those diagnosed "other," but the differences are not statistically significant. Whether the patient with morbid depressive symptoms is, or is not, diagnosed as depressed seems to make no difference with respect to the frequency of early improvement (i.e., discharge from the hospital within three months and remaining out of it for a year). Compared to the London sample, fewer of the patients in the United States received antidepressant treatment. Since the London outcome figures are not given, one cannot determine whether the administration of appropriate treatment really affects outcome. Judging from the high rate of good outcome in the American series (65 to 78 per cent), the London figures could not be much higher. This suggests that, in fact, the form of treatment does not make too much difference with this group. Although antidepressant treatment and electroshock therapy are probably the treatments of choice, the spontaneous remission rate is high and some patients with depressive symptoms respond well to phenothiazines. Taken together, these may obscure the possible advantages of appropriate antidepressant treatment.

I fully concur with the authors that more cross-cultural consistency would be achieved by classifying psychiatric patients in terms of syndromes rather than disease entities. This would clearly benefit research because research data cannot cumulate unless researchers agree on the labels they apply to the phenomena they are studying. Although it might not affect therapy with this particular group of patients, the value of using target complaints rather than clinical entities in guiding pharmacological treatment of psychotics has been amply demonstrated. One obstacle to the use of syndromes rather than clinical entities in the past may have been the greater labor involved, but this today is obviated by the computer.

We must all be grateful to Dr. Gurland and his colleagues for undertaking the laborious, painstaking task of cleaning out the Augean stables of psychiatric diagnosis. It is good to know that they are making tangible headway.

Reference

1. May, Philip R. A., Treatment of Schizophrenia. New York: Science House, 1968.

2

PRIMARY AND SECONDARY AFFECTIVE DISORDERS*

ELI ROBINS, M.D., RODRIGO A. MUNOZ, M.D.,
SUE MARTIN, M.D., AND KATHYE A. GENTRY, B.A.**

In a previous paper (23) the histories of the concepts of manic-depressive illness, depressive illness, endogenous depression, reactive depression, neurotic depression (depressive neurosis), psychotic depression, and involutional melancholia were briefly reviewed.

The current difficulties in the terms used for discussing depression were also discussed (23). Many of the problems are related to conceptual questions such as reactive versus endogenous depresssion, neurotic versus psychotic depression and agitated versus retarded depression.

Is reactive depression a different syndrome from endogenous depression?

Is stress causally related or even relevant to the precipitation of an affective episode in endogenous depression?

Can meaningful distinctions be made between neurotic and psychotic depression or is the question merely one of severity?

Are agitated, retarded, paranoid, and self-pitying depression (8, 9, 26) fundamentally different disorders or merely clinical variants of a single fundamental disorder?

Are bipolar affective disorders (attacks of manic and depressive episodes) fundamentally different from unipolar affective disorders (recurrent depressions only) or are these clinical variants of the same disorder? (2, 20, 21)

Does the term *depression* designate a transient mood state, a symptom, or a syndrome?

Other difficulties are related to empirical questions. Can the occurrence of a life stress (10) to which to react be determined reliably and, if so, can its causal relation to the ensuing affective episode be determined?

---

*Supported in part by grants MH 13002, MH 05804, and MH 04591 from the National Institute of Mental Health.
**Washington University, School of Medicine, St. Louis.

Can the first attack of psychotic depressive reaction (DSM - II) (1) be distinguished as a single attack, from the first attack of a series of recurrent depression?

Is the affective disorder a primary disorder only, a primary disorder associated with another nonaffective illness, or a secondary disorder?

To approach this problem of the classification of mood disorders requires both conceptual changes and an empirical and theoretical extension of previous studies. It has been pointed out that the establishment of the validity of a psychiatric diagnosis can be described in five phases (22): clinical description of the syndrome, laboratory studies, delimitation from other syndromes, follow-up studies, and family studies. To obtain a wide spectrum of cases, inpatients, outpatients, and emergency room patients should be studied. Ideally, a population survey should also be done, but in an illness subject to exacerbations, total remissions, and recurrences, a population survey is difficult and, in the absence of specific laboratory tests for identifying cases, may be more misleading than helpful.

The chief purposes of the present report are to suggest a basis for classifying affective disorders that avoids etiologic implications by using the concepts of primary and of secondary affective disorder, and to present preliminary data on patients seen in an emergency room.[1] There have been three studies of inpatients in which cognizance of the concepts of primary and secondary affective disorders have been taken into account (3, 28, 29); one outpatient clinic study is in progress;[2] the emergency room study is presented here. It will eventually be possible to cover a full spectrum of treatment and diagnostic locations when these studies are completed.

Definitions

Primary affective disorder is an appropriate diagnosis for a patient who presents with an affective episode if the patient's previous history may be

---

[1] A number of investigators have collaborated in the present project: Drs. Earle Dick, William Clendenin, Leticia Lacson, William Lovejoy, Somporn Bussaratid, Gary Kulak, and Nongyao Udomponsanontha, and Mrs. Susan Dick and Mrs. Susan LeVine. The results presented are preliminary because the initial interviews for the non-affective patients have not been fully analyzed and because, although there is a one to two-year follow-up on 95 per cent of all patients (affective and non-affective disorders) already completed, the follow-up interviews were done without knowledge of the initial interview and none of the follow-up findings has been analyzed. The data presented in this paper are, therefore, subject to some, but probably only slight, revision when the analysis of the entire study is completed. One of the ways in which the data will probably change is that a number of undiagnosed affective disorders—those who do not meet the probable or definite criteria—will probably be included in the overall number of affective disorders, regardless of whether they are thought to be primary or secondary.

[2] This study is being done by Drs. Robert A. Woodruff, Samuel B. Guze, and Paula Clayton on 500 outpatients and their families.

described in one of three ways: he has been psychiatrically well; he has had a previous episode of mania or depression and no other psychiatric illness; he has had a previous episode of mania or depression preceding the development of any other psychiatric or serious medical illness. Secondary affective disorder is an appropriate diagnosis for a patient who presents with an affective episode but who has had a pre-existing, diagnosable psychiatric illness, other than a primary affective disorder. The presence or absence of an apparent life stress is not crucial to either definition. The key is *chronology*. Primary affective disorder occurs in a patient previously well or with previous attacks of depression or mania only, regardless of the presence or absence of an apparent life stress. Secondary affective disorder occurs in a psychiatrically ill person, by history or currently, when the previous or current illness is diagnosable, and regardless of the presence or absence of an apparent life stress.

There are three chief areas of ambiguity in determining whether a given affective episode is primary or secondary. Since the key in the definition is time of onset, chronology, there will be a small group of patients in whom the time of onset of an affective illness relative to a non-affective illness will not be possible to determine. A second ambiguity occurs when there are pre-existing symptoms that suggest a psychiatric disorder, but, from the nature of the symptoms or failure in accurate recall, the symptoms do not form a diagnosable psychiatric illness. Pre-existing medical illness that is life-threatening or that forces the patient to change his way of life significantly requires clinical judgment to an uncomfortable degree for research purposes. Of these patients who develop an affective episode, some might be diagnosed primary, others secondary, and others undiagnosed. It is suggested that all patients with pre-existing medical illness be placed in an undiagnosed or uncertain group with respect to whether they are primary or secondary affective disorder, noting the presence of an affective episode.

The diagnosable illnesses that may pre-exist and lead to a diagnosis of secondary affective disorder are those that have been studied sufficiently well to provide information about most of the five phases of diagnostic validity noted previously. These illnesses include organic brain syndromes, schizophrenia, anxiety neurosis, hysteria, phobic neurosis, obsessive compulsive neurosis, antisocial personality, homosexuality and certain other forms of sexual deviation, alcoholism, drug addiction or abuse, and mental retardation. The symptoms of the pre-existing disorder may merge temporally with those of the affective episode or there may be a hiatus of days to years between the pre-existing disorder and the affective episode. The personality disorders, with the exception of antisocial personality (25), have been insufficiently studied with regard to the five phases noted above, even though there has been a recent first follow-up study of passive aggressive personality (27). Antisocial personality, on the other hand, has been studied in sufficient detail to justify its diagnostic use (25), even though more work is needed on family studies. In the presence of a pre-existing diagnosis of antisocial personality, a depressive episode would be diagnosed as a secondary depression. The psychophysiologic disorders have also been studied insufficiently in relation to diagnosable psychiatric illness.

Affective episodes in patients with medical illness are probably different from primary affective disorder. A study from this laboratory (24) showed that suicide is rare as a terminal event in seriously or even fatally ill medical patients, suggesting that such affective episodes differ from those primary affective episodes usually seen by psychiatrists in which there is a considerable risk of suicide. The reported study does not resolve the dilemma of properly classifying the medical patient who develops an affective episode, but it does indicate that the questions raised are not simple.

It is not to be assumed that all primary affective disorders represent a single disease entity; e.g., bipolar manic depressive illness may be fundamentally different from unipolar illness and not merely a clinical variant. The term primary as used in this study is meant, however, to sharply differentiate primary disorders from secondary disorders. It is highly probable that secondary affective disorders do not represent a single diagnostic entity, because there are a large number of pre-existing conditions during which a secondary depression may supervene (e.g., alcoholism, hysteria, antisocial personality, homosexuality). It is possible that an occasional secondary depression is, in fact, primary, in the sense that it is totally independent of the pre-existing illness. In the latter instance, a patient would then have two independent illnesses, the pre-existing one and an independent primary depression, but we believe this circumstance to be unusual. The not insignificant prevalence of secondary affective disorders compared with primary affective disorders (see below) supports the suggestion that it is unusual to have two independent illnesses. How frequently an independent primary affective disorder occurs in association with another unrelated disorder will be estimated in this study and the other studies now being conducted and referred to above.

Description of the Study

A total of 314 patients who presented themselves or were brought to the Malcolm Bliss Mental Health Center emergency room was studied. The case selection was random; patients who appeared after eight in the morning each day were interviewed consecutively and the number of interviews completed depended on the number of research psychiatrists working that day, which varied between one and four. Interviews were done Monday through Friday. On a given day the number of patients interviewed ranged from one to six. The reason that on some days more than four patients were interviewed was that if the first or second psychiatrist had finished his morning interview, he (or they) would interview the first, or first and second, patient(s) seen in the afternoon. Patients admitted directly to St. Louis City Hospital as a consequence of a suicide attempt were also interviewed, so that our sample would be as representative as possible. (A pilot study showed that patients interviewed at the times noted above did not differ demographically or diagnostically from patients seen in the evening or on weekends.)

The interview was a systematic one in which the same information was obtained from each patient. There were 819 items in the interview, which required an average of about three hours to complete. The emergency room clinical work-up for each patient interviewed was also systematic. Consequently, the involvement and concern of the physician with the patient were assured despite the length of the interview.

The three criteria that had to be met to receive a diagnosis of affective disorder, whether primary or secondary, were the occurrence of a dysphoric or euphoric mood, the presence of a certain number of somatic and psychological symptoms, and a definite onset. For depression, presence of a dysphoric mood was noted when the patient expressed feeling "blue," sad, depressed, worried, discouraged, low, despondent, disgusted, gloomy, guilty, hopeless, fearful, anxious, or irritable. The occurrence of a dysphoric or euphoric mood for mania was noted when the patient expressed feeling happy, "tops," high, irritable, or "never better."

The symptom criteria for mania were straightforward and relatively uncomplicated and included euphoria or irritability, hyperactivity, push of speech, flight of ideas, grandiosity, distractibility, and insomnia. Euphoria or irritability was requisite to the diagnosis. If the patient also exhibited three or more of the six additional symptoms the diagnosis was "definite"; two additional symptoms resulted in a "probable" diagnosis.

The symptom criteria for depression were much more complex to deal with because the classification of depressive disorders has given rise to so much controversy that comparing studies from different investigators is difficult (4, 5, 8, 9, 11, 12, 13, 14, 16, 17, 18, 19, 38, among others). We decided that three different sets of criteria should be used as criterion symptoms for a depressive episode until further study shows the superiority of one set over the others, the interchangeability of any two or all three of the sets, or that some other set of symptoms should be used as criterion symptoms.

The S set has relatively more emphasis on "somatic" symptoms, modified only very slightly from Cassidy et al. (6) and includes:

Anorexia	Constipation
Weight loss	Slow thinking
Insomnia	Poor concentration
Feelings of fatigue	Suicidal ideas
Decreased sex interest	Agitation

If the patient exhibited six or more of these ten symptoms, the diagnosis was "definite"; five of the ten symptoms resulted in a "probable" diagnosis.

The E set has a more or less equal emphasis on somatic and psychological symptoms and includes:

Anorexia or weight loss	Agitation or retardation
Insomnia	Slow thinking or poor
Feelings of fatigue	concentration
Loss of interest in job,	Suicidal ideas or wish
social activity, or sex	to be dead
	Guilt feelings

A "definite" diagnosis was made when the patient exhibited five or more of these eight symptoms while a "probable" diagnosis was made when four of the eight were present.

The P set has relatively more emphasis on psychological symptoms and includes:

Loss of interest in job, family	Feelings of incapacity
social activities, or sex	Worthlessness
Agitation or retardation	Gloomy future
Slow thinking, poor memory,	Irritability
or poor concentration	Boredom or disgust
Suicidal ideas, plans, attempts,	Reduced social
or wish to be dead	relationships
Guilt or self-reproach	Job disability
Hopelessness, feel or fear	
never get well	

The patient who presented seven or more of these thirteen symptoms was diagnosed as "definite" and the patient presenting six of the thirteen symptoms received a "probable" diagnosis. In this last set, however, we did insist on the presence of anorexia, weight loss, or insomnia because otherwise the ubiquity of dysphoric symptoms, 72 percent of our total sample of 314, would vitiate what we were attempting. Without requiring the presence of at least one of the three specific symptoms just mentioned, we would have ended up with a large number of patients with dysphoric mood who would not qualify by clinical criteria for affective disorder. A comparison of the differences between the present and past requisite components of an affective cluster (episode) for mania and depression is shown in Table 1.

Results of the Study

There were 314 patients seen in the emergency room during the course of this study. Complaining of a dysphoric mood was not synonymous with being diagnosed affective disorder. Of the total group of 314 patients, 72 per cent

Table 1

An Affective Cluster

Mania	Depression
1. A *current* affective cluster requires *a* plus at least three symptoms from *b* plus *c*:	1. A *current* affective cluster requires *a* plus *b*:
(a) Euphoria or irritability	(a) Meeting the S, E, or P criteria (definite or probable).
(b) Hyperactivity	(b) An onset that can be dated within ± six months.
Push of speech	2. A *past* affective cluster requires all three:
Flight of ideas	1) a, b, or c; 2) d; 3) f:
Grandiosity	(a) Met the checklist criteria (definite or probable).
Distractibility	(b) Hospitalization for primarily affective symptoms.
Insomnia	(c) Suicide attempt during which period the patient exhibited primarily affective symptoms.
(c) An onset that can be dated within ± six months.	(d) An onset that can be dated within ± one year.
2. A *past* affective cluster requires all three:	(e) An offset leading to a loss of all affective symptoms or having three or less such symptoms.
1) *a, b,* or *c*; 2) *d*; 3) *e*:	
(a) See 1*a* and 1*b*.	
(b) See 1*a* and 1*b*.	
(c) Hospitalization for primarily manic symptoms.	
(d) An onset that can be dated within ± one year.	
(e) An offset leading to disappearance of all affective symptoms or having two or less such symptoms.	

complained of dysphoric mood, but this preliminary paper will concentrate on only the 39 per cent of these patients who were diagnosed as primary or secondary affective disorder (Table 2). Inclusion in this group required meeting any one of the "probable" or "definite" criteria in sets S, E, or P.

Table 2

Overall Sample: Dysphoric Mood
or Affective Disorder

Total N = 314	
Total dysphoric mood	*72%*
Total affective disorder (maximum)*	*39%*
Total affective disorder (minimum)**	*24%*
Total primary affective disorder	*21%*
Affective disorder patients with another primary diagnosis 45/236***	19%

*Meeting any one of the probable or definite symptom criteria (S, E, or P).

**Meeting all three of the probable or definite symptom criteria (S, E, and P). There were nine patients diagnosed as mania or mixed mania and depression, regardless of whether the manic or mixed episode was current or past.

***The figure 236 was the number of patients with a primary diagnosis other than affective disorder. The figure 45 was the number of secondary affective disorders.

All patients diagnosed affective disorder met the criteria of having a dysphoric mood and a clustering of symptoms. Approximately 55 per cent of patients met at least one of the symptom criteria (S, E, or P) and were primary; another one-third of the patients met these same criteria but were secondary; and in the remaining one-ninth of the patients, we were uncertain whether they were primary or secondary (Table 3). The important finding is that the ratio of primary to secondary affective disorders was 5 to 3. The secondary affective disorders occurred subsequent to the onset of many different disorders (to be discussed in detail in later publications), including alcoholism, hysteria, antisocial personality, and drug abuse.

Since approximately the same proportions of patients were considered as primary, secondary, or uncertain, and a different number of patients met criteria S, E, and P, it was important to look at the kinds of overlap among patients meeting the various criteria (Table 4). The E criteria were the least stringent. Of the 91 patients meeting the S criteria, all met the E criteria. Of the patients meeting the P criteria virtually all (98 per cent) met the E criteria. The obverse of these two findings was not true. Meeting the E criteria signified meeting the S or P criteria in only three-quarters to four-fifths of patients. This finding, that criteria E was the least stringent, was further

Table 3

Primary and Secondary Affective Disorder
Classified According to Individual
Criterion Met

	S (N = 91)	E (N = 122)	P (N = 96)
Primary	55	54	55
Secondary	32	35	32
Uncertain	13	11	13
	100%	100%	100%

Ratio primary to secondary = 5:3

Table 4

Frequency of Meeting Additional
Criteria When One Is Met

Additional Criteria	Criteria Met		
	S (N = 91)	E (N = 122)	P (N = 96)
S	—	75%	77%
E	100%	—	98%
P	81%	77%	—
Both others	81%	61%	77%

supported by the finding that only 61 per cent of patients meeting criteria E met both criteria S and P, whereas meeting criteria S or P signified that about three-quarters to four-fifths of the patients met both the other criteria. The usefulness or validity of any of these criteria will depend upon the findings at follow-up and on comparisons with the inpatient and outpatient study. The number of patients meeting criteria E (N = 122) was significantly higher than the number meeting criteria S (N = 91) or P (N = 96) (Table 4). Approximately 34 per cent more patients met criteria E than met criteria S and 27 per cent more met criteria E than criteria P.

Discussion

The present study was of patients seen in the emergency room of the Malcolm Bliss Mental Health Center (MBMHC), a state hospital that is part of the Washington University Medical School — Barnes Hospital - Renard Hospital program in psychiatry. The patients seen at MBMHC are, for the most part, medically indigent. MBMHC serves the inner city of St. Louis and the eastern one-third of Missouri. It is one of three acute treatment centers established by the state. Last year MBMHC had an average patient stay of 30 days. The reason for emphasizing the characteristics of the hospital where the study was conducted and the kinds of patients served is to point out that affective disorder, contrary to the beliefs of many (7), is a frequent syndrome among such patients, most of whom are medically indigent.

The decision to study a group of patients using the concepts of primary and secondary affective disorder was made because of the continuing discussions and the failure of replications of many studies of affective disorder that have used concepts such as reactive depression, endogenous depression, neurotic depression, psychotic depression, paranoid depression, retarded depression, and agitated depression. This general topic has been reviewed by Kendell (12), who concludes, "Yet there remains a substantial body of well conducted investigations which yield no clear answer," referring to problems of classification of depressive disorders. The use of these older concepts may explain some of the failures of replication and agreement among various investigators studying depressive disorders. Each of these classification schemes implies an etiologic judgment, uses a chief clinical manifestation for classifying as the same disorder what may be different disorders, or does not take into account pre-existing illness in the patient who may develop an affective (depressive) cluster of symptoms. The latter may explain some of the differences found in studies of therapy and differences found in the results of follow-up studies. A chronic course of some patients with an affective episode may mean only that the patient's pre-existing chronic psychiatric illness is once again more evident after the affective episode has disappeared.

The initial advantage in using primary and secondary is its simplicity. For instance, no etiologic judgments or clinical estimates of severity are necessary. A second advantage, because of the emphasis on time of onset, is that the patient's pre-existing psychiatric illness must be as carefully described as the affective episode. The careful description of the pre-existing illness means that the pre-existing illness *must* be diagnosable, i.e., must be one that a good deal is known about when studying psychiatric illness. A diagnosable illness excludes such labels as the various "personality disorders" (excepting antisocial personality which is more than merely a label) and "psychophysiologic disorders" found in DSM-II. The terms are not useful diagnostic terms and are merely labels that indicate little concerning clinical picture, laboratory findings, delimitation from other illnesses, course, and family prevalence. If these non-diagnostic terms were included as possible pre-existing disorders, then it would be difficult ever to state that an affective episode was *not* preceded by some disorder. Such a statement would depend only on the unsupported (by studies of others) judgment of the psychiatrist evaluating the affective episode.

This restriction, that the pre-existing illness must be diagnosable, does not preclude the occurrence of an affective episode in a patient who has had a number and frequency of pre-existing symptoms that do not form a diagnosable pattern. It seems the soundest policy for the present to consider such a patient as an uncertain primary or secondary affective disorder, even though the affective episode itself may be clearly diagnosable.

A possible consequence of rigorously following the primary-secondary concept is that all primary affective disorders will turn out to be a single illness differing only in manifestations at given points in time. Another possibility is that primary affective disorders will turn out to be two or three or more specific disorders differing with regard to laboratory findings, course, and family patterning. To determine which of these possibilities is correct, requires a study in time to cover the course of the illness and a study of family members to ascertain if family patterning indicates one or more illnesses.

Since there is no specific test for a primary (or secondary) affective disorder, we thought it necessary to use more than one set of criteria, especially for depressive illness, to ascertain if one set is superior to another or if there is still a fourth or fifth set, other than the S, E, and P sets that we used, that would enable us to choose initially a more homogeneous group in order to make the last four phases of our five-phase approach most productive. It is clear from the criteria that we used that a different number of patients is obtained, depending on the criteria, and there is a differing amount of overlap. In the present study 75 patients met all three criteria, S, E, and P, and 124 patients met at least the probable category of at least one set of criteria. The usefulness and validity of these criteria will be determined only by further study.

It is instructive to point out that the ratio of primary to secondary affective disorder was 5 to 3, even when such affective disorder had to meet certain (minimal) criteria. This finding strongly suggests but does not prove that another difficulty in evaluating comparative studies of treatment, prognosis, and family patterns of depressive disorders may very well be contaminated by having a mixed group of primary and secondary affective disorders who may look much the same clinically with regard to their affective disorder (29), but differ significantly and substantially with regard to the presence or absence of a pre-existing illness.

There is sufficient variation in the results reported for affective disorders to suggest that our present classification system is in need of revision. This contrasts with the situation in schizophrenia in which a number of studies are converging to give a convincing picture of the necessity for separating poor prognosis from good prognosis schizophrenia (22, 23).

Summary

A new classification system for affective disorders is proposed in which these disorders are divided into primary affective disorder and secondary affective disorder. The basis of the division is chronology: a primary affective disorder is one in which the first evidence of diagnosable psychiatric illness is an affective epiosde; a secondary affective disorder is one in which the affective episode was preceded by another diagnosable psychiatric illness.

A total of 314 patients from an emergency room was studied and depending on the criteria used for inclusion, from 91 to 122 patients were diagnosed as affective disorder; the ratio of primary to secondary affective disorder was 5 to 3. It was suggested that many of the controversies concerning affective disorder may be resolved by using the concept of primary and secondary in a rigorous manner. Work is now in progress or has been completed on inpatients, outpatients, and emergency room patients to enable us within the near future to assess the validity and productivity of this classification system.

References

1. American Psychiatric Association: Diagnostic and Statistical Manual of Mental Disorders, 2nd ed. (DSM-II). Washington, D. C., 1968.

2. Angst, J., and Perris, C.: Zur nosologie endogener depression. Vergleich der ergebnisse zweier untersuchunger. Arch. f. Psychiatrie u. Nervenkrank. 210:373–386, 1968.

3. Baker, M., Dorzab, J., Winokur, G., and Cadoret, R. J.: Depressive disease: Classification and clinical characteristics. Submitted for publication.

4. Bratfos, O., and Haug, J. O.: The course of manic-depressive psychosis. A follow-up investigation of 215 patients. Acta Psychiat. Scand. 44:89–112, 1968.

5. Carney, M. W. P., Roth, M., and Garside, R. F.: The diagnosis of depressive syndromes and the prediction of E.C.T. response. Brit. J. Psychiat. 3:659–674, 1965.

6. Cassidy, W. L., Flanagan, N. B., Spellman, M., and Cohen, M. E.: Clinical observations in manic-depressive disease. A quantitative study of one hundred manic-depressive patients and fifty medically sick controls. J.A.M.A. 164:1535–1546, 1957.

7. Dohrenwend, B. P., and Dohrenwend, B. S.: Social Status and Psychological Disorder. Wiley-Interscience: New York, 1969.

8. Gillespie, R. D.: The clinical differentiation of types of depression. Guy. Hospital Rep. 79:306–344, 1929.

9. Grinker, R. R., Sr., Miller, J., Sabshin, M., Nunn, R., and Nunnally, J. C.: The Phenomena of Depressions. New York: Paul B. Hoeber, Inc., 1961.

10. Hudgens, R. W., Robins, E., and DeLong, B. W.: The reporting of recent stress in the lives of psychiatric patients. A study of 80 hospitalized patients and 103 informants reporting the presence or absence of specified types of stress. Brit. J. Psychiat. 117:635–643, 1971.

11. Kendell, R. E.: "The Problem of Classification. In A. Coppen and A. Walk (Eds.), Recent Developments in Affective Disorders. London: Headley Brothers Ltd., 1968.

12. Kendell, R. E.: The Classification of Depressive Illness. London: Oxford University Press, 1968.

13. Kessel, N., and Holt, N. F.: Depression—An analysis of a follow-up study. Brit. J. Psychiat. 3:1143-1153, 1965.

14. Kiloh, L. G., and Garside, R. F.: The independence of neurotic depression and endogenous depression. Brit. J. Psychiat. 109:451-463, 1963.

15. Lehmann, H. E.: Psychiatric concepts of depression: Nomenclature and classification. Canad. Psychiat. Assoc. J. 4:SI-SI2, 1959.

16. Lewis, A. J.: Melancholia: A clinical survey of depressive states, J. Ment. Sci. 80:277-378, 1934.

17. McConaghy, N., Joffe, A. D., and Murphy, B.: The independence of neurotic and endogenous depression. Brit. J. Psychiat. 113:479-484, 1967.

18. Mendels, J.: Depression: The distinction between syndrome and symptom. Brit. J. Psychiat. 114:1549-1554, 1968.

19. Mendels, J., and Cochrane, C.: The nosology of depression: The endogenous-reactive concept. Amer. J. Psychiat. 124:1-11, 1968 Suppl.

20. Perris, C. (Ed.): A study of bipolar (manic-depressive) and unipolar recurrent depressive psychoses. Acta Psychiat. Scand. 42:Suppl. 194, 1-189, 1966.

21. Perris, C.: The course of depressive psychoses. Acta. Psychiat. Scand. 44:238-248, 1968.

22. Robins, E., and Guze, S. B.: Establishment of diagnostic validity in psychiatric illness: Its application to schizophrenia. Amer. J. Psychiat. 126:983-988, 1970.

23. Robins, E., and Guze, S. B.: Classification of affective disorders: The primary-secondary, the endogenous-reactive, and the neurotic-psychotic concepts. Recent Advances in the Psychobiology of the Depressive Illnesses. Proceedings of a Workshop Sponsored by NIMH, Thomas A. Williams, Martin M. Katz, and James A. Shield, Jr. (Eds.), in press.

24. Robins, E., Murphy, G. E., Wilkinson, R. H., Jr., Gassner, S., and Kayes, J.: Some clinical considerations in the prevention of suicide based on a study of 134 successful suicides. Amer. J. Publ. Health. 49:888-899, 1959.

25. Robins, L. N.: Deviant Children Grown Up. Baltimore: The Williams & Wilkins Company, 1966.

26. Rosenthal, S. H., and Gudeman, J. E.: The self-pitying constellation in depression. Brit. J. Psychiat. 113:485-489, 1967.

27. Small, I. F., Small, J. G., Alig, V. B., and Moore, D. F.: Passive-aggressive personality disorder: A search for a syndrome. Amer. J. Psychiat. 126:973-983, 1970.

28. Winokur, G. W., Clayton, P. J., and Reich, T.: Manic Depressive Illness. St. Louis: The C. V. Mosby Co., 1969.

29. Woodruff, R. A., Murphy, G. E., and Herjanic, M.: The natural history of affective disorders - I. Symptoms of 72 patients at the time of index hospital admission. J. Psychiat. Res. 5:255-263, 1967.

DISCUSSION OF
DR. ROBINS' PAPER

HEINZ E. LEHMANN, M.D.
Douglas Hospital and McGill University, Montreal

Depression has been called the most common psychiatric disorder today. Whether or not this is justified, it is a fact that close to 2 million people in the United States are treated annually for depression. That is about 1 percent of the total population. Certainly, there have never been so many depressed patients under treatment at one time. Is the incidence of depression growing? Or is this simply a phenomenon of better case finding, because doctors have been taught to recognize more depressions, and depressed patients come forth more readily, since more effective treatments are now available? Be that as it may, if most physicians are better equipped today to recognize depressions or other affective disorders, they are still far from having produced a methodology for making accurate, valid, and consistent differential diagnoses. Researchers are painfully aware of the impossibility of obtaining homogeneous samples of depressed patients in whom to investigate the incidence of observable symptoms of depression in the behavioral, experiential, and autonomic fields or its nonobservable, physical and psychodynamic substrates. Clinicians are frustrated by the low predictability of therapeutic results, again because the depressed patients they are treating constitute an almost random collection of persons who have certain symptoms in common, but seem to differ widely with respect to the basic pathological entities they represent.

Dr. Robins has been for a long time in the forefront of sober and solid research in the hotly contested field of affective disorders, and now has tackled the old differential diagnostic puzzle in this area with admirable decisiveness and sensible pragmatism. He presents us with a no-nonsense approach to this problem which has become a redoubtable conversation piece whenever several psychiatrists want to engage in an argument.

The term "primary affective disorder" is proposed by Dr. Robins to cover the patient whose history reveals either no previous psychiatric disorder or a clearly manic or depressive illness; *secondary affective disorder* is the term proposed when the history shows that a non-affective psychiatric disorder has occurred in the past. One could hardly wish for a clearer operational definition. As, Dr. Robins points out, these terms eliminate the conflict between the concepts of reactive versus endogenous, neurotic versus psychotic, or involutional melancholia versus manic-depressive disorder. The conservative psychiatrists may react with an acute sense of loss at the sudden disappearance of several important pieces from the conceptual checkerboard; those of a more activist bent may say "good riddance." Where does all this leave us?

To establish diagnostic validity with psychiatric patients, Dr. Robins has previously described five phases. They are: (1) precise clinical description, (2) laboratory studies, (3) exclusion of other syndromes, (4) follow-up studies, and (5) family studies.

He has now suggested that when these phases are applied to affective disorders, the second phase, laboratory studies, be replaced by a precise clinical description of pre-existing psychiatric disorders—obviously, because laboratory studies, which can be of diagnostic help in the differentiation of affective disorders, are still a pipe-dream. In their absence a chronological differentiation seems to him to be the best method of filling the need for a systematic approach to affective disorders at the present time. The application of the criteria for the classification of affective episodes as either primary or secondary would almost certainly distinguish very successfully between those with good and with poor prognosis.

These five operating rules brought back recollections of the structural-analytic method of psychiatric diagnosis which was developed by my old teacher, Birnbaum, and which, I think, is still unmatched for conceptual precision and conciseness as a survey of factors which determine psycho-pathology. Birnbaum also proposed five steps; these were not operating rules, however, but were the basic factors of a conceptual framework and included: (1) pathogenic, (2) pathoplastic, (3) precipitating, (4) predisposing, and (5) preformative. As an illustration, the pathogenic factor of a depression might be the hypothesized disturbance of the biogenic-amine balance in the CNS; the pathoplastic factors, the personality make-up that determines the choice of specific symptoms; the precipitating factors, the traumatic life stresses that determine the point in time at which the depression manifests itself: the predisposing factors, the hereditary potential; and the preformative factors, the cultural environment that plays an important, though less specific role than the pathoplastic factors in the shaping of symptoms.

It should be noted, however, that neither was there in Birnbaum's time nor is there today, much reliable information available on the pathogenic factors (the real causes of the functional psychoses, including the affective disorders). Because of this, Dr. Robins has chosen to eliminate any reference

to etiological factors in his new classification of affective disorders. Throughout much of the last century, as psychiatry was gradually giving structure to
its schema of psychiatric diagnosis, an intellectual battle raged between those
who insisted that the only legitimate basis of psychiatric classification was
etiology and that without adequate knowledge of etiological factors, no
psychiatric classification should even be attempted, and those who were convinced that a realistic compromise had to be made and psychopathological
symptomatology had to be accepted as a basis for psychiatric diagnosis. A
further basis for classification, the consideration of the outcome of the illness, was subsequently introduced by Kraepelin as a new and important
development, and to this, the family history and, more significantly, the
patient's own medical and psychiatric history have now been added by Dr.
Robins.

The ever-recurring question of determining the occurrence of a traumatic
life stress and its causal relation, if any, to a depression, has been somewhat
arbitrarily, but effectively, solved for our hospital by the diagnostic rule that
a depression should be called reactive only if a convincingly traumatic life
stress, which is temporally related to the onset of the depression, is revealed
within the first five minutes of the diagnostic interview. Any depressive illness
for which no clearly traumatic cause is discernible by this method and which
is not related to another co-existing psychiatric condition, is diagnosed as
manic-depressive disorder or, at the involutional age, as involutional melancholia, irrespective of whether it is the first or a recurrent depression in a
patient's life. Our underlying assumption is, of course, that the depression is
endogenous unless proven otherwise.

Dr. Robins wants to eliminate completely the controversial endogenous-
reactive dichotomy, Kendell's endogenous to reactive continuum, and Weitbrecht's nice alloy, "endo-reactive." But Robins' unambiguous procedure,
classifying depressions as primary or secondary according to the presence or
absence of a previously diagnosable psychiatric disorder, seems to me to
present difficulties because the power of sampling has been sacrificed to
precision. With the ubiquitous, almost endemic distribution of psychiatric
disorders producing varied symptoms, but often little precise diagnosability in
Robins' strict scientific sense, and resulting in conditions referred to loosely
as emotional maladjustment, inadequacy, instability, insecurity, personality
disorder (other than anti-social), etc., a large number of depressions might
have to be classified as undiagnosed when Robins' stringent criteria are applied. This would possibly replace the qualitative problem of inhomogeneous
samples with another, equally limiting quantitative one of insufficient sample
size.

In conclusion, I would think that our first need today is to refine existing
practices of diagnosing depressive conditions. Hopes of achieving this through

new methods of statistical stratification of naturally occurring samples of depressed patients have not been fulfilled. Objective, external criteria for selecting samples (biochemical, neurophysiological or psychophysiological tests) do not exist. The only other way of assuring better diagnosis and greater homogeneity of depressed patients' samples would be to upgrade our training and sophistication in psychopathology and in the art and science of making a proper psychiatric diagnosis. Speaking realistically, in the antidiagnostic psychiatric climate, currently existing on this continent, this is a practical impossibility. As all other possible methods of reshaping and restructuring the diagnosis and classification of depressed patients have failed, I personally would welcome the introduction of Dr. Robins' radical, simple, and effective method of distinguishing between primary and secondary depressions.

Lothar B. Kalinowsky

3

Lothar B. Kalinowsky:
PAUL H. HOCH AWARD
LECTURER, 1970

FRITZ A. FREYHAN, M.D.

Lothar B. Kalinowsky's name has been linked with American and international psychiatry for over three decades. His interest in the somatic treatments of mental disorders and ECT in particular has made him an outstanding authority in clinical practice, professional councils, and scientific bibliography. This is a special occasion which affords me the privilege to reminisce about him in company such as this audience.

Perhaps the nicest thing about our speaker is the fact of originality which eludes any attempt of cliché or label. At a time of super-specialization and prestigious titles, he is proud to be first and last a private practitioner. Loyal to the tradition of his academic background and beliefs, he never separated psychiatry and neurology but maintained his scientific interest and clinical proficiency in both. In this sense he can be counted as parent of Biological Psychiatry.

I cannot enumerate nor do justice to his many accomplishments as clinician, author, and untiring participant in psychiatric affairs, whether national or international in scope. I believe that he has a secret weapon to account for his accomplishments: he is a virtuoso in the mastery of time. Nothing in his day is ever routine. Office hours, lunch, dinner, weekends, and vacation serve as parts of an intricate network of work, information gathering, debate, and diplomacy. Few foreign visitors have passed through New York, let alone understood American psychiatry, without Lothar Kalinowsky's unsparing efforts as guide and interpreter. He is a prodigious writer, lecturer, and discussant. If he has a passion, if not a vice, it is the irrepressible urge to attend meetings, whatever the topic, wherever the location. We find him seated in the front rows, listening intensely, and scribbling notes. As a speaker finishes, he is usually the first to raise his arm to start the debate. These qualities have kept him young, eminently knowledgeable, and made him friend and advisor to psychiatrists throughout the world.

Born and educated in Berlin, Germany, he studied medicine in the University of Berlin, Heidelberg, and Munich. After graduating in Berlin in 1922, he spent his graduate training years in Vienna, Hamburg, and Breslau. From 1927 to 1933 he worked in the Psychiatric University Clinic in Berlin. The next six years took him to Italy where he joined the staff of the University Hospital for Nervous and Mental Diseases in Rome. In November, 1937, at this University Hospital where Lothar Kalinowsky happened to be working, the first patient was treated with ECT. In 1940 he joined the New York State Hospital system and worked at the New York State Psychiatric Institute, the Pilgrim State Hospital, and the Neurological Institute of New York. Since 1960 he has been Clinical Professor of Psychiatry at the New York Medical College.

His role in contributing to the spread of ECT and other somatic treatments in the United States is a historical fact. His eminence in this field is as unique as it is durable.

I feel delighted to introduce our Award Speaker as a man of great knowledge, skill, friendship, and compassion.

The Paul H. Hoch Award Lecture:
DEVELOPMENTS IN THE TREATMENT OF MOOD DISORDERS*

LOTHAR B. KALINOWSKY, M.D.**

When Paul Hoch's and my generation entered the field of psychiatry in the 1920's, a lecture on developments in the treatment of mood disorders could not have been delivered. Today this is the most gratifying area of treatment in psychiatry and ranks among the greatest success stories in medicine in general.

Paul Hoch was one of the first to discuss active treatment of functional psychoses and in 1930 addressed the German Psychiatric Society on such a subject (1). His paper was limited to treatment attempts in schizophrenia—suggesting that the affective psychoses were already then somewhat neglected—but he found that only the mood changes in schizophrenic patients were favorably influenced by the currently available treatments. Such observations were indicative of future developments, as treatments, introduced for schizophrenia, were limited in their effect to the mood changes of schizophrenics, and later were recognized to produce much better results in the primary disorders of mood, the affective psychoses, rather than in schizophrenia. Hoch reported that only when disturbances such as manic excitement or depressive mood were prevalent in schizophrenics did the method of continuous sleep treatment, as described by Klaesi, yield therapeutic results. Contrary to Klaesi, who considered continuous sleep treatment a predominantly psychological approach, Paul Hoch even then emphasized its probably somatic mode of action. Of particular interest is his statement that "the removal of such mood changes in schizophrenics had to be followed by extensive psychotherapy and early discharge from the hospital," a suggestion which, 40 years ago, represented remarkable foresight.

---

*The Paul Hoch Award Lecture delivered before the APPA, February 13, 1970, at the New York Hilton Hotel, New York, N.Y.
**New York Medical College.

Paul Hoch continued his research, and soon after his arrival in the United States became a pioneer in metrazol convulsive treatment, which was introduced as a treatment for schizophrenia on the basis of certain chemical observations and the assumed antagonism between epilepsy and schizophrenia. Although Hoch was able to show that the effectiveness of metrazol convulsive treatment in schizophrenia was similar to that of insulin therapy, he soon realized, like many others, that convulsive treatment produced far more spectacular results in disorders of mood, particularly in depressions. In both his training and personal interest he struck a fortunate balance between psychological and biological approaches to psychiatry, but he always stressed the superiority of biological methods in disorders of mood and, in a Semmelweis Lecture (2) before the American-Hungarian Society and elsewhere, warned against futile psychotherapeutic attempts in depressions. During our later common interest in the field of psychosurgery he was the first to recognize that frontal lobe surgery was not as ineffective in depressions as originally thought. He described a group of chronic depressives unresponsive to convulsive therapy but responding extremely well to psychosurgery. In his last clinical efforts which were mainly concerned with pharmacotherapy he was greatly interested in antidepressant drugs and, although he realized more than others the limitations of the presently available antidepressants, he always expressed the conviction that one day pharmacotherapy would be the final answer to the treatment of all psychiatric illness. Considering his lifelong interest in the area of new methods of treatment, it seems quite appropriate to choose a discussion of the various treatments for disorders of mood as the topic for this Paul Hoch Award Lecture which I am greatly honored to deliver this year.

Today a great variety of therapeutic methods is at our disposal and it is our task to select the proper method for each individual patient. Disorders of mood occur in many psychiatric disorders and their treatment largely depends on the setting in which they occur. Prototypes of the affective psychoses, the primary disorders of mood, are depression and manic elation. Their phenomenology is entirely different and it is not surprising that some treatments, particularly pharmacological agents, differ in their effect on these two contrasting moods. There are, however, treatments that affect both types of mood swings and, since depression and elation may occur in the same patient in different phases of his illness as in manic-depressive psychosis, those treatments that are directed against—and more or less successful in—both phases of the disease are, of course, of particular practical and theoretical interest. There are also cases where depression and elation are intermingled and present at the same time; it is in such patients that all of our therapeutic modalities are particularly ineffective. Whenever we encounter treatments effective in both phases of mood changes, we feel that we are one step closer to an understanding of the manic-depressive illness. Historians have reported that Hippocrates applied the same substance extracted from the plant Hellebore for depressions and manic states alike. In modern psychiatry a bipolar therapeutic effect was soon noticed in convulsive therapy, although it is obvious that depressions respond better and faster than manic states. Even more convincing than the bipolar therapeutic effect is the prophylactic value of one monthly electric convulsive treatment for both depressive and manic phases. This prophylactic monthly ECT has become unnecessary in most cases since the introduction of lithium salts, but the theoretical implications of the bipolar effect of both these treatments should be stressed.

The most prevalent disorders of mood are the depressions. A brief list of methods used to treat this condition prior to convulsive therapy reflects the conceptual changes toward mental illness in the history of psychiatry, as therapeutic suggestions alternated between psychological and somatic methods. During the last three centuries since Boerhaave aimed at a removal of the "materia melancholica" postulated by him, somatic treatment dominated the field. The Hellebore extract of Hippocrates was revived and such historical methods as blood letting, emetics, etc. were used. Later, a sedative and hypnotic effect was aimed at in the treatment of mood disorders. Even in our time the sedating, and simultaneously euphorizing effect of opium made the use of tincture of opium one of the most popular treatments of depression. Other sedatives such as bromides were also used. These therapeutic attempts diminished the suffering of the patient but did not shorten the duration of a depression. Yet in the opinion of many clinicians such an essentially symptomatic effect repeats itself with the presently used antidepressant drugs, which in many patients must be given for the entire time a depressive episode would have lasted if untreated. Opium treatment of depressions raised an interesting side issue when it was noticed that depressed patients who had received opium for a long period of time never became addicted to it. It should be stressed, however, that both opium and the subsequently used prolonged sleep treatment with barbiturates and other hypnotic drugs had a purely sedative effect in contrast to the truly antidepressive effect of modern antidepressants.

Prior to any somatic treatment for disorders of mood psychotherapy was available; however, it always played a minor role in the treatment of depression, particularly of the endogenous type. This did not change even with the development of psychoanalysis which Freud himself did not find particularly applicable to the functional psychoses. Psychoanalysts like Abraham, who made the first analytical study on depressions, and Schilder were more interested in the psychodynamic and psychopathological aspects rather than in active psychotherapy. Even today, when psychoanalytical treatment of schizophrenia generates great interest, endogenous depressions are rarely treated with the aim of relieving an acute depressive state. Psychoanalytical psychotherapy is mostly done for the purpose of preventing future episodes of the disease. There is no proof that such attempts at prevention are successful. In my own opinion, based on my clinical experience of many referrals from psychotherapists for somatic treatment, whenever a new depression develops in spite of psychotherapeutic efforts, the value of this preventive psychotherapeutic approach is questionable. Psychotherapy has its main indication in reactive depressions. As in all psychoneuroses, the choice of the type of psychotherapy will depend on the total clinical picture or, more often, on the school to which the psychiatrist belongs. Today, even if psychotherapy is chosen as the primary treatment of such a patient, the symptom of depression can and should be relieved with pharmacotherapeutic means as an adjunct to psychotherapy. It may be mentioned that the true antidepressants in psychoneurotics are often less effective than the minor tranquilizers. The rejection of any psychotropic drugs by some psychoanalysts, even in severe mood changes, must be regretted. The usefulness of supportive psychotherapy was emphasized by Paul Hoch in endogenous depressions during somatic treatment with ECT or antidepressants. However, he warned against psychotherapy alone even in mild depressions because attempts at reassurance are often misinterpreted by the depressed patient as a demand which he cannot meet, and he may easily see in this a confirmation of his own conviction that he is unable to cope with life and should not live.

It is hardly questioned today that convulsive therapy is the most reliable treatment of depression and that any other treatment methods, like antidepressant drugs, must be measured against the effectiveness of convulsive treatment. The actual use of this treatment was definitely reduced by the availability of antidepressant drugs but it is quite apparent that in many countries, including the United States, the recourse to this treatment is again on the rise. The predictable disappearance of most symptoms of a typical endogenous depression after as few as three or four ECT's is a phenomenon which, aside from its practical therapeutic value, is of great theoretical significance. The response is reliable in all types of endogenous depressions. The response is identical in manic-depressive depression, whose spontaneous course is usually limited to a few months, and in cases of involutional melancholia which may last for two or three years if untreated. ECT is particularly effective in depressions of old age which are often misdiagnosed as senile brain disease. Martin Roth (3) was the first to recognize that even if senile changes are already present, the depression of such patients may be a functional psychosis which can be removed entirely with ECT. This identical response to treatment shows convincingly that these various types of depression are actually one and the same disease. This nosological concept is further corroborated by the frequent failure of ECT in some other depressions, such as neurotic and so-called atypical depressions which will be discussed later.

The introduction of antidepressant drugs has also benefited primarily the endogenous depressions which suggests that some common denominator in pharmacological and convulsive treatments may be effective. Of the two groups of antidepressant drugs, the tricyclic antidepressants are unquestionably the more effective ones. Mild depressions should always be treated first with drugs such as imipramine or amitryptiline. Psychiatrists today rarely see a patient who has not already been placed on one of these drugs by other physicians and has failed to improve. Our first step should then be to increase the dosage because most physicians, including many psychiatrists, are unfamiliar with the adequate dosage for these drugs. However, even with sufficient dosage results have not lived up to expectations. The main advantage of drugs over ECT is that the patient who is still functioning, can go on leading his normal life during medication. The side-effects of antidepressant drugs are slightly disturbing. The group of amitryptilines interferes with working ability because it often makes the patient tired. Imipramine is better, except for the patient in the older age group, where the hypotensive effect will frequently lead to sudden falls and perhaps to more dangerous cardio-vascular manifestations. The large group of monoamine oxidase inhibitors has increasingly fallen into disfavor since the most effective representatives of this group had to be withdrawn or limited in their application because of serious liver complications or hypertensive attacks. Several statistical surveys have shown that they all are less effective than the tricyclic antidepressants and both groups of antidepressants were found to be inferior to ECT.

Today, ECT is again used extensively, particularly in hospitals well equipped for this treatment and having the assistance of anesthesiologists, this is not so much due to the findings of statistical studies comparing the various treatments but due to the clinical experience of most psychiatrists. Suicides by depressed patients who had improved only partially, regaining their initiative without losing their depressive thought content, were probably the main reason for this changed attitude towards ECT. Non-medical factors might explain why ECT is used more in this country than in some others because hospital expenses are high, insurance coverage is often limited to a few weeks, and job protection is non-existent. These factors might also explain why frequently antidepressants are not, and cannot be given for an adequate period of time. The overriding consideration is the danger of suicide, even in hospitals, where they have occurred with greater frequency in recent years. However, the incomplete improvement often produced with antidepressants cannot alone be blamed for suicides in hospitals, because the introduction of the drugs coincided with the liberalization of hospital policies providing greater freedom and privileges to only partially improved patients. This increased risk of modern psychiatric hospital management is being accepted, but it should be weighed against the often exaggerated fear of the dangers of certain other treatments. For example, ECT is not an unduly dangerous treatment in a patient threatened by suicide, which is a danger that exists in every patient suffering from an endogenous depression, especially in the older age group, where all the statistics show a steep increase in the suicide rates. During the years of unmodified ECT, danger to life was practically unknown with this treatment. Although anesthesia techniques have not diminished the danger of anesthesia, it is recognized more and more that even cardio-vascular disease is no longer a contraindication to ECT if applied with such precautions as avoiding anesthesia with barbiturates and using, as anesthesia, a short subconvulsive stimulation until muscle relaxation sets in. There is no proof that antidepressant drugs are less dangerous than ECT because the risk of their hypotensive effect must be considered in older and hypertensive patients.

When the neuroleptic drugs were first introduced, both the phenothiazines and the rauwolfia drugs were recommended in depressed patients. The use of the rauwolfia drugs was soon recognized as erroneous but the use of phenothiazines is still frequent in large mental institutions, where too often all newly admitted patients are placed on one or more phenothiazines even before any diagnosis had been made. This is not only wrong, but dangerous, because the fact is overlooked that neuroleptics have depressive symptoms as a psychiatric side-effect. This was further illustrated by a recent British report (4) on the occurrence of depressions during treatment with fluphenazine depots resulting in several suicides. Such drug-induced depressions may have to be interrupted by ECT in the same way as other drug-induced mood changes. Similar experiences had been made in treatment with ACTH or cortisone, where such drug-induced depressions were characterized by a less deep depressive affect and by a poorer response to ECT than endogenous depressions usually show.

Changes of mood in psychoneurotic patients are more difficult to treat. Biological treatments have little to offer this group of neurotic or "reactive" depressives for whom psychotherapy remains the treatment of choice. Soon after the introduction of ECT it was recognized that these patients do not show a good response even when intensive, so-called regressive ECT was tried. If psychiatrists less experienced in ECT use it as a "last resort," or, as frequently happens, if neurotic patients themselves request a trial with ECT, the outcome can be quite disheartening. The neurotic patient in whom depression is always combined with anxiety, often becomes seriously disturbed by the temporary memory impairment due to ECT and may also add other physical side-effects to his already existing psychosomatic complaints. It is this type of patient who may feel that he was permanently damaged by ECT. This does not occur in endogenous depressions; it was demonstrated by the Swedish psychiatrists Cronholm and Ottosson (5) that longer-lasting complaints of memory loss are absent in those depressions responsive to ECT. Similarly negative results, partly explained by various physical side-effects, are also frequently seen from the use of the more potent antidepressant drugs in this group of neurotic depressives, and it was already mentioned that minor tranquilizers are often more helpful in these patients. A special group are those whom West and Dally (6) classified as "atypical" depressives, characterized by hysterical and schizoid features. In these patients iproniazid (Marsalid) has an almost specific effect and is still used in Britain. It is all the more helpful as these patients, who are not suitable for psychotherapy, also respond poorly to tricyclic antidepressants and ECT.

There are psychoneurotics who experience changes of mood of an episodic nature. They probably also suffer from a second illness (an affective psychosis) which clears up under the same drug or electroconvulsive shock treatment as any other endogenous depression, while the psychoneurosis remains untouched. Mood changes, associated with an episodic occurrence of neurotic symptoms, and many acute psychosomatic complaints can also occur in some patients and were described by Foster Kennedy (7) as "manic-depressive equivalents"—a well-defined but little known disease entity which responds well to ECT.

Disorders of mood may be the predominant symptom in schizophrenics. Manic syndromes may disguise a catatonic excitement and should be treated as such. Depressed mood of a certain flatness might hide an underlying schizophrenic syndrome, and when the depressive overlay is removed with a single ECT, an acute schizophrenic symptomatology may become manifest. The same uncovering of an acute paranoid or other schizophrenic syndrome probably appears under antidepressant drugs and may explain some cases, where imipramine seems to have produced a toxic delirium but has most likely only uncovered an underlying schizophrenic psychosis.

Some disorders of mood are essentially unresponsive, both to pharmacotherapy and to convulsive therapy. There are several fairly well defined groups of patients whose treatment still remains to be discussed. In younger patients a depressive mood super-imposed on pan-anxiety may be a symptom of pseudoneurotic schizophrenia, a disease entity, delineated by Hoch and Polatin (8), which has not lost its significance, although the concept has been overextended by some psychiatrists. Pseudoneurotic schizophrenics represent a group of patients in whom an extremely chronic course of the disease often cannot be prevented by any of the available psychotherapeutic and somatic treatments. Paul Hoch demonstrated that psychosurgery was useful with these patients and their prognosis was excellent. In recent times this indication revived the use of surgical interventions in psychiatry. The effect of frontal lobe surgery on depressions had not been immediately recognized. Originally, depression had been thought to be unaffected by psychosurgery and otherwise greatly benefited psychiatric patients were reported to have committed suicide, when long after surgery a depression occurred. Later on, it was seen that so-called chronic depressives of the middle or older age group, who showed no lasting response to ECT or pharmacotherapy, lost their chronic depression after psychosurgery. Today these patients represent a definite indication for this therapeutic approach. This groups differs from other disorders of mood, especially from the affective psychoses, by showing a rather superficial depressive mood and some paranoid and particularly hypochondriacal admixture. It might be that these hypochondriacal symptoms are responsible for the good response to frontal lobe surgery. However, quite recently, the effect of these operations on depressive mood changes was underlined by an observation of Post et al. (9). They found that patients with obsessive-compulsive neuroses respond best to psychosurgery when their neurosis is accompanied by a depressive mood, while obsessive-compulsives without coexistence of depression do less well.

Since the first active treatment of disorders of mood became available with the introduction of convulsive therapy, questions have been raised about its mode of action. Today, with the variety of drugs and other treatments available, answers to these questions are as remote as ever. All somatic treatments in psychiatry were discovered empirically on the basis of certain clinical observations, such as the disappearance of psychotic symptomatology after spontaneous convulsions, the euphorizing effect of drugs used in treating tuberculosis, etc. The supposed antagonism between epilepsy and schizophrenia led to the development of convulsive therapy as a treatment for schizophrenia. Later, A. E. Bennett (10) reported its much more spectacular effect on mood disorders as depressions. The reason for this antidepressive effect remains unclear. The same must be said about the mode of action of the antidepressants. The attempt to explain the therapeutic effect of one group of antidepressants by their property of monoamine oxidase inhibition failed when the more effective tricyclic antidepressants turned out to have entirely different biochemical properties. Many different theories were postulated on the mode of action of convulsive therapy in depressions. All psychological theories could soon be disproven, when, for instance, the psychological situation of ECT application was duplicated by subconvulsive, so-called petit mal responses which remained completely ineffective if no full convulsion with tonic and clonic phase occurred. Biological theories were also disproven. At one time, when anoxemia was thought to explain the therapeutic effect of all so-called shock treatments, nitrogen treatment was unsuccessfully tried. Today all attempts to link the effect of ECT to anoxemia, muscular contractions, or a physical or psychological shock effect are disproven because present techniques of anesthesia and muscle relaxation eliminate most of these factors. Amnesia and other organic cerebral manifestations indicated by EEG changes may prove that something occurring in the brain during a convulsion is responsible for the clinical effect on disorders of mood. Many clinical and basic science research efforts have been directed toward a solution of this problem but without success. The most recent attempt consists of the study of unilateral ECT over the non-dominant hemisphere which eliminates some of the organic manifestations of ECT but is also less effective in the removal of a depression. In the absence of any explanation of the predictable effect of convulsions on depression, old theories of the epileptic seizure as a detoxifying device of the organism come to mind. It is strange that modern brain research has not picked up this old concept which is clinically so well illustrated by the mood disturbances that manifest themselves in some epileptics quite regularly for several days before one or two spontaneous seizures miraculously clear up the mood disorder until the same cycle of mood disorder and seizure sets in again. Artificially induced seizures in such epileptic mood disorders have been shown to be equally successful as spontaneous attacks in removing this organic type of depression. It is hardly possible to explain the improvement of mood disorders in terms of amnesia, in the sense of extinction of the disease-provoking, psychological experiences, because the deep depressive mood of a patient with endogenous depression normally clears up with as few as three ECT before an organic psychopathological syndrome sets in. The identical therapeutic response to electrically and pharmacologically induced seizures has been demonstrated again recently by the new inhalation convulsive treatment with Indoklon. Research studies on all convulsive treatments have become extremely rare. The study by Max Fink and his group on unilateral ECT and similar work by Cronholm and Ottosson are exceptions. In contrast, all the more research is being done in connection with pharmacotherapy in disorders of mood. Since much of this work will be discussed in other papers presented at this meeting, I will not list it here. However, I would like to make a plea that equal attention be paid to biochemical and other changes during ECT and during successful pharmacotherapy. Most promising seem to be studies on the same patient during treatment with antidepressant drugs and subsequent convulsive therapy, if this should become necessary, or identical laboratory work, when the same patient receives different types of treatment in subsequent episodes of depression.

I am aware of the heavy emphasis of my presentation on clinical experience, but I strongly feel that the differences in clinical response to the various treatments should stimulate the curiosity of research workers. There are many questions that will not be answered by large statistics but may be answered by long-term observation of individual cases studied both clinically and biochemically, in several of their episodes of mood disorders. The hope for a better understanding of the mode of action of our treatments and, even more significant, for a better understanding of the diseases we are treating with these methods, will never be fulfilled unless clinicians and basic scientists close ranks in studying all types of observation. Only such joint effort will remedy a situation expressed in a statement by Paul Hoch in 1947 as the final sentence in our first book on shock treatments. This statement, which unfortunately is still valid today, reads as follows: "At present we can say only that we are treating empirically disorders whose etiology is unknown, with methods whose action is also shrouded in mystery."

References

1. Hoch, P. H.: New trends in the treatments of schizophrenia. Allg. Ztschr. f. Psychiat., 1930.

2. Hoch, P. H.: "Depression." Proceed. Amer.-Hungar. Med. Soc. Vol. 1, 1965.

3. Roth, M.: Affective disorders arising in the senium. J. Ment. Sc. 102:141, 1956.

4. Alarcon, R. de: Severe depressive mood changes following slow-release intramuscular fluphenazine injection. Brit. Med. J. 3:564, 1969.

5. Cronholm, B., and Ottosson, J. O.: The experience of memory function after electroconvulsive therapy. Brit. J. Psychiat. 109:251, 1963.

6. West, E. D., and Dally, P. J.: Effects of iproniazid in depressive syndromes. Brit. Med. J. 1:1491 and 2:433, 1959.

7. Kennedy, F.: The neuroses. Med. Clin. N. America 28:452, 1944.

8. Hoch, P. H., and Polatin, P.: Pseudoneurotic forms of schizophrenia. Psychiat. Quart. 23:248, 1949.

9. Post, F., Rees, W. L., and Schurr, P. H.: An evaluation of bimedial leucotomy. Brit. J. Psychiat. 114:1223, 1968.

10. Bennett, A. E.: Convulsive (pentamethylenetetrazol) shock therapy in depressive psychoses. Am. J. M. Sc. 196:420, 1938.

PART II

ETIOLOGY OF
MOOD DISORDERS

4

NEUROPHARMACOLOGICAL STUDIES OF MOOD DISORDERS*

JOSEPH J. SCHILDKRAUT, M.D.**

In 1952, Sperry presented a paper on "The Biochemistry of Depressions" before this society. Impressed by the paucity of meaningful data available at that time, he discussed several possible avenues for the advancement of knowledge in this field. On the one hand, he predicted that "if a drug could be found with the ability to induce depression in human subjects, the mechanism of its action could be studied in experimental animals." Moreover, he noted, "another approach, widely used in experimental medicine, is that of studying the mechanism of action of drugs or procedures which have been shown to have a therapeutic action on patients afflicted with the disease under study (43)." Applying these approaches, in 1952, Sperry found himself limited to a discussion of some of the biochemical changes produced by benzedrine. Since then, however, the discoveries of numerous drugs which alter mood in man or are effective in the treatment of depressions have enabled investigators to apply the approaches suggested by Sperry to a wide range of pharmacological agents (31).

These studies have generated interest in the possible role of biogenic amines both in pharmacologically induced alterations of mood in man, as well as in the pathophysiology of the affective disorders—depressions and manias (29, 2, 36). This is currently a very active area of research and the extensive literature in this field has recently been reviewed elsewhere (31). At the present time it appears that the effects of drugs or electroconvulsive shock on the metabolism of biogenic amines (the catecholamines—norepinephrine and

*This work was supported in part by USPHS grant MH-15413 from the National Institute of Mental Health. I wish to thank Mrs. Carolyn Schwarz, Donna Graham and Gladys Rege for their assistance in the preparation of this manuscript.
**Harvard Medical School, Boston.

dopamine and the indoleamine–serotonin) in the brain of the experimental animal seem to correlate with the effects of these treatments on affective states in man. Of the several biogenic amines, norepinephrine has been studied most extensively, and the findings from these studies provide the most coherent body of data (31).

Antidepressants such as the monoamine oxidase inhibitors or the tricyclic compounds, stimulants such as cocaine or amphetamine, and electroconvulsive shock all cause changes in the metabolism of norepinephrine which suggest an increase of norepinephrine at central noradrenergic receptors. In contrast, reserpine-like drugs which can produce clinical depressions, or lithium salts which are effective in the treatment of manias may decrease the norepinephrine available to receptors in the brain (Table 1). These neuropharmacological findings have suggested the hypothesis that some, if not all, depressions may be associated with a functional deficiency of catecholamines, particularly norepinephrine at critical receptors in the brain, whereas manias may be associated with an excess of such amines. This formulation has been termed the "catecholamine hypothesis of affective disorders (29)."

In this paper I shall not attempt to provide another general review of the field, but instead I shall focus upon two aspects of the research in which my collaborators and I have been engaged in the past several years. First, I shall present some of our data on the effects of imipramine and other tricyclic antidepressants on the turnover and metabolism of norepinephrine in the animal brain. Emphasis will be given to the recent finding that the effects of acute and chronic administration of imipramine on norepinephrine turnover are different, as these differences may help explain the need for chronic administration of tricyclic compounds in order to obtain clinical antidepressant effects. I then shall summarize some of the findings from our clinical studies of norepinephrine metabolism in patients with affective disorders. A brief preliminary review of the metabolism and physiology of norepinephrine, therefore, may be useful.

Norepinephrine is synthesized in the neuron from the amino acid tyrosine, through the intermediates, 3, 4-dihydroxyphenylalanine (dopa) and dopamine; it is then stored in intraneuronal storage granules. Norepinephrine which is discharged onto the receptor by nerve impulses is thought to be removed from the synaptic cleft mainly by reuptake of the norepinephrine into the presynaptic neuron. A fraction of the norepinephrine present extraneuronally escapes reuptake, however, and is converted to normetanephrine by the enzyme catechol O-methyl transferase. Thus levels of normetanephrine may reflect the level of norepinephrine discharged extraneuronally onto receptors. Norepinephrine, which may be released intraneuronally (i.e., into the neuronal cytoplasm) either spontaneously or by pharmacological interference with the binding mechanism (e.g., by reserpine-

Table 1

Summary of Effects of Psychoactive Drugs and Electroconvulsive
Shock on Norepinephrine Metabolism and Mood

Drug or Treatment	Effects on Mood (Man)	Effects on Norepinephrine Metabolism in Brain (Animals)	Presumed Effect on Norepinephrine at Receptors
Monoamine Oxidase Inhibitors	Antidepressant	Inhibits deamination; increases NE; increases NMN; decreases DCM	Increase
Tranylcypromine		May discharge NE and inhibit cellular uptake of NE	
Tricyclic Antidepressants	Antidepressant	Inhibits cellular uptake of NE; increases NMN; decreases DCM	Increase
Amitriptyline		May not inhibit cellular uptake of NE; but increases NMN; decreases DCM	
Cocaine	Stimulant	Inhibits cellular uptake of NE; increases NMN; decreases DCM	Increase
Amphetamine	Stimulant	Inhibits cellular uptake of NE; discharges NE; increases NMN; decreases DCM	Increase
Electroconvulsive Shock	Counteract Depression	Increases neuronal discharge of NE; increases NMN	Increase
Reserpine	Cause Depression	Depletes NE (with intracellular deamination); decreases synthesis of NE	Decrease
Lithium Salts	Counteract Mania	Increases DCM; decreases NMN; High dose increases turnover of NE	Decrease

NE = norepinephrine; NMN = normetanephrine; DCM = deaminated catechol metabolites. Modified from Schildkraut, Schanberg, Breese, and Kopin. *Amer. J. Psychiat.* 124:600–608, 1967.

like drugs), appears to be inactivated by mitochondrial monoamine oxidase, forming the deaminated catechol metabolites, 3,4-dihydroxymandelic acid and 3,4-dihydroxyphenyl glycol, before leaving the cell. Monoamine oxidase may thus regulate tissue levels of norepinephrine without necessarily playing a role in terminating the physiological activity of norepinephrine at the receptor (Figs. 1 and 2) (1,15).

Normetanephrine and deaminated catechol metabolites may be further metabolized, and secondary deamination or O-methylation reactions involved

NORADRENERGIC NEURON AND RECEPTOR

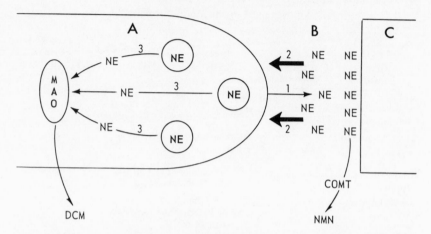

Fig. 1 Schematic representation of a noradrenergic nerve ending (A), synaptic cleft (B), and receptor (C). NE = norepinephrine, NMN = normetanephrine, DCM = deaminated catechol metabolites, COMT = catechol O-methyl transferase, MAO = monoamine oxidase (within a mitochondrion); 1 = discharge of norepinephrine into synaptic cleft and onto receptor, 2 = reuptake of norepinephrine from synaptic cleft, 3 = intracellular release of norepinephrine form storage granules into cytoplasm and onto mitochondrial monoamine oxidase. Reproduced from Schildkraut and Kety. *Science* 156: 21–30,1967.

in the formation of the deaminated O-methylated metabolites, 3-methoxy-4-hydroxymandelic acid (VMA) or 3-methoxy-4-hydroxyphenylglycol (MHPG), can occur in the central nervous system, as well as in the liver or kidney. Most MHPG present in urine is conjugated with sulfate (1). The sulfate conjugate of MHPG has recently been identified as the major metabolite of norepinephrine and normetanephrine in the rat brain (26), and studies in dogs of the origin of urinary MHPG support this finding (17).

The Effects of Imipramine and Other Tricyclic Antidepressants on the Uptake, Turnover, and Metabolism of Norepinephrine in the Rat Brain

Tricyclic antidepressants potentiate the peripheral effects of norepinephrine and serotonin under a wide variety of physiological conditions (14, 41, 24, 42, 44, 10). Various tricyclic antidepressant drugs have been found to inhibit the uptake of norepinephrine into peripheral noradrenergic neurons, and similar effects of tricyclic antidepressants on norepinephrine uptake in brain have been observed by many investigators with a variety of techniques (12, 6, 3, 28, 38). This literature has been reviewed elsewhere (31).

In our experiments we have utilized the technique of intracisternal injection in order to bypass the blood-brain barrier (27) and introduce radioactive

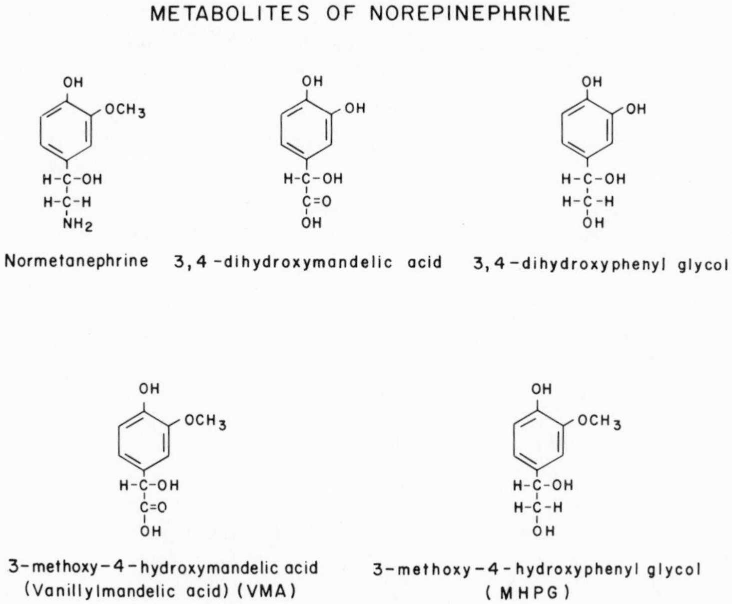

METABOLITES OF NOREPINEPHRINE

OH
OCH₃

H-C-OH
H-C-H
NH₂

Normetanephrine

OH
OH

H-C-OH
C=O
OH

3,4-dihydroxymandelic acid

OH
OH

H-C-OH
H-C-H
OH

3,4-dihydroxyphenyl glycol

OH
OCH₃

H-C-OH
C=O
OH

3-methoxy-4-hydroxymandelic acid
(Vanillylmandelic acid) (VMA)

OH
OCH₃

H-C-OH
H-C-H
OH

3-methoxy-4-hydroxyphenyl glycol
(MHPG)

Fig. 2 Metabolites of norepinephrine.

norepinephrine (norepinephrine-H^3) into the brain.* Tritiated norepinephrine injected intracisternally into the basal cisterns of the brain mixes with endogenous norepinephrine and appears to provide a representative, but not uniform, labelling of at least some stores of endogenous norepinephrine in the brain (27). After intracisternal injection of norepinephrine-H^3, the content of this amine in the brain is determined by initial neuronal uptake, as well as subsequent release and metabolism. In experiments in which drugs are administered before intracisternal injection of norepinephrine-H^3 and the animals sacrificed shortly (six minutes) thereafter, the content of tritiated norepinephrine in the brain primarily reflects the effects of the drugs on the initial neuronal uptake. It is assumed that such measurements of the uptake of exogenous norepinephrine-H^3 may provide information about the process of neuronal reuptake of endogenous norepinephrine. This process is of considerable physiological interest, since most norepinephrine which has been released from the presynaptic noradrenergic neuron is removed from the synaptic cleft (i.e., inactivated) by neuronal reuptake (see above and Fig. 1). The effects of drugs on the turnover and metabolism of norepinephrine-H^3 in the brain also

*This technique is similar to Glowinski's procedure for the intraventricular injection of norepinephrine-H^3 which he has used in his studies of the effects of psychoactive drugs on norepinephrine metabolism in brain (5).

may be studied with this technique by sacrificing animals at later times (e.g., in the present experiments animals were sacrificed 270 minutes after the intracisternal injection of norepinephrine-H^3).

When administered prior to the intracisternal injection of norepinephrine-H^3, various tricyclic antidepressant drugs inhibited the uptake of norepinephrine-H^3 in the brain, as evidenced by a lower content of cerebral norepinephrine-H^3 in animals sacrified six minutes after the intracisternal injection. At equal doses (25 mg/kg of the hydrochloride salts) acute administration of desmethylimipramine and protriptyline caused a greater inhibition of norepinephrine-H^3 uptake into the brain than did imipramine or nortriptyline (Table 2). Amitriptyline, in contrast, did not appear to inhibit norepinephrine-H^3 uptake under these conditions, but it is possible that ami-

Table 2

Effects of Tricyclic Antidepressants on the Uptake and Metabolism
of Norepinephrine-H^3 in Rat Brain

Drugs	NE-H^{3a}	NMN-H^{3b}	DCM-H^{3c}	Total DOM-H^{3d}	Free DOM-H^{3e}
	(Percent Control Mean ± SEM)				
Desmethylimipramine	71 ± 2***	196 ± 7***	52 ± 2***	102 ± 3	100 ± 6
Protriptyline	67 ± 5***	174 ± 11***	45 ± 4***	92 ± 5	98 ± 5
Imipramine	81 ± 5**	176 ± 8***	50 ± 3***	94 ± 7	100 ± 12
Nortriptyline	80 ± 3***	151 ± 6***	48 ± 2***	93 ± 3	102 ± 9
Amitriptyline	100 ± 2	123 ± 4***	74 ± 3***	95 ± 2	94 ± 5

A tricyclic antidepressant (25 mg/kg) or isotonic saline was administered 90 minutes before the intracisternal injection of norepinephrine-H^3, and animals were sacrificed 6 minutes after the intracisternal injection. In this series of experiments, the total number of animals administered each drug was: desmethylimipramine = 27; protriptyline = 6; imipramine = 6; nortriptyline = 15; amitriptyline = 29. Results for each drug were combined and are expressed as a percent of the matched control mean (100%) ± standard error of the mean.

a. NE-H^3 = norepinephrine-H^3
b. NMN-H^3 = normetanephrine-H^3
c. DCM-H^3 = tritiated deaminated catechol metabolites, i.e., 3,4-dihydroxyphenyl glycol and 3,4-dihydroxymandelic acid
d. Total DOM-H^3 = total tritiated deaminated O-methylated metabolites, i.e., 3-methoxy-4-hydroxymandelic acid (VMA), 3-methoxy-4-hydroxyphenyl glycol (MHPG), and the sulfate conjugate of MHPG
e. Free DOM-H^3 = free tritiated deaminated O-methylated metabolites, i.e., VMA and MHPG

*$p < 0.05$; **$p < 0.01$; ***$p < 0.001$ when compared with matched control mean values.

Reproduced from Schildkraut, Dodge, and Logue. *J. Psychiat. Res.* 7:29–34, 1969.

triptyline may have produced changes which were too small or too localized to be determined by the techniques used in these experiments.* In any case, since amitriptyline is metabolized to the demethylated derivative, nortriptyline, which does inhibit the uptake of norepinephrine, the inhibition of monoamine uptake may be of importance in the clinical antidepressant action of amitriptyline which requires chronic drug administration. The magnitude of the effects of these various tricyclic antidepressant drugs on norepinephrine uptake are inversely correlated with their relative sedative effects after acute administration clinically, i.e., amitriptyline is most sedative, whereas protriptyline and desmethylimipramine are least sedative (Table 2) (32).

All of the tricyclic antidepressant drugs studied under these conditions, including amitriptyline, caused statistically significant decreases in levels of tritiated deaminated catechol metabolites and increases in levels of normetanephrine-H^3 in the brain. The changes in metabolism of norepinephrine-H^3 produced by amitriptyline, however, were smaller than the changes produced by the other drugs (Table 2) (32). These findings suggest that tricyclic antidepressant drugs or their metabolites may prevent the deamination of norepinephrine by mitochondrial monoamine oxidase.

This possibility was first raised some years ago when, in clinical studies of depressed patients, we observed decreased urinary excretion of VMA, the major deaminated O-methylated metabolite of norepinephrine, during treatment with imipramine as well as with phenelzine (a monoamine oxidase inhibitor) (Table 3) (37, 35). There is some evidence from studies in vitro to suggest that tricyclic antidepressants may inhibit monoamine oxidase (23, 4, 20). While this could account for these findings, other possibilities must also be considered.

It has been suggested that tricyclic antidepressants might act at intraneuronal membranes (e.g., mitochondrial membranes) to prevent norepinephrine from interacting with monamine oxidase (37). Although this has not been directly demonstrated, it seems plausible that tricyclic antidepressants may exert actions at various neuronal membranes (presynaptic, postsynaptic, and intraneuronal) and that the effects of any given drug may depend upon the relative potencies of action at these various membrane sites (12, 3, 11, 19).

The effects of the tricyclic antidepressants on norepinephrine-H^3 uptake and metabolism in the rat brain, summarized in Table 2, were observed after the acute administration of these drugs. However, chronic administration (for about three weeks) is generally required before the initial antidepressant effects are observed in depressed patients treated with tricyclic antidepres-

---

*Some investigators have reported that norepinephrine-H^3 uptake is inhibited by amitriptyline (6). The factors which may possibly account for this discrepancy have been discussed elsewhere (33).

Table 3

Summary of Changes in VMA Excretion in Depressed Patients
during Treatment with Placebo, Phenelzine or Imipramine

Treatment Group	Number of Patients	Pretreatment (Mean VMA ± SEM)	Treatment (Mean VMA ± SEM)	P*
Placebo	5	4.54 ± 0.40	3.97 ± 0.81	N.S.
Phenelzine	6	3.54 ± 0.81	1.09 ± 0.23	<0.05
Imipramine	6	5.12 ± 0.92	2.36 ± 0.36	<0.05

In this study of VMA excretion in depressed patients, the initial "pretreatment" placebo period was followed by an "active" treatment period during which phenelzine, imipramine or placebo was administered. Mean urinary VMA excretion during each of the "active" treatments was compared with the corresponding pretreatment values. Levels of VMA excretion are reported in mg/24 hours.

*P = probability level for difference between pretreatment and treatment values.

Data from Schildkraut, Klerman, Hammond, and Friend. *J. Psychiat. Res.* 2: 257–266, 1964.

sants. It was, therefore, of interest to us to determine whether there might be differences between the effects of acute and chronic administration of tricyclic antidepressants on norepinephrine turnover and metabolism in brain that might possibly help to account for the delay in clinical effects. The following experiments were performed to study this (30, 39, 40).

In one series of experiments, imipramine hydrochloride (10 mg/kg) or isotonic saline (1 ml.) was administered by intraperitoneal injection twice daily for three weeks to male Sprague-Dawley rats. In another series of experiments, a single dose of imipramine hydrochloride (10 mg/kg) or isotonic saline (1 ml) was administered by intraperitoneal injection. Six hours after the intraperitoneal injection (the last intraperitoneal injection in the experiments on chronic drug administration), norepinephrine-H^3 was administered by intracisternal injection. Animals were sacrificed by cervical fracture six minutes after the intracisternal injection, in order to examine the effects of imipramine on the initial uptake and metabolism of norepinephrine-H^3, and 270 minutes after the intracisternal injection, in order to examine the effects of the drugs on the subsequent release and metabolism of norepinephrine-H^3 in the rat brain.

The inhibition of norepinephrine-H^3 uptake into the brain and the changes in levels of its metabolites (increased normetanephrine-H^3 and decreased tritiated deaminated catechol metabolites) were qualitatively similar after acute and chronic administration of imipramine, although some of these effects were more pronounced after chronic administration. In contrast, however, acute and chronic administration of imipramine had different effects on both the rate of disappearance of norepinephrine-H^3 from the brain and the content of endogenous norepinephrine in the brain (Tables 4 and 5).

Acute administration of imipramine appeared to slow the rate of disappearance of norepinephrine-H^3 from the brain, since animals treated with a single dose of imipramine had lower levels of norepinephrine-H^3 in the brain when compared with matched control values at the earlier time (six minutes), but higher levels of norepinephrine-H^3 than controls when examined at a later time (270 minutes) (Table 4). With chronic administration of imipramine, animals sacrificed six minutes after the intracisternal injection also had lower levels of norepinephrine-H^3 in the brain when compared with matched control values. Residual levels of norepinephrine-H^3 in the brain, however, were even lower (relative to control values) in animals treated chronically with imipramine and sacrificed 270 minutes after the intracisternal injection, indicating that after chronic administration of imipramine, the rate of disap-

Table 4

The Effects of Acutely Administered Imipramine on the Uptake
Release and Metabolism of Norepinephrine in Rat Brain

Treatment Group	Time of Sacrifice (min.)	NE-H^{3a}	NMN-H^{3b}	DCM-H^{3c}	Total DOM-H^{3d}	Free DOM-H^{3e}	Endog-enous NE
			(Percent of Control Mean ± SEM)				
Control	6	100 ± 2	100 ± 3	100 ± 4	100 ± 4	100 ± 4	100 ± 2
Imipramine	6	89 ± 3**	121 ± 6**	60 ± 3**	84 ± 4**	85 ± 5*	104 ± 3
Control	270	100 ± 3	100 ± 7	100 ± 7	100 ± 3	100 ± 4	100 ± 2
Imipramine	270	112 ± 4*	139 ± 10**	71 ± 4**	106 ± 4	96 ± 4	101 ± 2

Imipramine hydrochloride (10 mg/kg) or isotonic saline (1 ml) was administered by intraperitoneal injection. Six hours later norepinephrine-H^3 was administered by intracisternal injection. Animals were sacrificed 6 or 270 minutes after the intracisternal injection of norepinephrine-H^3. Results represent the mean of 13-16 determinations and are expressed as percents of the control means (100%) ± standard errors of the means. Control mean values (uncorrected for recoveries) from animals sacrificed 6 minutes after the norepinephrine-H^3 injection: NE-H^3 = 570 mμc/brain; NMN-H^3 = 240 mμc/brain; DCM-H^3 = 16 mμc/brain; Total DOM-H^3 = 220 mμc/brain; Free DOM-H^3 = 51 mμc/brain; Endogenous NE = 600 mμg/brain. Control mean values (uncorrected for recoveries) from animals sacrificed 270 minutes after the norepinephrine-H^3 injection: NE-H^3 = 88 mμc/brain; NMN-H^3 = 5 mμc/brain; DCM-H^3 = 2 mμc/brain; Total DOM-H^3 = 99 mμc/brain; Free DOM-H^3 = 7 mμc/brain; Endogenous NE = 590 mμg/brain.

a, b, c, d and e are defined in Table 2.

*p < 0.05 when compared with control values

**p < 0.01 when compared with control values

Reproduced from Schildkraut, Winokur, and Applegate, *Science* 168: 867-869, 1970.

Table 5

The Effects of Chronically Administered Imipramine on the Uptake, Release and Metabolism of Norepinephrine in Rat Brain

Treatment Group	Time of Sacri- fice (min.)	NE-H³ᵃ	NMN-H³ᵇ	DCM-H³ᶜ	Total DOM-H³ᵈ	Free DOM-H³ᵉ	Endog- enous NE
				(Percent of Control Mean ± SEM)			
Control	6	100 ± 3	100 ± 3	100 ± 8	100 ± 3	100 ± 3	100 ± 2
Imipramine	6	85 ± 4**	132 ± 6**	44 ± 4**	86 ± 3**	78 ± 5**	85 ± 3**
Control	270	100 ± 3	100 ± 8	100 ± 8	100 ± 4	100 ± 5	100 ± 2
Imipramine	270	80 ± 6**	118 ± 8	45 ± 5**	93 ± 4	83 ± 4*	84 ± 2**

Imipramine hydrochloride (10 mg/kg) or isotonic saline (1 ml.) was injected twice daily for three weeks. Six hours after the last drug injection, norepinephrine-H^3 was administered by intracisternal injection. Animals were sacrificed 6 or 270 minutes after the intracisternal injection of norepinephrine-H^3. Results represent the mean of 17–20 determinations and are expressed as percents of the control means (100%) ± standard errors of the means. Control mean values (uncorrected for recoveries) from animals sacrificed six minutes after the norepinephrine-H^3 injection: NE-H^3 = 650 mµc/brain; NMN-H^3 = 290 mµc/brain; DCM-H^3 = 15 mµc/brain; Total DOM-H^3 = 280 mµc/ brain; Free DOM-H^3 = 79 mµc/brain; Endogenous NE = 690 mµg/brain. Control mean values (uncorrected for recoveries) from animals sacrificed 270 minutes after the norepinephrine-H^3 injection: NE-H^3 = 136 mµc/brain; NMN-H^3 = 7 mµc/brain; DCM-H^3 = 2 mµc/brain; Total DOM-H^3 = 105 mµc/brain; Free DOM-H^3 = 8 mµc/brain; Endogenous NE = 660 mµg/brain.

a, b, c, d and e are defined in Table 2.

*p < 0.05 when compared with control values

**p < 0.01 when compared with control values

Reproduced from Schildkraut, Winokur, and Applegate. *Science*, 168: 867–869, 1970.

pearance of norepinephrine-H^3 from the brain was not slowed and possibly may have been accelerated (Table 5). Moreover, the content of endogenous norepinephrine in brain was lower after chronic administration of imipramine than after chronic administration of saline, whereas the content of endogenous norepinephrine in brain was not altered by acute administration of imipramine (Tables 4 and 5) (30, 39). We have observed similar differences in experiments comparing the effects of acute and chronic administration of the tricyclic antidepressant protriptyline (40).

The effects on the turnover of norepinephrine in brain have also been found to be different after acute and chronic administration of other drugs (13). Therefore, differences in the duration of drug administration may possibly account for some of the apparent discrepancies in the findings of various studies of the effects of tricyclic antidepressants on the turnover of norepinephrine in brain (5, 38, 18).

The effects of chronic administration of imipramine appear to develop gradually since imipramine hydrochloride (10 mg/kg), administered by intraperitoneal injection twice daily for ten days, caused changes in the turnover and content of norepinephrine in the brain which were similar to, but less pronounced than the changes seen after three weeks of treatment with this drug. Thyroid hormone, when combined with imipramine, has been reported to produce more rapid clinical improvement in depressed patients than imipramine alone (21, 22). Our preliminary experiments suggest that thyroid hormone may also accelerate the development of the changes in turnover and content of norepinephrine in the brain which are produced by chronic administration of imipramine. Norepinephrine-H^3 disappeared from the brain more rapidly and the content of endogenous norepinephrine in the brain was lower after ten days of treatment with imipramine hydrochloride (10 mg/kg, twice daily) in combination with thryoxine (375 μg/kg, daily) than after ten days of treatment with imipramine alone (Fig. 3) (40). These changes were approximately equal to or greater than the changes seen after three weeks of treatment with imipramine.

The changes in norepinephrine uptake, turnover, and metabolism (increased normetanephrine-H^3 and decreased tritiated deaminated catechol metabolites) in the rat brain after chronic administration of imipramine suggest that more norepinephrine may be made available to receptors despite the reduction in brain levels of this amine. In depressed patients (who may have a relative deficiency of norepinephrine at critical receptors in brain) (29) chronic administration of imipramine may, therefore, facilitate the restoration of normal functioning, in spite of relatively reduced levels of endogenous norepinephrine or decreased rates of discharge from presynaptic noradrenergic neurons. The decrease in the rate of disappearance of norepinephrine-H^3 from the rat brain after acute, but not after chronic administration of imipramine may also help to account for such side effects as sedation and postural hypotension which often occur during the initial period of administration of this drug and which gradually diminish with continued treatment. While further experiments will be required to explore these possibilities, the present findings do indicate that there are differences between the effects of acute and chronic administration of imipramine on norepinephrine turnover. Moreover, these findings suggest the hypothesis that, in addition to thyroxine (21, 22), other hormones and pharmacological agents or physiological and behavioral techniques (31, 34, 35), which increase the turnover of norepinephrine in the brain when administered in combination with tricyclic antidepressant drugs, may also accelerate and enhance the clinical antidepressant effects of these drugs.

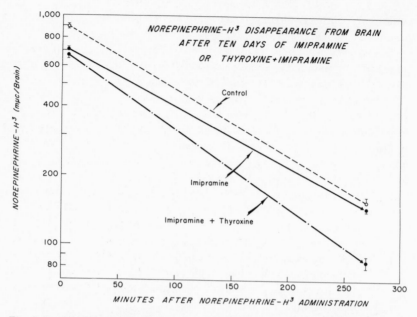

Fig. 3 Norepinephrine-H³ disappearance from brain after 10 days of imipramine or thyroxine plus imipramine. Three groups of animals were used in these experiments. All drugs were administered by intraperitoneal injection and throughout the ten day period all animals received three injections daily (of either the active drugs or the appropriate injection vehicles). One group of animals was treated with imipramine hydrochloride (10 mg/kg, twice daily) and thyroxine (375 µg/kg, once daily). Another group of animals received imipramine hydrochloride (10 mg/kg, twice daily) but no thyroxine. The control received no active drugs but only the appropriate injection vehicles. Six hours after the last drug injection, norepinephrine-H³ was administered by intracisternal injection. Animals were sacrificed 6 or 270 minutes after the intracisternal injection of norepinephrine-H³. Each point represents the mean ± SEM of 7 to 11 determinations. From Schildkraut, Winokur, Draskoczy, and Hensle. *Amer. J. Psychiat.* 127: 1032–1039, 1971.

Studies of Norepinephrine Metabolism in Patients with Depressions and Manias

In a series of longitudinal studies, the urinary excretion of catecholamines and metabolites has been examined in relation to changes in clinical state in patients with depressions or manias (35, 34, 9, 8). A gradual rise in the excretion of normetanephrine, the metabolite of norepinephrine which may reflect the level of noradrenergic activity, occurred during the period of definitive clinical improvement in a group of patients with endogenous depressions treated with imipramine (Fig. 4) (35, 34). Patients with retarded depressions had lower levels of normetanephrine excretion when depressed than after

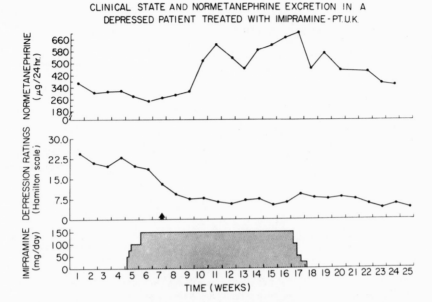

Fig. 4 Weekly change in clinical state and normetanephrine excretion in a depressed patient treated with imipramine. The arrow ↑ denotes the week of onset of definitive clinical improvement determined by each of three independent raters. Reproduced from Schildkraut, Green, Gordon, and Durell. *Amer. J. Psychiat.* 123: 690–700, 1966.

clinical remission (Table 6) (34). In contrast, increased excretion of catecholamines and metabolites including normetanephrine have been observed in manic and hypomanic patients, and the magnitudes of the normetanephrine elevations appeared to be related to the clinical severity of the hypomanic symptomatology (Tables 6 and 7) (34, 9). It thus appears from these findings that normetanephrine levels in urine are decreased in patients with retarded depressions and increased in patients with hypomania or mania.

Because of the relatively effective blood-brain barrier to normetanephrine, as well as to norepinephrine (45, 7, 26), it is probable that only a small fraction of urinary normetanephrine derives from the brain. In studies of the metabolism of normetanephrine in the rat brain we found that normetanephrine had to be deaminated in order to leave the brain. Prior treatment with pargyline, a monoamine oxidase inhibitor, almost completely prevented the conversion of normetanephrine-H^3 to other metabolites and markedly diminished the rate of disappearance of the unaltered amine in brain (Fig. 5). In these studies, the sulfate conjugate of 3-methoxy-4-hydroxyphenylglycol (MHPG) was shown to be the major metabolite of normetanephrine (as well as norepinephrine) in rat brain (Fig. 6) (26).

Table 6

Affective State and Normetanephrine Excretion

Patient	Clinical State	N (Weeks)	Mean Depression Rating	Normetanephrine Excretion (Mean ± SEM)
E.J.	Markedly Depressed	3	24.8	321 ± 9
	Normal	4	3.6	561 ± 73*
U.K.	Markedly Depressed	4	22.1	327 ± 16
	Normal	5	6.4	432 ± 39**
N.B.	Severely Depressed	2	23.6	277 ± 49
First Admission	? Trace Hypomanic	3	3.3	531 ± 23***
			Mean Mania Rating	
N.B.	Markedly Hypomanic	6	16.3	777 ± 49
Second Admission	Moderately Hypomanic	4	6.3	650 ± 43****

Normetanephrine excretion was studied in patients with retarded depressions before and after successful treatment with imipramine. Patients were receiving no psychoactive drugs at the times these data were collected. In one of these patients, a subsequent episode of hypomania occurred, and this was treated without drug administration. The patient was markedly hypomanic during the first six weeks and moderately hypomanic during the next four weeks. Levels of urinary normetanephrine excretion are reported in $\mu g/24$ hours.

*Different from pretreatment placebo (Pt. E.J.) – $p < 0.05$ (two-tailed)

**Different from pretreatment placebo (Pt. U.K.) – $p < 0.03$ (one-tailed)

***Different from pretreatment placebo (Pt. N.B.) – $p < 0.02$ (two-tailed)

****Different from markedly hypomanic and trace hypomanic periods (Pt. N.B.) – $p < 0.05$ (one-tailed)

Reproduced from Schildkraut, Green, Gordon, and Durell. *Amer. J. Psychiat.* 123: 690-700, 1966.

Other investigators have found that, in dogs, most norepinephrine originating in the brain is excreted in the urine as MHPG (17). While technical difficulties have prevented comparable studies of these routes of metabolism of norepinephrine in human brain, we have found the sulfate conjugate of MHPG to be present in the cerebrospinal fluid of man (25). The urinary excretion of MHPG may, therefore, provide a more direct index of central noradrenergic activity in man, than does any other metabolite of norepinephrine; urinary MHPG may, however, also derive in part from norepinephrine coming from the peripheral sympathetic nerves.

MHPG excretion has been reported to be lower in a diagnostically heterogeneous group of depressed patients than in a nondepressed control popula-

Table 7

Normetanephrine Excretion in Hypomanic Patients

| Patients | Drugs | Normetanephrine Excretion | | Difference* | P** |
| | | Hypomanic Period | Normothymic Period | | |
		(Mean ± SEM)			
A	Placebo-Lithium	421 ± 62 (5)	338 ± 25 (5)	+ 83	–
B	Placebo-Lithium	558 ± 75 (3)	363 ± 25 (4)	+195	<.05
C	Placebo-Lithium	556 ± 50 (8)	420 ± 50 (8)	+136	<.10
D	Placebo-Placebo	340 ± 80 (3)	208 ± 22 (3)	+132	<.20

Normetanephrine excretion was studied in hypomanic patients before (hypomanic period) and after (normothymic period) clinical remission of the hypomanic symptomatology. All patients received placebo medication during the hypomanic study period. Patient D remained on placebo throughout the study; patients A, B and C were receiving lithium carbonate during the normothymic study period. The number of 24-hour urine specimens analyzed is given in parentheses. The values for normetanephrine excretion are expressed in $\mu g/24$ hr and reported as the means ± SEM.

*Difference = hypomanic mean minus normothymic mean

**P = level of statistical significance of the difference between the hypomanic and normothymic means and is indicated only for P < 0.20.

Reproduced from Greenspan, Schildkraut, Gordon, Levy, and Durell. *Arch. Gen. Psychiat.* 21: 710–716, 1969.

tion (16). In a recent longitudinal study of a small group of depressed patients, we have found levels of MHPG in urine to be lower during the depression than after clinical remission and these values were also considerably lower than MHPG levels observed in any of the other patients in this study. Hypomanic patients, in contrast, had higher levels of MHPG excretion prior to clinical remission (Table 8) (8). The possibility that measurement of urinary MHPG may help to distinguish central from peripheral noradrenergic activity was, moreover, supported by the findings in this study that MHPG excretion was decreased during depressive episodes even in those patients with agitated depressions who may have had increased peripheral sympathetic and adrenomedullary activity, as evidenced by increased urinary levels of norepinephrine, normetanephrine, epinephrine, and metanephrine (8). These findings are thus compatible with the hypothesis that some depressions may be associated with a decrease in central noradrenergic activity (29).

Conclusions

In focusing our research on the possible role of norepinephrine in disorders of mood, we have adopted an admittedly reductionist approach to the

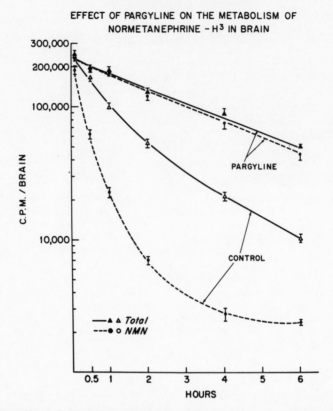

EFFECT OF PARGYLINE ON THE METABOLISM OF
NORMETANEPHRINE – H³ IN BRAIN

Fig. 5 The effect of pargyline (a monamine oxidase inhibitor) on the metabolism of normetanephrine-H³ in brain. Pargyline (75 mg/kg) or saline (control) was injected intraperitoneally 45 minutes before the intracisternal injection of normetanephrine-H³. Total radioactivity and normetanephrine-H³ were determined at various times after the intracisternal injection. Each point represents the mean ± SEM of eight determinations. Reproduced from Schanberg, Schildkraut, Breese, and Kopin. *Biochem. Pharmacol.* 17: 247–254, 1968.

problem (29). Almost invariably drugs or procedures that alter the metabolism of norepinephrine will alter the metabolism of the other biogenic amines (e.g., dopamine and serotonin), suggesting that important interactions of the biogenic amines may occur within the brain. These could occur as a result of either common chemical and pharmacological properties of the monoamines or the neuroanatomical interconnections of the monoaminergic neuronal systems (e.g., synaptic connections between noradrenergic and serotonergic neurons). Moreover, alterations in the metabolism of indoleamines as well as catecholamines have been observed in depressed patients (31).

METABOLISM OF NORMETANEPHRINE-H^3 IN BRAIN

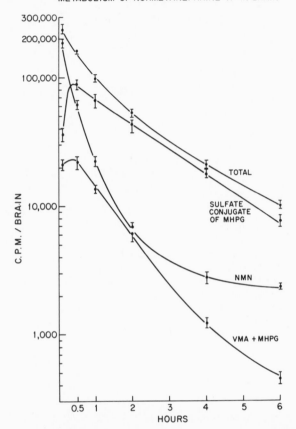

Fig. 6 Metabolism of normetanephrine-H^3 in brain. Normetanephrine-H^3 was administered by intracisternal injection and normetanephrine-H^3 and its metabolites were determined in brain at various times thereafter. Each point represents the mean ± SEM of eight determinations. NMN = normetanephrine; VMA and MHPG are defined in the text. Reproduced from Schanberg, Schildkraut, Breese, and Kopin. *Biochem. Pharmacol.* 17: 247–254, 1968.

While alterations in monoamine metabolism do seem to be associated with at least some types of affective disorders, it is unlikely that such changes in the metabolism of the biogenic amines or the activity of the monoaminergic neurons will provide a sufficient explanation for such complex biological states as these disorders of mood. It, therefore, seems reasonable to anticipate that many other concomitant biochemical, physiological, and psychological factors will have to be included in any truly comprehensive formulation (36). In the present state of our knowledge, however, it may be premature to

Table 8

MHPG Excretion in Patients Treated with Lithium Carbonate

Patients	MHPG Excretion		Difference*	P**
	Pretreatment Period	Treatment Period		
	(Mean ± SEM)			
Hypomanic Patients				
A.C.	2,750 ± 290 (4)	2,210 ± 80 (3)	+540	<.20
O.E.	2,810 ± 230 (5)	2,170 ± 200 (5)	+640	<.10
Normothymic Patients				
H.B.	2,470 ± 280 (3)	2,240 ± 290 (4)	+230	–
G.S.	2,720 ± 140 (5)	2,730 ± 370 (5)	–10	–
Agitated Depressed Patients				
W.J.	1,330 ± 210 (5)	1,580 ± 270 (5)	–250	–
C.S.	1,520 ± 50 (5)	1,940 ± 220 (5)	–420	<.20
C.O.	1,590 ± 110 (5)	2,130 ± 170 (4)	–540	<.05

MHPG excretion was studied in patients who were initially hypomanic, normothymic or depressed (agitated). All patients received placebo during the pretreatment period and lithium carbonate during the treatment period. During the treatment period all patients were clinically normothymic. The number of 24-hour urine specimens analyzed is given in parentheses. The values for MHPG excretion are expressed in μg/24 hr. and reported as the means ± SEM.

*Difference = pretreatment mean minus treatment mean

**P = level of statistical significance of the difference between the pretreatment and treatment means and is indicated only for p < 0.20.

Reproduced from Greenspan, Schildkraut, Gordon, Baer, Aronoff, and Durell, *J. Psychiat. Res.* 7:171–183, 1970.

attempt to develop such comprehensive syntheses; and, until this is possible, reductionistic hypotheses such as the catecholamine hypothesis of affective disorders (29) will continue to be of considerable heuristic value.

References

1. Axelrod, J.: Methylation reactions in the formation and metabolism of catecholamines and other biogenic amines. Pharmacol. Rev. 18:95–113, 1966.

2. Bunney, W. E., Jr., and Davis, J. M.: Norepinephrine in depressive reactions. Arch. Gen. Psychiat. 13:483–494, 1965.

3. Carlsson, A., and Waldeck, B.: Mechanism of amine transport in cell membrane of adrenergic nerves. Acta Pharmacol. 22:293–300, 1965.

4. Gabay, S., and Valcourt, A. J.: Biochemical determinants in the evaluation of monoamine oxidase inhibitors. In: Wortis, J. (Ed.): Recent Advances in Biological Psychiatry. New York, Plenum Press, 1968, Vol. 10, pp. 29–41.

5. Glowinski, J., and Axelrod, J.: Effects of drugs on the disposition of H^3-norepinephrine in the rat brain. Pharmacol. Rev. 18:775–785, 1966.

6. Glowinski, J., and Axelrod, J.: Inhibition of uptake of tritiated noradrenaline in the intact rat brain by imipramine and related compounds. Nature 204:1318–1319, 1964.

7. Glowinski, J., Kopin, I. J., and Axelrod, J.: Metabolism of [H³] norepinephrine in rat brain. J. Neurochem. 12:25–30, 1965.

8. Greenspan, K., Schildkraut, J. J., Gordon. E. K., Baer, L., Aronoff, M. S., and Durell, J.: Catecholamine metabolism in affective disorders III. MHPG and other catecholamine metabolites in patients treated with lithium carbonate. J. Psychiat. Res. 7:171–183, 1970.

9. Greenspan, K., Schildkraut, J. J., Gordon, E. K., Levy, B., and Durell, J.: Catecholamine metabolism in affective disorders II. Norepinephrine, normetanephrine, epinephrine, metanephrine and VMA excretion in hypomanic patients. Arch. Gen. Psychiat. 21:710–716, 1969.

10. Gyermek, L.: Effects of imipramine-like antidepressant agents on autonomic nervous system. In: Efron, D. H., and Kety, S. S. (Eds.): Antidepressant Drugs of Non-MAO Inhibitor Type. Workshop of Pharmacology Unit, NIMH, 1966, No. 1, pp. 41–62.

11. Haefely, W. v., Hurlimann, A., and Thoenen, H.: Scheinbar paradoxe beeinflussung von peripheren noradrenalinwirkungen durch einige thymoleptica. Helv. Physiol. Acta 22:15–33, 1964.

12. Hertting, G., Axelrod, J., and Whitby, L. G.: Effect of drugs on uptake and metabolism of H³-norepinephrine. J. Pharmacol. Exp. Ther. 134:146–153, 1961.

13. Javoy, F., Thierry, A. M., Kety, S. S., and Glowinski, J.: The effects of amphetamine on the turnover of brain norepinephrine in normal and stressed rats. Communicat. Behav. Biol. 1 (Part A): 43–48, 1968.

14. Klerman, G. L., and Cole, J. O.: Clinical pharmacology of imipramine and related antidepressant compounds. Pharmacol. Rev. 17:101–141, 1965.

15. Kopin, I. J.: Biochemical aspects of release of norepinephrine and other amines from sympathetic nerve endings. Pharmacol. Rev. 18:513–523, 1966.

16. Maas, J. W., Fawcett, J., and Dekirmenjian, H.: 3-methoxy-4-hydroxyphenylglycol (MHPG) excretion in depressive states: A pilot study. Arch. Gen. Psychiat. 19:129–134, 1968.

17. Maas, J. W., and Landis, D. H.: In vivo studies of the metabolism of norepinephrine in the central nervous system. J. Pharmacol. Exp. Ther. 163:147–162, 1968.

18. Neff, N. H., and Costa, E.: Effect of tricyclic antidepressants and chlorpromazine on brain catecholamine synthesis. In: Garattini, S., and Dukes, M.N.G. (Eds.): Antidepressant Drugs. Amsterdam, Excerpta Medica, 1967, pp. 28–34.

19. Pletscher, A.: Pharmacologic and biochemical basis of some somatic side effects of psychotropic drugs. In: Brill, H., et al. (Eds.): Neuropsychopharmacology. Amsterdam, Excerpta Medica, 1967, pp. 571–577.

20. Porter, C. C.: Personal communication.

21. Prange, A. J., Jr., Wilson, I. C., Rabon, A. M., and Lipton, M. A.: Enhancement of imipramine by triiodothyronine in unselected depressed patients. In: Cerletti, A. (Ed.): The Present Status of Psychotropic Drugs: Proceedings of the VI International Congress of the C.I.N.P., Tarragona, April, 1968. Amsterdam, Excerpta Medica International Congress Series, 1969, No. 180.

22. Prange, A. J., Jr., Wilson, I. C., Rabon, A. M., and Lipton, M. A.: Enhancement of imipramine antidepressant activity by thyroid hormone. Amer. J. Psychiat. 126:457–469, 1969.

23. Pulver, R., Exer, B., and Herrmann, B.: Einige wirkungen des N-(γ-dimethylamino-propyl)-iminodibenzyl-HC1 und seiner metabolite auf den stoffwechsel von neurohormonen. Arzneim Forsch. 10:530–533, 1960.

24. Ryall, R. W.: Effects of cocaine and antidepressant drugs on nictitating membrane of cat. Brit. J. Pharmacol. 17:339–357, 1961.

25. Schanberg, S. M., Breese, G. R., Schildkraut, J. J., Gordon, E. K., and Kopin, I. J.: 3-methoxy-4-hydroxyphenylglycol sulfate in brain and cerebrospinal fluid. Biochem. Pharmacol. 17:2006–2008, 1968.

26. Schanberg, S. M., Schildkraut, J. J., Breese, G. R., and Kopin, I. J.: Metabolism of normetanephrine-H³ in rat brain—identification of conjugated 3-methoxy-4-hydroxyphenylglycol as the major metabolite. Biochem. Pharmacol. 17:247–254, 1968.

27. Schanberg, S. M., Schildkraut, J. J., and Kopin, I. J.: The effects of pentobarbital on the fate of intracisternally administered norepinephrine-H[3]. J. Pharmacol. Exp. Ther. 157:311–318, 1967.

28. Schanberg, S. M., Schildkraut, J. J., and Kopin, I. J.: The effects of psychoactive drugs on norepinephrine-H[3] metabolism in brain. Biochem. Pharmacol. 16:393–399, 1967.

29. Schildkraut, J. J.: The catecholamine hypothesis of affective disorders: A review of supporting evidence. Amer. J. Psychiat. 122:509–522, 1965.

30. Schildkraut, J. J.: Changes in norepinephrine-H[3] (NE-H[3]) metabolism in rat brain after acute and chronic administration of tricyclic antidepressants. Federat. Proc. 28:795, 1969.

31. Schildkraut, J. J.: Neuropsychopharmacology and the Affective Disorders, Boston, Little, Brown and Co., 1970.

32. Schildkraut, J. J., Dodge, G. A., and Logue, M. A.: Effects of tricyclic antidepressants on the uptake and metabolism of intracisternally administered norepinephrine-H[3] in rat brain. J. Psychiat. Res. 7:29–34, 1969.

33. Schildkraut, J. J., Dodge, G. A., and Logue, M. A.: Preliminary findings on the effects of amitriptyline on norepinephrine-H[3] metabolism in rat brain. Dis. Nerv. Syst. (Suppl.) 30:44–46, 1969.

34. Schildkraut, J. J., Green, R., Gordon, E. K., and Durell, J.: Normetanephrine excretion and affective state in depressed patients treated with imipramine. Amer. J. Psychiat. 123:690–700, 1966.

35. Schildkraut, J. J., Gordon, E. K., and Durell, J.: Catecholamine metabolism in affective disorders I. Normetanephrine and VMA excretion in depressed patients treated with imipramine. J. Psychiat. Res. 3:213–228, 1965.

36. Schildkraut, J. J., and Kety, S. S.: Biogenic amines and emotion. Science 156:21–30, 1967.

37. Schildkraut, J. J., Klerman, G. L., Hammond, R., and Friend, D. G.: Excretion of 3-methoxy-4-hydroxymandelic acid (VMA) in depressed patients treated with antidepressant drugs. J. Psychiat. Res. 2:257–266, 1964.

38. Schildkraut, J. J., Schanberg, S. M., Breese, G. R., and Kopin, I. J.: Norepinephrine metabolism and drugs used in the affective disorders: A possible mechanism of action. Amer. J. Psychiat. 124:600–608, 1967.

39. Schildkraut, J. J., Winokur, A., and Applegate, C. W.: Norepinephrine turnover and metabolism in rat brain after long-term administration of imipramine. Science 168: 867–869, 1970.

40. Schildkraut, J. J., Winokur, A., Draskoczy, P. R., and Hensle, J. H.: The effects of chronically administered imipramine and protriptyline on the turnover and metabolism of norepinephrine in rat brain. Amer. J. Psychiat. 127: 1032–1039, 1971.

41. Sigg, E. B.: Tricyclic thymoleptic agents and some newer antidepressants. In: Efron, D. H. (Ed.): Psychopharmacology: A Review of Progress, 1957–1967: Proceedings of the sixth annual meeting of the American College of Neuropsychopharmacology. San Juan, Puerto Rico, December 12–15, 1967. Washington, D.C.: U.S. Government Printing Office, 1968. U.S. Department of Health, Education and Welfare, Public Health Service, Publication No. 1836, pp. 655–669.

42. Sigg, E. B., Soffer, L., and Gyermek, L.: Influence of imipramine and related psychoactive agents on effect of 5-hydroxytryptamine and catecholamines on cat nicitating membrane. J. Pharmacol. Exp. Ther. 142:13–20, 1963.

43. Sperry, W. M.: The biochemistry of depressions. In: Hoch, P. H., and Zubin, J. (Eds.): Depression. New York, Grune and Stratton, 1954, pp. 83–92.

44. Thoenen, H., Hurlimann, A., and Haefely, W.: Mode of action of imipramine on 5-(3'-methyl-aminopropyliden)-dibenzo [a,e] cyclohepta [1,3,5] trien hydrochloride (Ro 4–6011), new antidepressant drug, on peripheral adrenergic mechanisms. J. Pharmacol. Exp. Ther. 144:405–414, 1964.

45. Weil-Malherbe, H., Axelrod, J., and Tomchick, R.: Blood-brain barrier for adrenaline. Science 129:1226–1227, 1959.

DISCUSSION OF
DR. SCHILDKRAUT'S PAPER

ARTHUR J. PRANGE, JR., M.D.

University of North Carolina, Chapel Hill

Dr. Schildkraut's presentation today has embellished a substantial structure, the role of catecholamines in affective disorders, and Dr. Schildkraut is surely its most able spokesman. When I criticize it to some extent I criticize myself, for over the years our group has added a board here and a nail there (1, 2, 3, 4). But a critic must criticize, even when the price is self-criticism. In appraising this structure, I find that my comments can be arranged under either of two questions. First, does this intellectual edifice need remodeling? Should we add a room or change the pitch of a roof? Second, have we, or may we soon outgrow this structure altogether? Should we take its materials, all of which are in excellent condition, add some new ones, and build a larger accommodation?

Let me speak first about remodeling. For four reasons I think we should direct more attention to indoleamines. First, evidence for the catecholamine hypothesis (1, 5, 6) is still largely indirect and circumstantial, and most of it can be understood as evidence for indoles as well (7, 8, 9). Second, while I am not especially troubled by the inefficacy of racemic DOPA as an antidepressant (10)—it has limited value in Parkinsonism as well (11)—I am troubled by the low potency of the laevo form (12). Over and against this is the value of L-tryptophan as an antidepressant, and not only when combined with a MAO inhibitor (13, 14). Recently Coppen, Whybrow, and I have been able to show in a double-blind trial that L-tryptophan alone, 9 g daily, is as effective as 150 mg of imipramine (15). Perhaps tryptophan exerts effects on catecholamines, but I am bound to believe that an indole precursor will have a greater effect on indoles than on catechols. A third reason to suggest an increased appreciation for indoleamines is that from several sources there is evidence of synergism between the two amine families. They may serve neuron nets that have complementary effects on functions, such as sleep, that are disordered in

85

depression (16). Serotonergic and noradrenergic terminals may synapse with the same nerve cell (17). My fourth reason, which has only teleology to recommend it, is the unlikelihood that nature would place all her affective eggs in one amine basket. Without evidence to the contrary, a biologist looks for redundancy.

Still under the rubric of remodeling, I should like to speak more explicitly about the data that Dr. Schildkraut has just presented. He poses some tantalizing problems. The facts are that acute imipramine diminishes norepinephrine (NE) reuptake, diminishes turnover (and presumably synthesis), and has no effect on endogenous levels. Chronic imipramine diminishes reuptake, turnover is restored to normal, and endogenous levels decrease. These facts must somehow be made to match the clinical and pharmacological data. There are several possibilities.

In the acute situation diminished turnover and normal endogenous levels should lead to less NE at the post-synaptic junction. This may or may not be offset by diminished reuptake inactivation. If a reuptake block overshadows other factors, then there should be increased NE at the receptor and imipramine should begin to exert its antidepressant activity. But if this takes place in the brain, it should be true in the periphery as well. However, there are hypotensive effects. Are they perhaps due to other actions of imipramine such as its anticholinergic property? The alternative is that the balance between reuptake and diminished synthesis is negative, and that less NE reaches the receptor. This could explain peripheral hypotension, but then centrally it should lead to depression.

The solid lines in Figure 1 show the mean Hamilton Rating Scale scores over time of groups of depressed patients being treated with imipramine plus placebo. Notice that the three groups of ten patients receiving imipramine alone show a slow, steady improvement. But the point is not their improvement; the point is their failure to become worse early in treatment.

The interpretation of Dr. Schildkraut's chronic imipramine data are equally complex, and there is simply no obvious noradrenergic way at present to reconcile them with the clinical and pharmacological phenomena.

The only way out of this tangle, I think, is to adopt a point of view. A plausible one is this: that peripheral events do *not* reflect central ones. This notion can be defended on the following grounds: 1) Early in treatment when imipramine is apt to produce hypotension it does not worsen depression. 2) Later, when the drug most clearly manifests its antidepressant qualities, it does not cause hypertension. 3) MAO inhibitors are both antidepressant and antihypertensive. If our theory is right, they are proadrenergic in the brain and antiadrenergic in the periphery.

As long as we follow this assumption of brain-periphery discordance, we must disregard findings concerned with urinary normetanephrine (18),

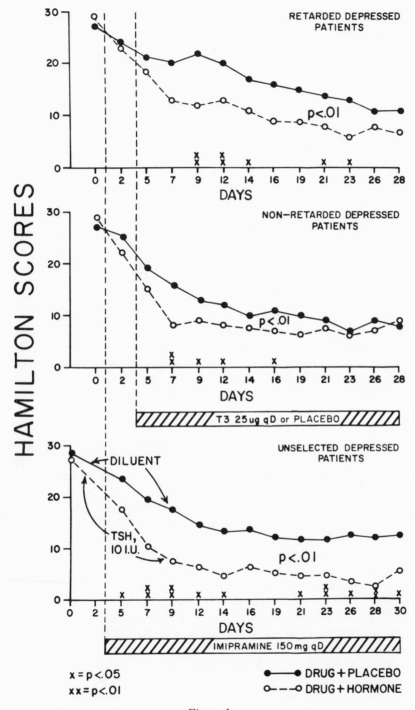

Figure 1

because all or nearly all of it comes from the periphery (19), and findings concerned with 3-methoxy-4-hydroxy phenylglycol (20), because most of it comes from the periphery (19). To my own regret, we must discount the value of NE infusion data (3). What we gain from the assumption of brain uniqueness is the right, so to speak, to assume further that after both acute and chronic imipramine administration, reuptake blockage overrides other factors. In the acute situation it overrides diminished NE synthesis; in the chronic, it overrides diminished endogenous levels. We can say that imipramine is a slow but steady antidepressant owing to its overriding proadrenergic effects. I would quickly add that this convenient interpretation is based on two assumptions, and the assumption of complete brain uniqueness is surely simple minded. What we need to know are the aspects of the brain that resemble the periphery and the aspects of brain that are different.

In any case, in the course of imipramine administration we are left to ponder the significance of early diminished NE synthesis and later diminished NE amount. These I would look upon as compensatory changes—compensatory for increased NE activity caused by the block in reuptake inactivation. The noradrenergic system says, as it were, "you are pushing too hard," and it tries to slow down. That the system can compensate seems clear. We have shown, for example, that grossly hyperthyroid animals can partly "turn off" NE, while remaining in a state of obvious hyperadrenergy (21). Conversely, hypothyroid animals can turn it on (22). In the former connection, it is interesting that thyroid hormone will augment the clinical effects of imipramine (see Figure 1) (23, 24, 25, 26). However, if low endogenous NE does represent a compensation, will there come a time when compensation is complete, when imipramine no longer produces an overall central noradrenergic push, and when patients become refractory to the drug? Moreover, when a system seems to oppose an attempt to augment its function, does this not suggest that the system itself was not hypoactive initially? When we manipulate amines are we only forcing more gasoline into a faulty engine?

All these complexities, I think, are not reasons to doubt the truth of the amine concepts, but rather their sufficiency. I would give them high grades for heuristic and explanatory value but a low grade for prediction. For example, no amine concept could have predicted some results obtained by Dr. George Breese in our laboratory.

Breese gives 6-hydroxydopamine intracisternally to rats. Three days later he finds that their brains contain only 10 per cent of normal endogenous dopamine and only 10 per cent of normal endogenous NE (27). The striking thing about these animals' behavior is that they show little change; they show no lethargy whatever. I should also remind you that if one wanted to produce depression in man by amine manipulation, one would not have a very good way of doing it. Reserpine is probably the best agent—it depletes both NE and serotonin—but it is only 15 per cent effective (28). And my final point about the probable insufficiency of amine hypotheses is that a skilled interviewer can often force a manic to abandon his flight, stop, weep, and wring his hands in anguish. This depressive episode, if I may call it such, can come and go in much less time than the half-life of any amine. Amine metabolism is simply too sluggish to account for what we observe.

This brings me to the second major consideration: the possibility that aminocentric concepts require more than remodeling, that we may need to fashion a more inclusive structure. Dr. Lipton will speak on this point in detail when he presents the paper by himself, Wilson and me later this afternoon. To pave the way, I should like to submit for your consideration what I consider to be clinical facts. You may not accept them, but we are bound to state our premises. These are among the phenomena that a comprehensive theory of affective disorders must govern.

1. There are sudden changes in patients with affective disorder—principally from mania to depression—and these changes can be momentary.
2. Affective disorders usually remit without treatment, and then they usually recur. Is this an exclusive, or even an important function of the amine processes? We have reported that depressed patients who recover on placebo treatment show an enhanced cardiovascular response to NE (3). However, we have no reason to believe that this is more than a consequence of recovery, and then only a peripheral manifestation.
3. Depressed patients are refractory to experience, good and bad, but principally good. That is why many psychiatrists are discouraged about offering them, without other treatment, their special kind of beneficently intended experience, psychotherapy. Does this inability to record experience bear any analogy to an inability to learn? If so, certain observations about the biology of learning processes might have relevance for depression.
4. Childhood bereavement seems to predispose to later depression (29). Does this observation alone require us to think of protein chemistry? Does protein chemistry furnish a link between remote experience and present malfunction?
5. The incidence of affective disorders, especially depression, is quite high in a number of endocrinopathies (30, 31, 32). Some of these endocrinopathies are not without amine effects. But when an endocrinopathy has produced electrolyte change, must we necessarily look to electrolyte effects on amines, or can we ask about direct effects of electrolytes on central neurons?
6. If mania and depression are amine opposites, why does one find in bipolar patients (33), who show the greatest genetic loading, that the patient is depressed on one occasion and manic on another?

Do patients have alternately opposite physiologic states or only alternate manifestations, perhaps through cortical elaboration, of the same midbrain disorder?

7. Just as happiness seems less readily sustained than sadness, mania is less frequent than depression. Does the relative infrequency of mania offer any clues about its relation to depression and the nature of affective disorders generally?

8. A lesson of clinical observation is that mood and cognition are inseparably linked. Thus, a frequent harbinger of impending mood disorder is the inability to concentrate. A frequent concomitant of the thought disorders, the schizophrenias, is a disorder of mood and sometimes this symptom nearly engulfs the diagnosis. In organic brain syndrome mood is labile and memory is untrustworthy. In certain endocrinopathies, notably hypothyroidism, depression and faults of cognition develop, and with treatment are relieved, pari passu (32). The term, affective disorders, emphasizes a salient complaint but one that is not invariably present (34). A theory of the syndrome will have to govern all the usual phenomena that the syndrome encompasses.

In my opinion we will not achieve a comprehensive theory until we untangle some accumulated semantic problems and until we appreciate the cybernetic aspects—i.e., the controlling functions as opposed to the doing functions—of the brain circuits that concern us. What studies of amines and of amine-active drugs have contributed is a wedge into an enormously complicated system. Students of this maze are indebted to Dr. Schildkraut for having demonstrated the complexity of their subject and for having clarified a key segment of it.

References

1. Prange, A. J., Jr.: The pharmacology and biochemistry of depression. Diseases of the Nervous System 25:217, 1964.

2. Prange, A. J., Jr., Pustrom, E., and Cochrane, C. M.: Imipramine enhancement of norepinephrine in normal humans. Psychiatry Digest 25:27, 1964.

3. Prange, A. J., Jr., McCurdy, R. L., and Cochrane, C. M.: The systolic blood pressure response of depressed patients to infused norepinephrine. Journal of Psychiatric Research 5:1, 1967.

4. Perez-Reyes, M., and Cochrane, C.: Differences in sodium thiopental susceptibility of depressed patients as evidenced by the galvanic skin reflex inhibition threshold. Journal of Psychiatric Research 5:335, 1967.

5. Schildkraut, J. J.: The catecholamine hypothesis of affective disorders: a review of supporting evidence. American Journal of Psychiatry 122:509, 1965.

6. Bunney, W. E., Jr., and David, J. M.: Norepinephrine in depressive reactions. Archives of General Psychiatry 13:483, 1965.

7. Coppen, A.: The biochemistry of affective disorders. British Journal of Psychiatry 113:1237, 1967.

8. Lapin, I. P., Oxenkrug, G. F.: Intensification of the central serotoninergic processes as a possible determinant of the thymoleptic effect. Lancet 1:132, 1969.

9. Glassman, A.: Indoleamines and affective disorders. Psychosomatic Medicine 31:107, 1969.

10. Klerman, G. L., Schildkraut, J. J., Hasenbush, L. L., Greenblatt, M., and Friend, D. G.: Clinical experience with dihydroxyphenylalanine (DOPA) in depression. Journal of Psychiatric Research 1:289, 1963.

11. Yahr, M. D., and Bering, E. A., Jr.: Parkinson's Disease: Present status and research trends. Pub. No. 1491. Washington, D.C.: Government Printing Office, 1966.

12. Bunney, W. E., Janowsky, D. S., Goodwin, F. K., Davis, J. M., Brodie, H. K. H., Murphy, D. L., and Chase, T. N.: Effect of L-DOPA on depression. Lancet 1:885, 1969.

13. Coppen, A., Shaw, D. M., Farrell, J. P.: Potentiation of the antidepressive effect of a monoamine-oxidase inhibitor by tryptophan. Lancet 284:79, 1963.

14. Glassman, A. H, and Platman, S. R.: Potentiation of a monoamine oxidase inhibitor by tryptophan. Journal of Psychiatry Research 7:83, 1969.

15. Coppen, A., Prange, A. J., Jr., and Whybrow, P. C.: In preparation.

16. Jouvet, M.: Biogenic amines and the states of sleep. Science 163:32, 1969.

17. Hillarp, N. A., Fuxe, K., Dahlström, A.: Demonstration and mapping of central neurons containing dopamine, noradrenaline, and 5-hydroxytryptamine and their reactions to psychopharmacology. Pharmacology Review 18:727, 1966.

18. Schildkraut, J. J., Gordon, E. K., Durell, J.: Catecholamine metabolism in affective disorders: normetanephrine and VMA excretion in depressed patients treated with imipramine. Journal of Psychiatric Research 3:213, 1965.

19. Maas, J. W., Landis, D. H.: In vivo studies of the metabolism of norepinephrine in the central nervous system. Journal Pharmacol. Exp. Ther. 163:147, 1968.

20. Maas, J. W., Fawcett, J., Dekirmenjian, H.: 3-methoxy-4-hydroxy phenylglycol (MHPG) excretion in depressive states. Archives of General Psychiatry 19:129, 1968.

21. Prange, A. J., Jr., Meek, J. L., and Lipton, M. A.: Catecholamines: Diminished rate of synthesis in rat brain and heart after thyroxine pretreatment. Life Sciences 9:901, 1970.

22. Lipton, M. A., Prange, A. J., Jr., Dairman, W., and Udenfried, S.: Increased rate of norepinephrine biosynthesis in hypothyroid rats. Fed. Proc. 27:399, 1968.

23. Prange, A. J., Jr., Wilson, I. C., Rabon, A. M., and Lipton, M. A.: Enhancement of imipramine by triiodothyronine in unselected depressed patients. Excerpta Medica International Congress Series, No. 180—Proceedings of the VI International Congress of the C.I.N.P., Tarragona, April 1968.

24. Prange, A. J., Jr., Wilson, I. C., Rabon, A. M., and Lipton, M. A.: Enhancement of imipramine antidepressant activity by thyroid hormone. American Journal of Psychiatry 126:457, 1969.

25. Wilson, I. C., Prange, A. J., Jr., McClane, T. K., Rabon, A. M., and Lipton, M. A.: Thyroid hormone enhancement of imipramine in non-retarded depressions. New England Journal of Medicine 282:1063, 1970.

26. Prange, A. J., Jr., Wilson, I. C., Knox, A., McClane, T. K., and Lipton, M. A.: Enhancement of imipramine by thyroid stimulating hormone. American Journal of Psychiatry 127:191, 1970.

27. Breese, G. R., and Traylor, T. D.: Effect of 6-Hydroxydopamine on brain norepinephrine and dopamine: Evidence for selective degeneration of catecholamine neurons. Journal of Pharmacology and Experimental Therapeutics 174:413, 1970.

28. Lemieux, G., Davignon, A., and Genest, J.: Depressive state during rauwolfia therapy for arterial hypertension. Canadian Medical Association 74:522, 1956.

29. Bowlby, J.: The Adolf Meyer Lecture: Childhood mourning and its implications for psychiatry. American Journal of Psychiatry 118:481, 1961.

30. Michael, R. P., and Gibbons, J. L.: Interrelationships between the endocrine system and neuropsychiatry. International Rev. Neurobiology 5:243, 1963.

31. Petersen, P.: Psychiatric disorders in primary hyperparathyroidism. Journal Clin. Endo. & Metab. 28:1491, 1968.

32. Whybrow, P. C., Prange, A. J., Jr., and Treadway, C. R.: Mental changes accompanying thyroid gland dysfunction. Archives of General Psychiatry 20:48, 1969.

33. Perris, C.: A study of bipolar (manic depressives) and unipolar recurrent depressive psychoses. Acta Psychiatrica Scandinavica 42:7, 1966.

34. Beck, A. T.: Depression. New York: Haeber Medical Division, Harper and Row, 1967.

5

CNS EFFECTS OF CONVULSIVE THERAPY: *Significance for a Theory of Depressive Psychosis**

MAX FINK, M.D.**

Theories of the biochemical changes in the central nervous system underlying functional psychoses are difficult to study in man since these changes can be measured only indirectly. The usual behavioral measures of brain function, such as memory, perception, mood, and language, are also indirect. They are difficult to record and to quantify, are discontinuous, and are either sensitive to education and to social differences or relatively invariant and insensitive to changes in brain function. Electrical activity of the central nervous system, however, is continuous, recordable, quantifiable, relatively insensitive to social and educational differences, and is sensitive to changes in alertness, thought, and attention. Of many measures of brain electrical activity, the scalp-recorded EEG has been most studied in man, and it is these data that are reviewed here and related to prevailing biochemical theories of depressive psychoses and the convulsive therapy process.

Activated EEG for Classifications of Depression

Despite much interest, neurophysiological studies of depressive illnesses fail to define characteristic signs in the resting electroencephalogram (6, 14, 82). But measures of responsivity (reactivity) of the central nervous system show extensive and characteristic differences among patients with depressive disorders, and between depressive patients and those with other mental dis-

*Supported in part by USPHS grants MH-13358 and 15561. I am indebted to the collaboration of my present associates Drs. Richard Abrams, Rhea Dornbush, Jan Volavka, Jiri Roubicek and Stanley Feldstein for the data of our ongoing studies; and to Drs. Robert L. Kahn, Max Pollack and Joseph Jaffe for much of the data from earlier studies.

**New York Medical College and the International Association for Psychiatric Research, Inc.

orders and normal states. The most studied "activation" measures are the EEG response to barbiturates and to sleep (e.g., sedation, pentothal, and sleep thresholds) and to repetitive tactile and visual stimulations (e.g., the evoked response and the recovery cycle) (4, 12, 24, 25, 26, 27, 28, 33, 34, 35, 43, 58, 70, 71, 72, 73, 74, 75, 76, 77, 78, 79).

Each index changes more rapidly and more extensively in psychotic depressive patients than in either normal subjects or neurotic depressive patients. Shagass reports that intravenous sodium amobarbital at a rate of 0.5 mg/kg/40 seconds (sedation threshold) yields an increase in EEG beta rhythm in psychotic depressive patients at less than 3.5 mg/kg amobarbital, but requires 4.0 mg/kg or more for neurotic depressive subjects. In addition, patients with low sedation thresholds improve with convulsive therapy more frequently than those with high values (70, 71, 74, 76, 77). Similar results are reported by Itil (33, 34, 35), Goldman (25, 26, 27, 28) and Claridge (4), using other EEG indices, different drugs, and different rates of administration for sedation. Studies of alphachloralose (58, 59) and methamphetamine (24), while not as striking as studies of barbiturates, exhibit similar classifications of depressed populations.*

Depressive populations assume a bimodal distribution in these studies, with psychotic depressive and neurotic depressive patients at the poles and normal subjects between. Schizophrenic patients behave more like those with neurotic depression and require larger amounts of amobarbital or pentothal for the defined neurophysiologic response, while patients with organic psychoses require lesser amounts, more like patients with psychotic depression. Perez-Reyes confirmed the sedation threshold classifications using intravenous sodium pentothal (60, 61). He reports that neurotic depressed patients require 4.0 mg/kg pentothal for GSR inhibition and 4.9 mg/kg to induce sleep, while psychotic depressed subjects require much less, 1.6 mg/kg for GSR inhibition and 2.8–3.0 mg/kg for sleep induction.

Depressive states may be classified by the rate at which cerebral electrical activity is altered by sedatives. This separation reflects the differences in central biochemical processes in the depressive states usually described as endogenous and reactive. These differences are at the least, quantitative, if not necessarily qualitative. These populations also differ in their response to induced convulsions and to antidepressants. This differential rate of change must also be related to differences in central neurochemical mechanisms. One expression is seen in the alterations in the EEG patterns with treatment.

*Peripheral activation measures (e.g., the blood pressure response to methacholine or GSR inhibition after barbiturate) are also related to the type of illness that may respond to ECT. These indices also change with successful treatment (12).

EEG Effects of ECT

Each individual seizure follows a characteristic sequence and although varying in duration is usually similar, whether the seizure is idiopathic or artificially induced by electrical or chemical means. The electrical characteristics of individual seizures are also strongly patterned and show similar records for different modes of induction. Attempts to relate seizure characteristics to post-seizure behavioral effects have generally been unsuccessful.

By contrast, the interseizure EEG provides many measures with interesting relationships to clinical behavior. Early studies of the EEG in convulsive therapy found beta activity to increase in psychotic depressed women during acute phases of their illness, to decrease with the successful clinical response to ECT, and to reappear in those patients who relapsed (32). The alpha mean frequency also decreased with treatment and after treatment, increased in those patients who sustained clinical improvement.

It is the slowing of frequencies and the appearance of delta activity, however, that is the most characteristic interseizure response. Increasing theta and delta activity, increasing amplitudes, and the appearance of burst activity are directly related to the number and the frequency of induced seizures—the greater the number and the shorter the intervals between seizures, the greater the amount of slowing, the greater the amplitudes, and the longer each burst is sustained. In depressive patients receiving three grand mal seizures a week, delta activity percent time may increase to 40 per cent with voltages over 150 μv and an average frequency of 2.5 cps after seven to nine treatments (13, 15).

In successfully treated patients, delta and slow theta activity rapidly disappear following the last seizure. Within seven to fourteen days the records usually exhibit more alpha, less beta, and some theta activity with increased amplitudes and regularity (synchronization) when compared to pre-treatment records (15, 19).

The degree of slow wave activity is related to the duration of the seizure and to the intensity and the amount of the electrical current employed. Suprathreshold alternating current induces greater degrees of slowing more rapidly than unidirectional current or either current at threshold levels (13, 30, 31).

In subconvulsive therapy, in which electrical current is passed between bitemporal electrodes for extended periods without producing a seizure, no characteristic EEG changes are observed (15, 81).

Seizures developed by biochemical means, as with intravenous pentelenetetrazole (51) or PM-1090 (5) or after the inhalant Indoklon (18, 55, 80), exhibit the usual patterned motor and neurophysiologic patterns during the

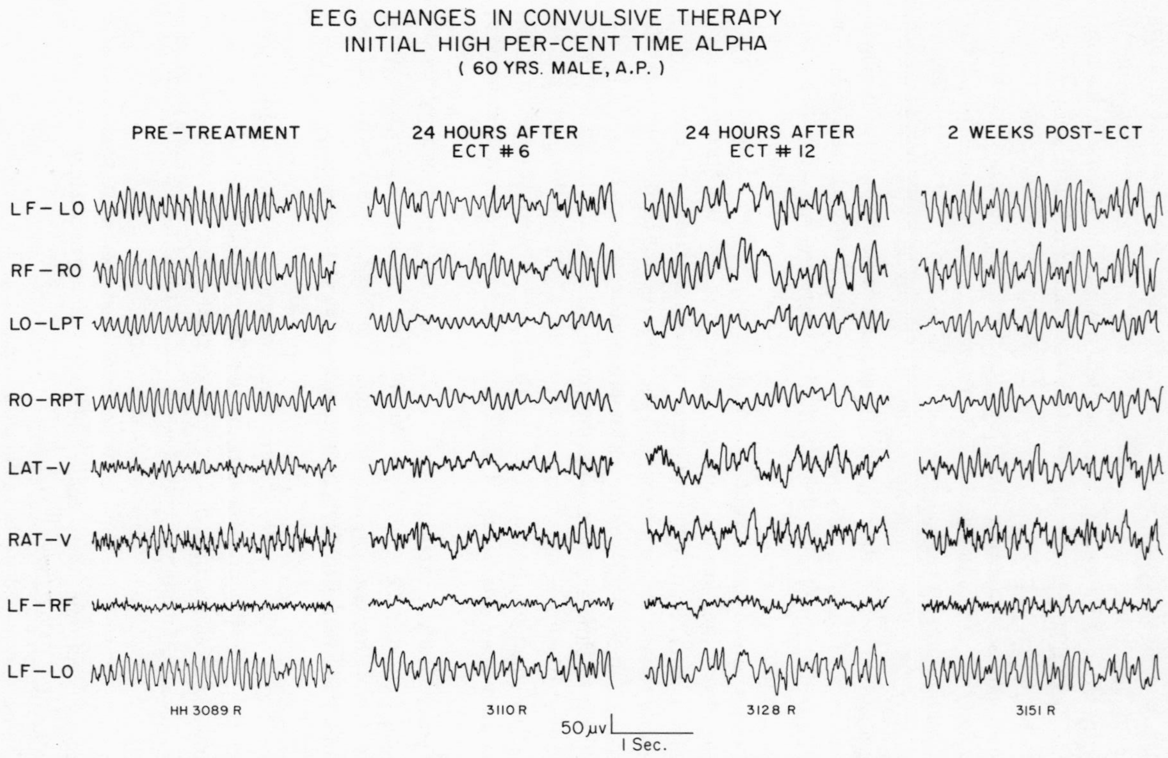

Fig. 1. EEG Changes in Convulsive Therapy. Increased slowing in all leads, with increased amplitudes. Changes are symmetric. Rapid return of alpha and decrease in slowing after two weeks.

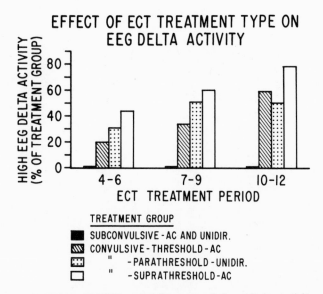

Fig. 2. Effect of ECT Electrical Current on Induced Delta Activity.

seizure.* Interseizure records are distinguishable only in degree, but not qualitatively from the electrically induced seizures. The interseizure EEG of an Indoklon convulsion is similar in the amount of slowing to a seizure induced by suprathreshold alternating currents applied bitemporally (18, 80).

An extension of these observations is seen in the electrographic studies of two recent modifications of the ECT process: unilateral electrode applications and multiple monitored seizures, In unilateral ECT, electrodes are placed over the non-dominant hemisphere and current is applied with sufficient intensity to induce a grand mal convulsion. The convulsion is usually shorter in duration than after bitemporal electrode placement and the amount of EEG slowing is less. An asymmetry in slow wave activity, with greater amplitudes and percent time theta on the side of the electrode application, has been reported.**

In multiple monitored ECT, four to eight seizures are induced at one to two minute intervals under hyper-oxygenated conditions. Blachly has described an abrupt ending to the electrical seizure in patients who have

*Although Metrazol and Indoklon both may have an initial myoclonic phase not seen with ECT (3).
**In this study a blind assessment of the laterality of interseizure records after bitemporal electrode placement exhibited 2/3 the records as asymmetric, lateralized with a greater amount of slow activity in the electrodes over the left anterior part of the head (1).

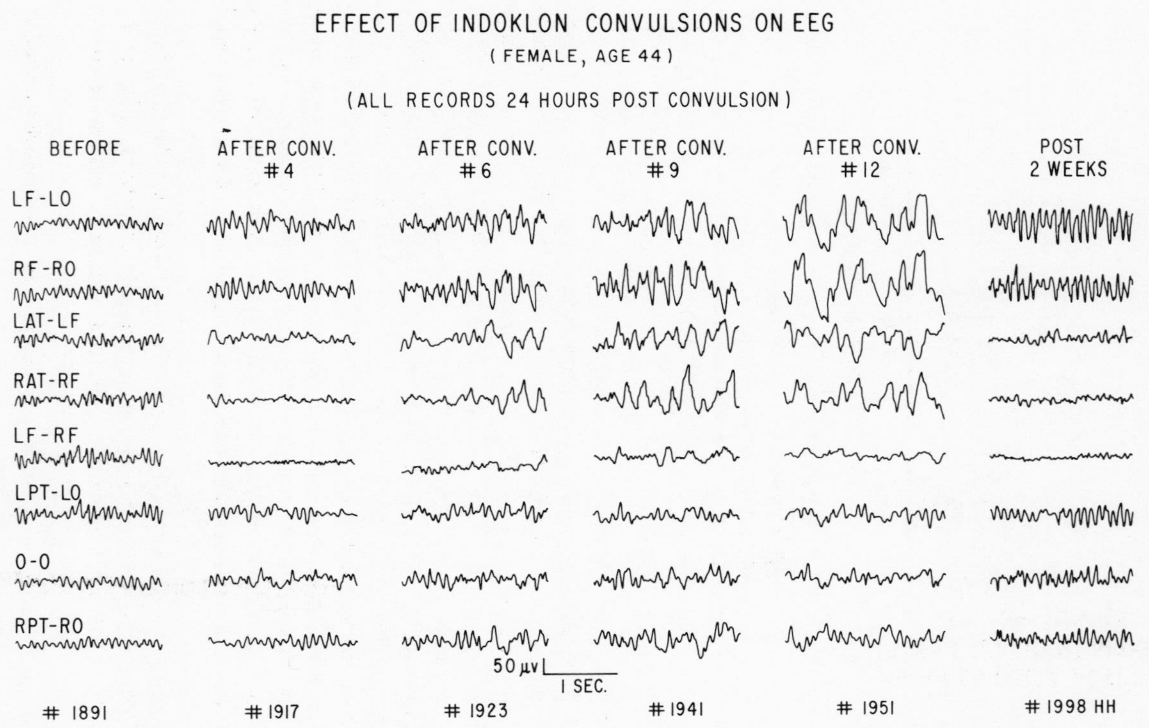

Fig. 3. Effect of Indoklon Convulsions on EEG. Changes are similar to Figure 1. Note again rapid resolutions of slowing after two weeks.

received an insufficient number of treatments, and a gradual decay of electrical activity in those who have improved. This "fit-switch" pattern is another index of altered electrical activity during treatment (2).

These studies indicate that repeated seizures yield characteristic patterns of EEG slowing and burst activity, directly related to the rate and intensity of the seizures and not to the specific mode of induction or the direct effects of the currents used (although these are contributory). But are these EEG changes, like the beta response to barbiturates, related to the behavioral effects of the therapy or to the clinical classification of subjects?

EEG Behavioral Relations

The behavioral consequences of repeated seizures are as extensive as the post-seizure EEG changes. From the point of view of treatment and clinical response, the changes in mood, thought, and the vegetative processes of sleep and appetite are the most salient and most commonly described. There are widespread changes in speech patterns, perception, memory, affect, motor activity, and libido. Indeed, almost any aspect of behavior that can be measured shows systematic changes (39, 40, 42, 54). But not all behavioral changes are observed in all subjects, for the outward expressions of the central events seem to vary with each individual personality (37, 46, 47, 62, 63). The habitual modes of adaptation, particularly the usual psychological defense mechanisms, provide a tapestry of responses to altered brain function that make up the distinguishable responses of each subject (17, 36, 37, 44). In one study of the behavioral patterns after convulsive therapy, we described four principal patterns of behavior, subsumed under the terms "euphoric-hypomanic," "somatization," "paranoid-withdrawal," and "panic" (17). These related to pretreatment psychological test performances, particularly the California "F" scale (10, 41, 48) and a "denial" score (21, 40), Rorschach characteristics (16, 41, 42, 45), and to errors on the embedded figures test (21, 39, 49). Thus, patients who exhibited the euphoric-hypomanic adaptation had higher F scale and denial scale scores, made more errors on the embedded figures tests, and reported no human movement, more color, and more popular responses on the Rorschach test than subjects with other adaptations. Paranoid-withdrawal and panic modes were associated with low F scale and denial scale scores, few errors on the embedded figures tests, and human movement and form-color responses on the Rorschach test.

The changes in behavioral response are consistent accompaniments of repeated seizures; but are the electrical and behavioral consequences directly related, or are the electrical events epiphenomena, unrelated to the behavioral expressions?

In a comparison of the amount of interseizure slow wave activity with various behavioral measures at weekly intervals during treatment, we found

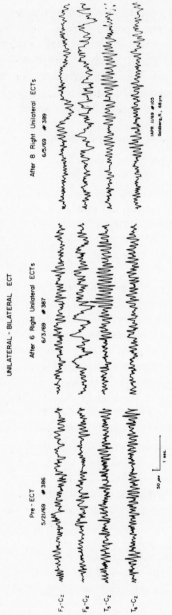

Fig. 4. Effect of Unilateral Electrode Placement on EEG. Slowing is asymmetric, and less in amount compared to bilateral electrode placement (Fig. 1).

patients with the earliest onset and the greatest amount of EEG change to exhibit the best behavioral change ratings, with the greatest increases in denial language, impairment in memory tasks, and perceptual errors (20). More refined tasks of visual stimuli, threshold electrical stimulations, (52, 53) and the attitudes reflected by the California F Scale also exhibit alterations in perceptual performance, related to the number and frequency of induced seizures, and to the degree of interseizure EEG electrical activity. These relationships may be seen not only in ECT, but in comparisons of ECT and Indoklon seizures (19). The changes in task scores are not distinguishable for the treatment types, but are related to the number of seizures. (19, 80).

But are these aspects of behavior relevant to the question of EEG-behavioral association? We did not relate measures of mood and euphoria directly to electrical events, but I would anticipate that the desired mood changes, for which ECT is usually administered, are directly associated with the observed changes in electrical activity. This association requires more study. From these experiments, we concluded that the behavioral changes accompanying repeated seizures and the interseizure EEG activity are derived from common changes in the central nervous system, with specific patterns of behavioral change dependent on the subject's adaptive repertoire or life style.

Biochemical Correlates

Is there a set of neurohumoral changes common to the convulsive therapy process, and how do these changes relate to the etiology of mood disorders?

The association between increased EEG slow wave activity and behavioral improvement should lead to an understanding of the central nervous system changes in depressive psychosis, if we had an understanding of the biochemical or neurohumoral significance of electrographic slow wave activity. Unfortunately, we have no chemical theory of EEG frequencies or frequency pattern changes that is viable, leaving the significance of these observations to be interpreted by extrapolation.

Intravenous barbiturates augment the amount, amplitude, and duration of interseizure EEG slow wave activity (29). Roth reported these changes to be predictive of behavioral improvement with ECT, noting that if pentothal augmentation of EEG slowing is not observed, behavioral improvement either fails to occur or is unsustained (67, 68).

Using amobarbital, we confirmed Roth's report of an increase in EEG slowing in successful treatment, noting in addition, characteristic changes in mood and language (40, 44). Euphoria and feelings of well-being increase, motor restlessness decreases, and denial, displacement, minimization, and repetitiveness increase. Denial adaptation patterns are clearly augmented. These observations were reported at the 1956 meeting of this Association (40).

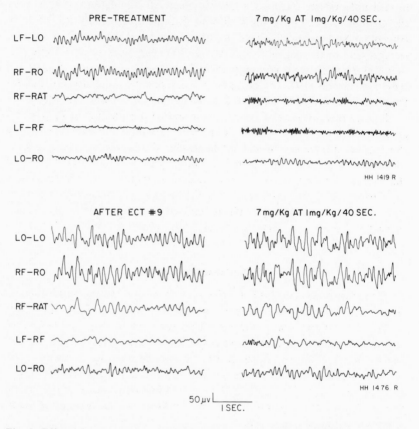

EFFECT OF INTRAVENOUS AMOBARBITAL ON EEG SLOWING
PRE-TREATMENT AND POST-CONVULSIVE
(25 YRS., FEMALE, P.C.)

PRE-TREATMENT   7 mg/Kg AT Img/Kg/40 SEC.

LF-LO

RF-RO

RF-RAT

LF-RF

LO-RO

HH 1419 R

AFTER ECT #9   7 mg/Kg AT Img/Kg/40 SEC.

LO-LO

RF-RO

RF-RAT

LF-RF

LO-RO

HH 1476 R

50 μv ⌐
I SEC.

Fig. 5. Effect of Intravenous Amobarbital. Before ECT, amobarbital elicits beta spin-dling in frontal (LF-RF) leads. After ECT (#9), spindling not seen, but slowing is augmented and amplitudes increased.

With other compounds, we observe different EEG, behavior, and language changes. Intravenous diethazine reduces EEG slowing and this change is accompanied by restlessness, discomfort, anxiety, paranoia, crying, and irrita-bility. In some subjects, the pre-ECT patterns of illness emerge (7). After benactyzine, procyclidine, imipramine, atropine, lysergide, amphetamine, and the experimental compounds, WIN-2299, JB-318 and Ditran, EEG slowing is reduced in amount and the behavioral and linguistic patterns of the illness increase (8, 9). Reductions are also seen after diphenhydramine, and antihistamine, but the principal antagonists to EEG slowing are compounds with anticholinergic potency.

The blockage of the EEG and behavioral consequences of ECT by anticholinergic drugs led to a review of the pharmacology of the central effects of seizures (11). Repeated seizures are accompanied by increased levels of acetylcholine and the cholinesterases in the cerebrospinal fluid, reflecting increased levels of these substances in interstitial fluids. These changes also occur after spontaneous seizures and after craniocerebral trauma. In an extensive review of the cholinergic aspects of convulsive therapy, I concluded, ". . . that induced convulsions, like craniocerebral trauma and spontaneous seizures, are associated with an increase in free acetylcholine in intercellular fluids, altering cerebral permeability and enhancing the appearance of cholinesterases. The level of free acetylcholine is maintained by repeated induced seizures. EEG hypersynchrony is one reflection of altered levels of acetylcholine and the altered permeability of electrolytes and other substances, including cholinesterases. The changes in interceullular electrolytes, including acetylcholine, provide the biochemical substrate for the per-

EFFECT OF IV LSD ON EEG DELTA
(FEMALE, AGE 44-24 HOUR POST CONVULSION #9)

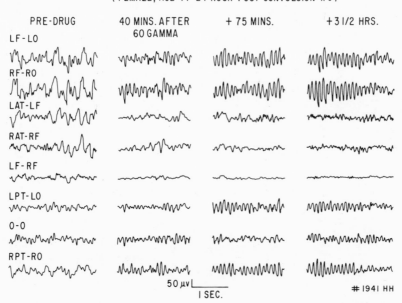

Fig. 6. Effect of LSD on EEG Slowing. Rapid decrease in slow activity and re-establishment of high voltage alpha record.

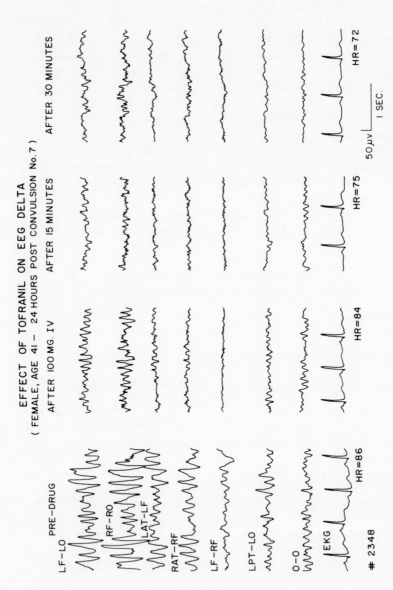

Fig. 7. Effect of imipramine on EEG Slowing. Decrease in amplitudes and in slowing without re-establishment of alpha activity. Note also fast frequencies in frontal (LF-RF) leads.

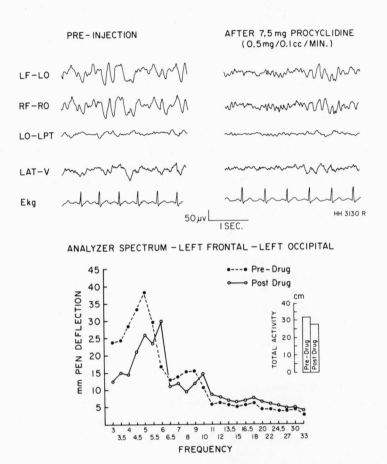

Fig. 8. Effect of Procyclidine on EEG Slowing. Similar to imipramine. Analyzer spectrum shows shift to faster frequencies (delta to theta) without amplitude increase.

sistent behavioral changes and EEG hypersynchrony following induced convulsions." (11)

This focus on cholinergic mechanisms is probably too limited. The cholinergic basis for the therapeutic effects of induced seizures may also be criticized from the vantage of the mode of action of antidepressants, particularly imipramine and desipramine. These compounds are pharmacologically described as anticholinergic, and indeed, in our essays of imipramine after

ECT, we observed that post-seizure EEG slow wave activity was inhibited by imipramine (8). A logical explanation for this apparent discrepancy is lacking.

LSD and amphetamine also reduce EEG slowing and their anticholinergic activity has not been defined (56). In spinal fluid studies, serotonin was also reported to increase after ECT (69), and it is probable that, as other neurohumors are studied, they will be found to be altered by ECT. Repeated seizures are such a massive assault on the central nervous system and have such ubiquitous effects on behavior, that it would not be surprising to find many neurohumoral systems markedly affected. The data on cholinergic mechanisms may be the result largely of the focus of the early experiments, much as the present focus is on the catecholamines.

Can these observations be related to the prevailing views of the roles of catecholamines in depressive illness? The EEG data are derived from studies in man and the chemical data from pharmacologically and physiologically distinct species, with doses of drugs that frequently far exceed the doses tolerated by man. Theories of depression focus on central norepinephrine, suggesting that the depressive state is characterized by reduced levels of norepinephrine with low turnover rates; is mimicked by reserpine; and is reversed by monoamine oxidase inhibitors and tricyclic drugs. Repeated seizures are reported to increase norepinephrine turnover rates (50, 66), sympathetic reactivity (23), and serotonin levels (22). Kety recently reported that the increase in tyrosine hydroxylase activity in the brain persisted at least 24 hours after a series of induced convulsions. These data are inconsistent with the classical views of catecholamines and acetylcholine acting in opposite directions on central receptors, and a simplistic view of competing neurohumors is undoubtedly incorrect. If we postulate a massive, nonspecific increase in various neurohumors in response to induced seizures, norepinephrine levels would increase, as has been observed for acetylcholine. Such increases in catecholamines may also be accompanied by increased EEG slow wave activity, particularly in successful treatment. A possible relation of acetylcholine and brain amine levels is found in the report of increased acetylcholine in the spinal fluid of amphetamine addicts prior to detoxification (38). The amphetamine release of norepinephrine from synaptic terminals may provide a model for acetylcholine-norepinephrine relations. Assuming ECT affects the central nervous system after its administration, these views may be tested by direct CSF measurements, studies of the EEG, and behavioral effects of a centrally active adrenergic blocking agent, such as alpha-methyldopa.

There is also the possibility that neither the cholinergic nor the catecholamine changes are critical in either the depressive process or in the effects of convulsive therapy. The criticisms of the amine hypothesis by Lipton (57) and Prange (64) are particularly cogent. The marked behavioral changes and apparent specificity of lithium in mania and studies of electrolyte changes in depression suggest that other systems must be investigated.

Discussion

In this review, I have focussed on the systematic nature of the interseizure electrical changes accompanying convulsive therapy, on the relation of these changes to clinical, behavioral, and task performance indices, and to recent biochemical views of the convulsive therapy process.

From an experimental point of view, induced convulsions act as a stressor in the "activation" paradigm, and may be used in subdividing populations for clinical and biochemical studies. In addition to the use of ratings of overt phenotypic behavior and historical data to classify depressive states, the clinical and/or the electrographic response to repeated seizures provides an important genotypic classification. Thus, I would expect subjects who exhibit distinctive interseizure EEG changes and/or clinical improvement after three to four ECT to comprise a neurophysiologically distinct group from those subjects requiring more than eight seizures for a similar neurophysiologic response. The sedation threshold, the inhibition of GSR, or the sleep threshold are useful alternatives. It is surprising that so few studies have used these activation tasks as classification devices, for their use allows the definition of more homogeneous populations for studies.

From a clinical point of view, interseizure EEG records provide a convenient and quantifiable measure of the adequacy of the course of treatment. In the absence of typical electrographic responses, the usual clinical responses may not appear, suggesting that a change in the type or rate of treatment is needed.

From a theoretical point of view, these data are consistent with two interpretations: that increased cholinergic activity is an accompaniment of the relief of psychotic depression after ECT in man and ought to be examined further in the mechanism or etiology of depressive psychosis; and, that theories of the mode of action of ECT be justified by tests of the neurophysiologic changes described here. Neurohumoral and neurophysiologic changes alone are insufficient to explain the variety of behavioral adaptations accompanying the ECT process (11, 46, 47). In our earlier reports, the psychological and sociological contributions to these expressions were encompassed in a neurophysiologic-adaptive view of the ECT process. In this view, the central nervous system biochemical changes accompanying repeated seizures are seen as necessary for the behavioral response, but not sufficient. The behavioral expressions of the induced changes in brain chemistry, such as changes in mood, affect, thought, and memory, are clearly dependent on the subject's usual modes of behavior and adaptation, expressed or exaggerated by the massive changes in neurochemistry. The neurohumoral change most implicated in the ECT process is at least an increase in interstitial acetylcholine. Continued study of this system and its relation to catechol and indole amines, as well as alterations in protein and electrolytes, is indicated.

The image of convulsive therapy parallels recent experiences and prevailing views of lithium therapy. Both ECT and lithium treatments are nonspecific, eliciting extensive neuropharmacological effects which are viewed over-simply for study purposes. Therapy is effective for a well-defined population, but proponents insist on extending the population of study and then criticize the therapy as inadequate for the complications that ensue or for expectations that are unfulfilled (i.e., ECT in schizophrenia and lithium in depression). Both therapies are accompanied by an increase in EEG slow frequencies, although the degree of change is more marked with induced seizures. For lithium therapy, perhaps, more extensive pharmacological and psychological studies are needed to provide a hypothesis parallel to the neurophysiologic-adaptive view of the ECT process. In the historical perspective of both therapies, we need longitudinal biochemical, neurophysiologic, and psychological studies focussed on the most responsive populations. Such studies will improve our understanding of the relation of brain function and behavior, particularly the unique, subtle aspects of clinical psychopathology. Ideally, more focussed and specific ways of altering brain function must be sought, which are less massive in their biochemical effects than repeated seizures or gross ionic disequilibria.

SUMMARY

Studies of the persistent electrical changes in the central nervous system accompanying repeated induced seizures for the therapy of depressive mood disorders are reviewed. Characteristic changes in EEG activity (e.g., increased slowing, amplitudes, and burst activity; decreased beta activity) accompany successful convulsive therapy. The rate and degree of EEG change is directly related to the number and frequency of seizures but less to the type of induction or to the underlying neurohumoral organization of the central nervous system. Differences in central organization may be identified by activated electroencephalography, with barbiturates as the most common stressor. Repeated convulsions are suggested as an activation stressor to separate distinctive depressive populations, a classification usually described clinically as "endogenous" and "reactive" depressions. Observations on the influence of a wide variety of "antagonists" on the interseizure EEG suggest that an increase in central cholinergic activity is a necessary, though not sufficient, condition for improvement in ECT. The relation of changes in other neurohumors to changes in acetylcholine and to clinical behavior requires study for an understanding of the convulsive therapy process. The relation of EEG changes to personality and social characteristics of subjects is described in the neurophysiologic-adaptive view of the mode of action of that process.

References

1. Abrams, R., Volavka, J., Roubicek, J., and Fink, M. Lateralized EEG Changes after Unilateral and Bilateral Electroconvulsive Therapy. Dis. Nerv. Syst. 31 (Suppl.) 28–33, 1970.

2. Blachly, P., and Gowing, D. Multiple Monitored Electroconvulsive Treatment. Comp. Psychiat., 7: 100–109, 1966.

3. Chatrian, G. E., and Peterson, M. C. The Convulsive Patterns Provoked by Indoklon, Metrazol and Electro-shock. Some Depth Electrographic Observations in Human Patients. Electroenceph. clin. Neurophysiol., 11: 844–845, 1959.

4. Claridge, G. S. Personality and Arousal. Pergamon Press, Oxford, 1967.

5. Edwalds, R. M. Experimental Studies with PM 1090. Int. Rec. Med. G. P. Clin., 169: 469–472, 1956.

6. Ellingson, R. J. Brain Waves and Problems of Psychology. Psychol. Bull., 53: 1–34, 1956.

7. Fink, M. Effects of Anticholinergic Agent, Diethazine, on EEG and Behavior: Significance for Theory of Convulsive Therapy. Arch. Neurol. Psychiat. (Chic.), 80: 380–387, 1958.

8. Fink, M. Electroencephalographic and Behavioral Effects of Tofranil. Canad. Psych. Assn. Jour., 4: 166S–171S, 1959.

9. Fink, M. Effect of Anticholinergic Compounds on Post-Convulsive EEG and Behavior of Psychiatric Patients. Electroenceph. clin. Neurophysiol., 12: 359–369, 1960.

10. Fink, M. Prediction of Individual Patient Response to Convulsive Therapy. VA Cooperative Chemotherapy Studies in Psychiatry, 6: 317–324, 1961.

11. Fink, M. Cholinergic Aspects of Convulsive Therapy. J. Nerv. Ment. Dis., 142: 475–484, 1966.

12. Fink, M. Neurophysiological Response Strategies in the Classification of Mental Illness, In The Role of Methodology of Classification in Psychiatry and Psychopathology, Katz, M. M., Cole, J. O., and Barton, W. E. (eds.), Government Printing Office, Washington, D.C., pp. 535–540, 1968.

13. Fink, M., and Green, M. Electroencephalographic Correlates of the Electroshock Process. Dis. Nerv. Syst., 19: 277, 1958.

14. Fink, M., Itil, T., and Clyde, D. Classification of Psychosis by Quantitative EEG Measures. In Recent Advances in Biological Psychiatry, Wortis, J. (ed.), Plenum Press, New York, 8: 305–312, 1966.

15. Fink, M., and Kahn, R. L. Relation of EEG Delta Activity to Behavioral Response in Electroshock: Quantitative Serial Studies. Arch. Neurol. Psychiat. (Chic.), 78: 516–525, 1956.

16. Fink, M., and Kahn, R. L. Prognostic Value of Rorschach Criteria in Clinical Response to Convulsive Therapy. J. Neuropsychiat., 1: 242–245, 1960.

17. Fink, M., and Kahn, R. L. Behavioral Patterns in Convulsive Therapy. Arch. gen. Psychiat., 5: 30–36, 1961.

18. Fink, M., Kahn, R. L., and Green, M. Experimental Studies of the Electroshock Process, Dis. Nerv. Syst., 19: 113–118, 1958.

19. Fink, M., Kahn, R. L., Karp, E., Pollack, M., Green, M., Alan, B., and Lefkowits, H. J. Inhalant Induced Convulsions: Significance for the Theory of the Convulsive Therapy Process. Arch. gen. Psychiat., 4: 259–266, 1961.

20. Fink, M., Kahn, R. L., and Korin, H. Relation of Tests of Altered Brain Function to Behavioral Change Following Induced Convulsions. In The First International

Congress of Neurological Sciences, VanBogaert, L., and Radermecker, J. (eds.), Pergamon, London, pp. 613-619, 1959.

21. Fink, M., Kahn, R. L., and Pollack, M. Psychological Factors Affecting Individual Differences in Behavioral Response to Convulsive Therapy. J. Nerv. Ment. Dis., 128: 243-248, 1959.

22. Garattini, S., Kato, R., and Valzelli, L. Biochemical and Pharmacological Effects Induced by Electroshock. Psychiat. Neurol. (Basel), 140: 190-206, 1960.

23. Gellhorn, E. Physiological Foundations of Neurology and Psychiatry. Univ. Minn. Press, Minneapolis, 1953.

24. Giberti, F., and Rossi, R. Proposal of a Psychopharmacological Test ("Stimulation Threshold") for Differentiating Neurotic from Psychotic Depressions. Psychopharmacologia, 3: 128-131, 1962.

25. Goldman, D. Specific Electroencephalographic Changes with Pentothal Activation in Psychotic States. Electroenceph. clin. Neurophysiol., 11: 657-667, 1959.

26. Goldman, D. Differential Response to Drugs Useful in Treatment of Psychoses Revealed by Pentothal-Activated EEG. In Recent Advances in Biological Psychiatry, Wortis, J. (ed.), Grune and Stratton, New York, pp. 250-267, 1960.

27. Goldman, D. Electroencephalographic Changes Brought to Light Under Pentothal Activation in Psychotic (Schizophrenic) Patients, with Particular Reference to Changes Produced by Pharmacologic Agents. Ann. N.Y. Acad. Sci., 96: 356-374, 1962.

28. Goldman, D. Electroencephalographic Manifestations Associated with Psychotic Illness: Pentothal Activation Technique and Pharmacologic Interrelationships. Comp. Psychiat., 5: 80-92, 1964.

29. Gottlieb, J. S., Ashby, M. C., and Kinble, L. L. Pharmacologic Study of Schizophrenia and Depression. IV. Influence of Electric Convulsive Therapy on the Sodium Amytal Response of the Electroencephalogram. Amer. J. Psychiat., 104: 686-696, 1948.

30. Green, M. A. Significance of Individual Variability in EEG Response to Electroshock. J. Hillside Hosp., 6: 229-240, 1957.

31. Green, M. A. Relation Between Threshold and Duration of Seizures and Electrographic Change During Convulsive Therapy. J. Nerv. Ment. Dis., 130: 117-120, 1960.

32. Hoagland, H., Malamud, W., Kaufman, I. C., and Pincus, G. Changes in Electroencephalogram and in the Excretion of 17-Ketosteroids Accompanying Electroshock Therapy of Agitated Depression. Psychosom. Med., 8: 246-251, 1946.

33. Itil, T. Elektroencephalographische Studien Bei Psychosen Und Psychotropen Medikamenten. Monograph, Ahmet Sait Matbaasi, Istanbul, 128 pp., 1964.

34. Itil, T. Pentothal Induced Changes in EEG as Prognostic Index in Drug Therapy of Psychotic Patients. Amer. J. Psychiat., 121: 996-1002, 1965.

35. Itil, T. Relation of Resting and Pentothal-Activated EEG to Drug Therapy in Depressed Patients. In Pharmacotherapy of Depression, Cole, J., and Wittenborn, J. R. (eds.), C. C Thomas, Springfield, pp. 112-126, 1966.

36. Jaffe, J., Esecover, H., Kahn, R. L., and Fink, M. Modification of Psychotherapeutic Transactions by Altered Brain Function. Amer. J. Psychotherap., 15: 46-55, 1961.

37. Jaffe, J., Fink, M., and Kahn, R. L. Changes in Verbal Transactions with Induced Altered Brain Function. J. Nerv. Ment. Dis., 130: 235-239, 1960.

38. Jönsson, L., Schuberth, J., and Sundwall, A. Amphetamine Effect on the Choline Concentration of Human Cerebrospinal Fluid. Life Science, 8: 977-981, 1969.

39. Kahn, R. L., and Fink, M. Perception of Embedded Figures after Induced Altered Brain Function. Amer. Psychol., 12: 361, 1957.

40. Kahn, R. L., and Fink, M. Changes in Language During Electroshock Therapy. In Psychopathology of Communication, Hoch, P., and Zubin, J. (eds.), Grune & Stratton, pp. 126-139, 1958.

41. Kahn, R. L., and Fink, M. Personality Factors in Behavioral Response to Electroshock Therapy. J. Neuropsychiat., 1: 45-49, 1959.

42. Kahn, R. L., and Fink, M. Prognostic Value of Rorschach Criteria in Clinical Response to Convulsive Therapy, J. Neuropsychiat., 1: 242-245, 1960.

43. Kahn, R. L., Fink, M., and Weinstein, E. A. The Amytal Test in Patients with Mental Illness. J. Hillside Hosp., 4: 3-13, 1955.

44. Kahn, R. L., Fink, M., and Weinstein, E. A. Relation of Amobarbital Test to Clinical Improvement in Electroshock. Arch. Neurol. Psychiat. (Chic.), 76: 23-29, 1956.

45. Kahn, R. L., and Pollack, M. Prognostic Application of Psychological Techniques in Convulsive Therapy. Dis. Nerv. Syst., 20: 180-184, 1959.

46. Kahn, R. L., Pollack, M., and Fink, M. Social Factors in Selection of Therapy in a Voluntary Mental Hospital. J. Hillside Hosp., 6: 216-228, 1957.

47. Kahn, R. L., Pollack, M., and Fink, M. Sociopsychologic Aspects of Psychiatric Treatment in a Voluntary Mental Hospital: Duration of Hospitalization, Discharge Ratings and Diagnosis. Arch. gen. Psychiat., 1: 565-574, 1959.

48. Kahn, R. L., Pollack, M., and Fink, M. Social Attitude (California F Scale) and Convulsive Therapy. J. Nerv. Ment. Dis., 130: 187-192, 1960.

49. Kahn, R. L., Pollack, M., and Fink, M. Figure-Ground Discrimination after Induced Altered Brain Function. Arch. Neurol. Psychiat. (Chic.), 2: 547-551, 1960.

50. Kety, S., Javoy, F., Thierry, A. M., Julou, L., and Glowinski, J. A Sustained Effect of Electroconvulsive Shock on the Turnover of Norepinephrine in the Central Nervous System of the Rat. Proc. Natl. Acad. Sci., 58: 1249-1254, 1967.

51. Knott, J. R., Gottlieb, J. S., Leet, H. H., and Hadley, H. D. Changes in the Electroencephalogram Following Metrazol Shock Therapy. Arch. Neurol. Psychiat. (Chic.), 50: 529-534, 1943.

52. Korin, H., and Fink, M. Role of Stimulus Intensity in Perception of Simultaneous Cutaneous Electriccal Stimuli. J. Hillside Hosp., 6: 241-250, 1957.

53. Korin, H., and Fink. M. The Role of Set in the Perception of Simultaneous Tactile Stimuli. Amer. Psychol., 72: 384-392, 1959.

54. Korin, H., Fink, M., and Kwalwasser, S. Relation of Changes in Memory and Learning to Improvement in Electroshock. Conf. Neurol., 16: 88-96, 1956.

55. Kurland, A. A., Hanlon, T. E., Esquibel, A. J., Krantz, J. C., and Sheets, C. S. A Comparative Study of Hexafluorodiethyl Ether (Indoklon) and Electroconvulsive Therapy. J. Nerv. Ment. Dis., 129: 95-98, 1959.

56. Lennox, M. A., Ruch, T. C., and Guterman, B. The Effect of Benzedrine on the Post-Electroshock EEG. Electroenceph. clin. Neurophysiol., 3: 63-69, 1951.

57. Lipton, M. Proceedings this meeting.

58. Monroe, R. R. Episodic Behavioral Disorders—Schizophrenia or Epilepsy. Arch. gen. Psychiat., 1: 205-214, 1959.

59. Monroe, R. R., Kramer, M. D., Goulding, R., and Wise, S. EEG Activation of Patients Receiving Phenothiazines and Chlordiazepoxide. J. Nerv. Ment, Dis., 141: 100-107, 1965.

60. Perez-Reyes, M. Differences in Sedative Susceptibility Between Types of Depression. Arch. gen. Psychiat., 19: 64-71, 1968.

61. Perez-Reyes, M., and Cochrance, C. Differences in Sodium Thiopental Susceptibility of Depressed Patients as Evidenced by the Galvanic Skin Reflex Inhibition Threshold. J. Psychiat. Res., 5: 335-347, 1967.

62. Pollack, M., and Fink, M. Sociopsychological Characteristics of Patients Who Refuse Convulsive Therapy. J. Nerv. Ment. Dis., 132: 153-157, 1961.

63. Pollack, M., Siegel, N., Kahn, R. L., and Fink, M. Social Aspects of Psychiatric Treatment in Three Hospitals: Methodological Problems. VA Cooperative Chemotherapy Studies in Psychiatry, 6: 202-206, 1961.

64. Prange, A. Proceedings this meeting.

65. Rose, J. T. Reactive and Endogenous Depressions - Response to E.C.T. Brit. J. Psychiat., 109: 213-217, 1963.

66. Rosenblatt, S., and Chanley, J. D. Differences in the Metabolism of Norepinephrine in Depression. Arch. gen. Psychiat., 13: 495-502, 1965.

67. Roth, M. Changes in the EEG Under Barbiturate Anesthesia Produced by Electro-Convulsive Treatment and Their Significance for the Theory of ECT Action. Electroenceph. clin. Neurophysiol., 3: 261–280, 1951.

68. Roth, M., Kay, D. W. K., Shaw, J., and Green, J. Prognosis and Pentothal Induced Electroencephalographic Changes in Electroconvulsive Treatment. Electroenceph. clin, Neurophysiol., 9: 225–237, 1957.

69. Sachs, E., Jr. Acetylcholine and Serotonin in the Spinal Fluid. J. Neurosurg., 14: 22–27, 1957.

70. Shagass, C. Sedation Threshold. A Neurophysiological Tool for Psychosomatic Research. Psychosom. Med., 18: 410–419, 1956.

71. Shagass, C. A Measurable Neurophysiological Factor of Psychiatric Significance. Electroenceph. clin. Neurophysiol., 9: 101–108, 1957.

72. Shagass, C. Effects of LSD on Somatosensory and Visual Evoked Responses and on the EEG in Man. In Recent Advances in Biological Psychiatry, Wortis, J. (ed.), Plenum Press, N.Y., 9: 209–227, 1967.

73. Shagass, C. Pharmacology of Evoked Potentials in Man. In Psychopharmacology—A Review of Progress, 1957–1967, Efron, D., Cole, J., Levine, J., and Wittenborn, J. R. (eds.), Government Printing Office, Washington, pp. 483–493, 1968.

74. Shagass, C., and Jones, A. L. A Neurophysiological Test for Psychiatric Diagnosis: Results in 750 Patients. Amer. J. Psychiat., 114: 1002–1010, 1958.

75. Shagass, C., Muller, K., and Acosta, H. B. The Pentothal "Sleep" Threshold as an Indicator of Affective Change. J. psychosom. Res., 3: 253–270, 1959.

76. Shagass, C., and Naiman, J. The Sedation Threshold as an Objective Index of Manifest Anxiety in Psychoneurosis. J. psychosom. Res., 1: 49–57, 1956.

77. Shagass, C., Naiman, J., and Mihalik, J. An Objective Test which differentiates Between Neurotic and Psychotic Depression. Arch. Neurol. Psychiat. (Chic.), 75: 461–471, 1956.

78. Shagass, C., and Schwartz, M. Evoked Potential Studies in Psychiatric Patients. Ann. N. Y. Acad. Sci., 112: 526–542, 1964.

79. Shagass, C., and Schwartz, M. Visual Cerebral Evoked Response Characteristics in a Psychiatric Population. Amer. J. Psychiat., 121: 879–987, 1965.

80. Small, J. G., Small, I. F., Sharpley, P., and Moore, D. F. A Double-Blind Comparative Evaluation of Fluorothyl and ECT. Arch. gen. Psychiat., 19: 79–86, 1968.

81. Ulett, G. A., Smith, K., and Gleser, G. C. Evaluation of Convulsive and Subconvulsive Shock Therapies Utilizing a Control Group. Amer. J. Psychiat., 112: 795–802, 1956.

82. Wilson, W. P. (ed.) Applications of Electroencephalography in Psychiatry. Duke Univ. Press, Durham, N.C., 1965.

DISCUSSION OF
DR. FINK'S PAPER

CHARLES SHAGASS, M.D.

*Temple University Medical School and
Eastern Pennsylvania Psychiatric Institute*

Although ECT no longer enjoys the popularity of twenty years ago, it remains the most reliable method for quick amelioration of severe depression. It is unfortunate for psychiatric knowledge that ECT declined in popularity before full advantage could be taken of this remarkable therapeutic modality as a tool for understanding brain function in affective disorders. Dr. Fink is one of the relatively few people who has devoted serious and sustained effort to exploiting the properties of ECT in the interest of understanding the mechanisms of depressive illness and its reversal.

I should like to highlight and comment on some of the main points made in Dr. Fink's paper. Subtypes of depression may be classified by means of EEG responses to drugs and external stimuli. My own work in this area has been cited by Dr. Fink. I should like, here, to draw attention to the sedation threshold work of Dr. Perez-Reyes at North Carolina who has confirmed our findings showing greater than normal barbiturate tolerance in neurotic depressions. His sedation threshold method appears to be more sensitive than mine, since he also shows clearly lower than normal tolerance in psychotic types of depression, whereas my technique showed only slightly reduced values in such patients. The fact that these types of depression respond differentially to ECT is well known.

ECT modifies the electrical activity of the brain and the ease of such modification is correlated with therapeutic response. In other words, when the electrical activity resists displacement, clinical change does not occur.

Modifications in the parameters of ECT result in different EEG changes. With unilateral ECT, the EEG changes are greater under the area to which current is applied. With multiple ECT, the EEG changes are more rapidly induced. With subconvulsive electrotherapy there are virtually no EEG changes. The manipulation of the parameters of the electrical current and the locus and timing of its application offer possibilities for experimentation that have never been fully exploited. Some years ago, a commonly used form of ECT involved applying a subconvulsive current through bitemporal leads for some minutes following the application of the usual bifrontal convulsive current dose. This so-called "combined convulsive-subconvulsive" treatment appeared to have the remarkable property of markedly reducing the memory deficit and anxiety accompanying the usual convulsive treatment. Again, this subconvulsive counteraction of convulsive current presented an opportunity for the investigation of brain function that was never properly explored. The experimental neurophysiologist varies his stimulation parameters systematically in order to obtain information. ECT offers some of these opportunities in affective disorders.

Behavioral changes with ECT appear to be a function of the number and frequency of seizures. Various neurohumors, such as acetylcholine, cholinesterase, norepinephrine and serotonin, change in amount after ECT. Dr. Fink has drawn special attention to the cholinergic effects. Dr. Fink sees the CNS changes accompanying repeated seizures as necessary, but not sufficient, for the behavioral response to ECT, the specific expression of which depends on previous personality.

An important issue raised by Dr. Fink's presentation concerns the question whether the gross electrical and biochemical changes that have been described represent essential actions of ECT or are merely incidental concomitant effects. Available evidence suggests that unilateral ECT provides about the same therapeutic effect in depression as bilateral ECT, and yet the EEG changes are less and are more or less restricted to the side of application of the current. This is important evidence, because it suggests that the gross EEG changes may be a little like the surgical wound that has to be inflicted on the way to repairing an internal organ. It used to be said that electrical convulsion was essential for the therapeutic effect and this may still be the case. However, since unilateral ECT is usually accompanied by a generalized convulsion, the fact that the EEG changes are localized means that the localized slow waves result from the initial passage of current and not from the ensuing generalized seizure. I would wonder whether the various neurohumoral changes may not also fall into the same category and reflect some general disturbances in brain metabolism resulting from the application of current, and remotely, if at all, related to the depressive state and its reversal.

My question about the significance of these various effects of ECT arises because I find it hard to view depression as resulting from total brain dysfunction. It seems more likely that some specific parts of the brain are not functioning normally. The most likely brain areas that ought to be functioning badly in affective disorder are, in my opinion, those concerned with regulatory activities. These are the ones that modulate sensory input, that maintain a balance between excitatory and inhibitory activities, and in general, oversee the fine tuning that is needed for well-regulated behavior. Among the mumerous candidates for this role, the reticular formation and the septal region are frequently mentioned. In recent experiments with chronically implanted cats, we showed that two seconds of electrical stimulation applied to the septal region can modify the amount and timing of cortical responsiveness for at least the succeeding 20 or 30 minutes. Although I have no idea whether the septal region is involved in depression, or in what way, it seems reasonable to me that brain regions that function in this manner are likely to play a key role in affective disturbance.

The clinical fact that ECT is good for both stupor and excitement also suggests that defective regulation, which may deviate in either direction, is being corrected by this treatment. I emphasize the possibility that dysfunction of some key regulatory structure may underlie affective disorder because such dysfunction can result in both over- or underactivity. Unlike diabetes mellitus, pathognomonic laboratory findings could be bidirectional rather than unidirectional.

6

SOURCES OF CONTRIBUTION TO THE UNDERSTANDING OF THE ETIOLOGY OF MOOD DISORDERS*

MORRIS A. LIPTON, Ph.D., M.D.,**
ARTHUR J. PRANGE, JR., M.D.,*** and
IAN C. WILSON, M.B., D.P.M.****

The state of knowledge of the mood disorders reflects one of the many paradoxes of contemporary psychiatry. On the one hand, depression, the most common of the mood disorders, appears to be on the increase. Rawnsley (1), studying first admission rates to psychiatric hospitals in England and Wales, noted a 75 per cent increase over the period 1952 to 1960, while first admission rates for schizophrenia remained constant. Hospital admissions represent only a small portion of the population of affective disorders, because most patients are not seen by psychiatrists, but are instead treated by general practitioners. A variety of studies from Britain cited by Rawnsley (1) suggest that the actual incidence is about ten times as high as the final admission rates. Schwab (2) predicts that present and continuing social unrest will lead to an epidemic of depression in the 1970's.

We must admit with Mendels (3) that "we do not know what causes depression, how to objectively define its presence, how to classify the various types of depression, and whether the differences between them are qualitative or quantitative." Yet, depressions are recognized to be generally self-limiting illnesses in which treatment is aimed at relieving suffering, preventing irreversible damage, and accelerating the rate of recovery. This is done with gratifying results even though we continue to have a confused nosology in which the term *depression* often describes a mood, a symptom, a syndrome, and a specific disease entity (4, 5). As with so many psychiatric entities, empirical

---

*Supported in part by Grants MH222536, MH15631, HD24585, MH16522, from U.S.P.H.S.
**University of North Carolina School of Medicine, Chapel Hill.
***University of North Carolina School of Medicine, Chapel Hill.
****North Carolina Department of Mental Health, Raleigh.

treatment has outstripped theory, and successful treatment has yielded data which have permitted the generation of new hypotheses.

All illnesses of unknown or ill-defined etiology attract researchers from many disciplines. Each of these tends to view the disorder in the light of his own investigational methods and results. Thus, depression has been and continues to be investigated by epidemiologists (1, 6), geneticists (7, 8), social psychologists (9, 10), experimental psychologists and ethologists (5, 11), psychoanalysts (12, 13, 14, 15, 16), clinical psychiatrists (3, 17, 18), psychopharmacologists (19, 20, 21, 22, 23, 24), and neurophysiologists (25, 26, 27, 28).

Sound data derived from such studies are gradually accumulating and may someday permit a unified and comprehensive concept of etiology. But this is not yet possible. Instead, there are isolated data which cannot be denied but which seek a broader rubric under which they can exist. There are also self-contained hypotheses which attempt to explain the data generated by a particular method of inquiry and tend to ignore the data from other disciplines. For example, genetic data show a concordance rate of 68 per cent for monozygotic twins and 23 per cent for dizygotic twins (7). Monozygotic twins reared apart, though rare, show a concordance rate similar to those reared together. Such results clearly show a genetic contribution, but equally clearly show that other factors must also play a part. Social psychiatrists like Wilson (29) have presented evidence for transmission by a family tradition of pressure to social conformity. Schwab et al. (9) found differences in the typical symptoms of depression in differing social classes and also differences in age, male-female ratios, and married-unmarried ratios depending upon social class. Psychodynamic hypotheses exist, but these, as well as the social psychological hypotheses, are unable to account for the data which come from the somatic therapies, just as biological hypotheses are unable to accommodate the wealth of data derived from intensive clinical observation. It is clearly beyond the scope of this essay to consider the contributions to concepts of etiology from all of these diverse sources. Instead, we shall selectively focus upon those areas which seem to offer some potential for the generation of bridging concepts to relate one type of data to another.

To psychiatrists, clinical depression presents as a syndrome characterized by a complex of symptoms and signs of varying proportions which involve feelings, thoughts, and somatic and visceral disturbances. The patient is dysphoric, sad, or sometimes wooden in his affect. He is frozen in this posture or is sometimes randomly overactive. He fails to respond to the kindness and understanding offered him or responds to them with even more depression. The world holds no pleasure for him and he feels trapped and hopeless. He is sometimes guilty and may feel that he deserves his fate. Suicide may be sought as a relief. There is a reduction in most of his drives so that there is a loss of interest in food and sex. Sleep is disturbed and diminished and cognitive functions are impaired or retarded. Frequently he is agitated and anxious, although he may also be apathetic or alternative between the two.

This syndrome or constellation of signs and symptoms, whose components vary in proportion from patient to patient, is called clinical depression. Although the disturbance of mood is usually prominent and we name the syndrome for this part, we must not forget that endocrine, visceral, autonomic, motor, and thinking disturbances also occur, and that depression is a disorder involving the whole organism.

How are these clinical data to be organized and explained? Kraepelin (30) explained them in terms of the 19th century models of disease. His models, based upon the new findings of pathology and bacteriology, saw disease as something new occurring in the life of a patient. The disease did not pre-exist or exist in latent form. Rather, it was something new added to him as a result of some pathological insult to his nervous system. The nature of the insult was not specified, nor could the specific pathology be found grossly or microscopically, but it was postulated for endogenous depression, the manic-depressive psychoses, and even the neurotic depressive reactions. All of these were distinct clinical entities in his classification system and each had a constitutional base. Even though Kraepelin recognized that depression could result from prolonged adversity, he felt that this occurred only in individuals who had a constitutional psychopathic disorder—a form of degenerative process.

In contrast to the concept of depression as an acquired disease, there has been since the time of Abraham (16), Freud (15), and Meyer (31) the concept of depression as a reaction based upon the total life experience of the individual and constituting a total psychobiological response to a uniquely intolerable situation. When the patient's typical coping mechanisms failed, he became ill and his symptoms were regarded as defensive and compensatory. Depression was seen as an attempt to bring about recovery. Viewed in this light, depression is a grossly quantitative intensification of normal emotional states which takes on autonomous features. Transient emotional states, like sadness, anxiety, hopelessness, and helplessness, common to all of us, become intensified and persistent, and this is called depression.

Much is owed to psychoanalysts who as clinical observers noted as far back as 1911 (16) that depression was not a disorder of affect solely along the sadness-elation axis, but that it also contained elements of anxiety and rage. Analysts have attempted psychological-etiological explanations of depression. Abraham emphasized that the difference between grief and melancholia was based upon the component of anger in the latter because of the initial ambivalence to the loved object. Introducing manic-depressive illness into psychoanalysis, Abraham felt that both phases contained the same complexes. In the depressed state the patient was overwhelmed, in the manic state he denied his unresolved complexes. Freud (15) compared and contrasted mourning and melancholia. Mourning is a grief reaction to the loss of a loved person or symbolic representation of one; it is a conscious and normal process. In melancholia the loss may not be perceptible and there is also a characteristic and marked loss of self-esteem which leads to feelings of worthlessness, self-reproach, and expectation of punishment. In psychoanalytic terms, the ego rather than the world is impoverished because of a narcissistic identification of the ego with the abandoning love object. Freud visualized a developmental defect based upon childhood disappointment and narcissistic injury which led to a personality structure characterized by excessive dependency and a basic defect in self-esteem. Such people become especially vulnerable to the consequences of adult disappointments. Real or symbolic love object losses in adults with such a diathesis led to regression to early oral-aggressive behavior patterns. Thus, the loss of self-esteem and self-punishing behavior was seen as an attempt to punish the incorporated but abandoning love object.

With the shift of the psychoanalysts' interests to ego psychology, emphasis was placed on the phenomenon of self-esteem and the coping of security operations aimed to guarantee it. Bibring (14), for example, saw anxiety as a reaction to internal or external changes in which the ego, challenged by the danger, prepared for fight or flight. In depression, by contrast, the ego was paralyzed and helpless. To Bibring, all depressions, whether associated with fatigue, physical illness, object loss, or circular psychoses, were characterized by an impoverished ego and a loss of self-esteem. Predisposition could be caused by any form of childhood experience which reinforced the helplessness of the infantile ego.

Spitz (32), Bowlby (13), and Engel (12) showed that infants and young children seek to gratify their needs initially by an activity pattern aimed at obtaining a response from the outer world. If this fails, they move toward apathy, reducing activity, and inhibiting stimulus input. The adult depressive exhibits a similar behavior pattern which reduces pain and frustration to a minimum (33).

Pribram, who has studied the neurophysiology of emotions in monkeys, sees emotion as a set of procedures that, first, "reflect the state of relative organization or disorganization of an ordinarily stable configuration of neural systems and, second, reflect those mechanisms which operate to redress an imbalance, not through action, but by the regulation of input (25)." Depression ensues when the organism is unable to fulfill its aspirations and needs and becomes frustrated and exhausted in its coping. At such a point it reduces input. Psychoanalytic observations suggest that depression subsides when the goals again appear within reach, when the goals are diminished or relinquished, or when the ego recovers from its narcissistic shock by regaining its self-esteem through a variety of psychological defenses without necessarily relinquishing the goal (14).

On the matter of self-esteem and its relation to depression, Sir Denis Hill states, "The gap which always exists in all of us between the self-image of what we know ourselves to be (the actual ego-state) and the image of what we would like to be, or feel we ought to be (the ideal ego-state) widens dangerously . . . At some point the 'credibility gap' . . . becomes so great as to be intolerable and a catastrophic lowering of self-esteem occurs. This, in the opinion of many observers, is the state which trips the depressive mechanism (18)."

The psychological constructs around which dynamic psychiatrists base their etiological hypotheses of the mood disorders correspond with clinical observations noted in many depressed patients. But they are unable to accommodate the results of somatic interventions. Here we enter into a totally different frame of discourse. What is the utility of the psychological hypotheses in explaining the effects of ECT or of the antidepressant drugs? Therapeutic effects of ECT were once explained as gratifying the punishment needs of the guilty patient, but this can hardly be true for swallowing pills. Psychological theorists of the affective disorders can no more afford to ignore the effects of somatic intervention than the exponents of the biochemical hypotheses can afford to ignore the rich clinical observations of the naturalists. The real problem is the integration of the two.

Modern biochemical models, whether pertaining to amines, electrolytes, or hormones lie, in a sense, within the Kraepelinian concept of depression as a disease state. They presume an insult to the CNS which leads to metabolic changes manifested as depression. The postulated Kraepelinian pathology need not be seen under a microscope, even an electron microscope. Changes in function may occur with alterations in metabolism, and this can result in a functional pathology better demonstrated by chemical techniques than by anatomical ones. An old example that comes to mind is the convulsions and opisthotonus seen in severe thiamine deficiency. There are no known anatomical lesions, but the loss of ability to metabolize pyruvic acid is readily demonstrable and the metabolic lesion is quickly reversed by administration of the vitamin (34). The catecholamine hypothesis (23, 35, 36, 37) postulates a biochemical lesion characterized by a deficiency of norepinephrine (NE) at critical receptor sites as etiologically related to depression. Why there is this deficiency and how it comes about is not known. The serotonin (5HT) hypothesis (19, 38, 39) resembles the catecholamine hypothesis, except for the choice of the critical amine, and is based upon similar types of evidence. For our purpose at this time they may be considered interchangeably.

Schildkraut (40) considered four possible interpretations of the data which support a relationship between NE and affective states. 1) Changes in NE metabolism are necessary and sufficient for alterations in mood. This, he feels, is logically possible but too simple for so complex an organ as the brain. 2) The correlations between NE metabolism and the drug-induced changes in mood are unrelated and purely a matter of chance. This seems unlikely. 3) Drugs which may lead to depression or which successfully alter it may produce a chain of effects of which a change in NE metabolism is one link which leads to a change in mood. 4) Drugs may produce a series of effects leading to a change in NE metabolism and this mirrors another series of effects leading to a change in mood. In this condition there is no causal connection between the changes in NE metabolism and alteration in mood despite their correlation. Dr. Schildkraut cautiously does not choose between these latter two alternatives.

Dr. Prange has discussed Dr. Schildkraut's presentation earlier in this symposium and has cited some clinical facts which an amine hypothesis, or any other hypothesis, must accommodate. In summary, affective disorders can vary in sign within the same individual from attack to attack and even from hour to hour. Like many psychophysiologic disorders, they can remit and recur without obvious cause. A family history of depression, or especially the death of one or both parents during a patient's childhood, predisposes him to depression, which unaccountably is more common than mania. Clinical observations also underscore a link between cognition and affect. These and other clinical facts raise issues concerning the amine hypotheses which warrant more detailed consideration.

The first is the problem of understanding the induction of the clinical state of depression with drugs. A corollary of this involves the acquisition of increased information about the role of central biogenic amines in the regulation of mood and behavior. Much is made of the fact that 15 per cent of patients receiving reserpine, which lowers at least two amines (NE and 5HT), become depressed (41), but less is said of the fact that 80 per cent do not become depressed even though their peripheral response, for example in hypertension, does not appear to differ. Does this imply that central amines are lowered in only 20 per cent of the reserpinized population, while peripheral amines are lowered in all of them, or does it imply that most individuals are able to tolerate a lowering of central amines without developing depression? We suspect that the latter is true, but we do not know and the problem is worth studying. Alpha-methyltyrosine, which lowers catecholamines selectively, has been used in patients and does not produce depression in most of them. Interestingly, it does produce a rebound anxiety when the drug is discontinued (42). Parachlorphenylalanine, which reduces serotonin selectively, also does not characteristically alter mood, though other mental changes and sleep disturbances ensue (43).

The whole problem of the role of the central aminergic systems is complex and confusing and has thus far been studied mainly in animals.

Recently, Dr. George Breese (44) from our laboratory has studied the effects of injecting 6-hydroxydopamine (6-OHD) into the cisterna magna of young rats. This compound selectively destroys adrenergic neurons. With two injections of 6-OHD, brain NE is reduced by at least 90 per cent and dopamine to a similar degree. Tyrosine hydroxylase, the enzyme necessary for the synthesis of these compounds, disappears from the caudate nucleus and elsewhere in the brain is reduced by 90 per cent. Direct measurement of the synthesis of NE from tyrosine by isotopic methods shows a reduction of at least 80 per cent.

These changes in brain NE are striking and are irreversible for at least 10 weeks. Yet the gross behavioral effects are minimal. The animals grow a bit more slowly, but they mature sexually and seem to show normal sexual activity, though we do not yet know whether they can breed. They appear to groom themselves a bit less and so look a bit dirtier than control rats, but one is very hard put to distinguish a control from a treated rat by their spontaneous behavior. There are no tremors, they tolerate cold stress as well as normals, and thus far, they do not seem to respond unusually to a variety of drugs, including amphetamine. After acute injection, a severe hypothermic response occurs in rats when placed in a cold environment; cats show this hypothermia at room temperature after intraventricular 6-OHD injection (45). The usual systematic tests of emotionality, acquisition, extinction, and short and long term memory have not been done.

These preliminary results are surprising because they appear so minimal. Superficially, it appears that the central noradrenergic system has no vital function, but this is hard to believe. Perhaps there is so much redundancy in this system that 90 per cent of it can be eliminated in animals without gross behavioral effects. Considerable redundancy apparently does exist with cholinesterase in the brain, which can be chronically reduced by 50 per cent without behavioral consequences (46), while 60 per cent reduction does not alter the behavior of rats except for slowing down the extinction of acquired behavioral responses. It is also possible there are "failsafe" mechanisms by which some other neuronal system takes over the functions of the adrenergic system. The implications of either of these possibilities for the catecholamine hypothesis are interesting. It is difficult to imagine that 90 per cent reduction of brain catecholamines occurs in human depression, for the brains from persons who have committed suicide show little change in NE and only about 30 per cent reduction in serotonin (47). It seems most likely that more than the adrenergic system is affected in depression. Indeed, we already know this to be true because the evidence for a disturbance in serotonin metabolism is quite as good as that for NE (20). Perhaps even more systems are disturbed, and here we are limited as much by our technology as by our concepts. With new methods we may find still other disturbances.

In summary, the role of central NE in animals is far from clear, and the mechanism for the pharmacological production of depression in man by agents which alter catecholamines is far from clear. Certainly a one-to-one concordance between levels of catecholamines and clinical depression does not exist.

A second point which requires accommodation by the catecholamine hypothesis, or a more generalized hypothesis relating amines to affective disorders, pertains to the temporal aspects of relief of depression. A strict interpretation of the hypothesis, implying a one-to-one concordance, requires that mood would fluctuate immediately and directly with amine levels at post-synaptic junctions. We have already seen that this is not the case in the pharmacological production of depression by reserpine, where peripheral drug action is quickly evident and alteration of mood is both slow and inconstant. Similar difficulties are encountered in the study of drug therapy. The clinical effects of imipramine are slow but constantly progressive. But if we can extrapolate from animals to man, the effects of the drug on inhibiting uptake takes place in hours. Since inhibition of inactivation by uptake is the proposed mechanism by which more NE is made available to post-synaptic neurons, the hypothesis cannot explain why depression does not lift quickly with imipramine. For those who prefer to relate indoleamines to affective disorder, we must point out that tryptophan, the serotonin precursor, works no faster clinically than imipramine, even though it is highly likely that serotonin levels are quickly elevated (48).

These and similar data raise serious problems for the catecholamine hypothesis, or for that matter any biogenic amine hypothesis. Schildkraut (40) suggests that drugs may produce a chain of effects, of which a change in NE metabolism is one link, which lead to an alteration in mood. We would prefer to say that drug-induced changes in amine metabolism may occur rapidly and that these slowly produce a series of consequences which ultimately alter the affective state. We might even suggest that by manipulating amines we enter the system at a point that is not at fault or is perhaps already overworking. Using Prange's analogy (49), we need to add new rooms to our conceptual house. What shall they be?

Our studies with the thyroid hormone add one such room. Clinically, the addition of triiodothyronine (22, 24, 50), or more recently of TSH (51), accelerates the therapeutic effectiveness of imipramine in both retarded and agitated depressed patients. Our animal studies suggest that the thyroid hormone acts primarily on the adrenergic receptors and sensitizes them. The evidence for this is the finding that hypothyroid animals, who are sluggishly responsive to infused NE, actually have a greater rate of synthesis than do normals (52). Hyperthyroid animals, who are exquisitely sensitive to administered NE, have a less than normal rate of synthesis (53). Evidence from other laboratories (54, 55) has shown that when receptors are pharmacologically blocked, increased synthesis takes place, apparently in an effort to overcome the block.

Still another room in the edifice may be built out of Kety's finding (56) that electroconvulsive shock and other forms of stress result in a sustained increase in turnover of NE, probably by the induction of new tyrosine hydroxylase, the rate-limiting enzyme. Such an increase should increase the capacity of the adrenergic system to respond when needed. Biological changes in the central nervous system following electroconvulsive therapy are by no means limited to NE. Changes in blood flow, electrolytes, and serotonin have been reported. But whether they are sustained, as with NE, is not known.

The question may be raised as to whether, under the conditions of coping with serious losses, the anxiety and stress result in so much activation of the central adrenergic systems that something resembling tachyphylaxis occurs— i.e., the receptor-effector complex diminishes in sensitivity and this is associated with depression. If this were so, diminished input might result in the restoration of receptor sensitivity. Perhaps hospitalization and enforced isolation from social and interpersonal stress accomplish this. One should also remember that phenothiazine tranquilizers are frequently reported to be of value in depression. Recent careful reports indicate that they work more quickly, but in the end, not so effectively as imipramine (57). The biological mode of action of phenothiazines is not entirely clear, but psychological measurements indicate that they decrease sensitivity to sensory input (55). A concept like tachyphylaxis may also explain the finding of Prange et al. (58) that depressed patients have a smaller pressor response to infused NE than they do when recovered. Moreover, Bunney et al. (59) described an inpatient subgroup of psychotically depressed patients who showed high urinary levels of NE and its metabolites. One wonders if they, like hypothyroid patients, are not producing more NE precisely because they are less able to use it effectively. In a similar way, Dr. Perez-Reyes (60) of our department has shown that psychotic depressed patients show a diminished ability to respond hormonally to a given level of induced hypoglycemia.

Consideration of the possibility of a tachyphylactic stage of depression leads to a novel interpretation of Schildkraut's recent experiments with acute and chronic imipramine (61). Imipramine diminishes NE inactivation by reuptake and tends to make more NE available at synaptic junctions. But acutely, it also diminishes turnover and if this is equated with synthesis, it might make less NE available. His data do not permit us to determine whether the actual balances of these forces are positive or negative, but if they were negative, it might permit the refractory system to become more sensitive and in this sense, share an action with phenothiazines. Then, as the inhibitory effects on synthesis wear off with chronic administration, the balance of NE effects might become positive, now in the presence of a more sensitive system. Such an interpretation could account for the slow therapeutic action of imipramine as well as the acceleration by thyroid hormone.

Beyond this we can venture only with speculations because there are no data. It may be worthwhile to speculate in the realm of the biology of learning and memory, because it may be possible to build a fanciful house which would accommodate both the naturalistic clinical observers and the experimental interventionists. Let us begin with the relation of emotions to memory, a subject to which Kety has recently addressed himself (62). This has long been a preoccupation of psychologists and psychoanalysts and it is clear that "emotional factors" interact strongly with memory. They not only quantitatively facilitate or inhibit remembering or forgetting, but they also organize the emerging memories, condensing, distorting, and symbolically replacing them (63). Let us focus merely on the facilitation.

Recent studies by the biologists of memory tend to differentiate short- and long-term memory (64). Short-term memory, which may last for seconds to hours, seems to be associated with neurophysiological and electrical nets, because such memory can be obliterated by anesthetics which diminish the electrical activity of the brain or by electroconvulsive shock which apparently disrupts these fields. The precise mechanism by which short-term memories are converted to long-term memories is not yet known. Kandel and Spencer (65) have reviewed the evidence for persistent neuronal changes in this process; Glassman (64) has summarized the evidence associating RNA and protein synthesis with increased neuronal activity associated with learning; and Roberts and Flexner (66) have suggested that more protein may be synthesized during learning than is required by newly established neuronal patterns, and that except for the protein required by repeatedly reinforced patterns, the remainder decays.

It is a commonplace observation that arousing or emotionally laden material is better remembered than neutral material. One can learn and remember a neutral seven digit number briefly, but will consolidate it as a long-term memory if it is emotionally arousing. Is it possible, then, that the biological mechanisms underlying emotion play a role in learning and remembering? In 1967 Kety speculated on this possibility (67). Since that time several lines of evidence have accumulated which suggest that this possibility may perhaps be probable. First, an anatomical basis for such a relationship seems to exist. Fluorescence microscopy has demonstrated that there are amine-containing neurons with cell bodies in the brain stem (68). The catecholamine neurons lie laterally to the midline raphe and have a high density in the Locus Cereleus; the serotonin neurons are in the midline raphe nuclei. Axons from these neurons descend into the spinal cord and ascend by way of the median forebrain bundle to innervate various hypothalamic nuclei, the cerebellar cortex, and the cerebral cortex (69, 70). These neurons are similar in distribution to the brain stem cells described by Scheibel (71) which synapse with thousands of neurons in the neuraxis. Thus, there seems to be no special problem in linking aminergic neurons arising in the brain stem with very large numbers of other neurons in the higher centers of the CNS. Second, pharmacological and neurophysiological evidence suggests an inter-action between amine systems and learning. Thus, lesions of the median forebrain bundle depress acquisition (72) and lower levels of telencephalic amines. Substances like amphetamine, which release NE, facilitate learning (73). The suppression of consolidation by cyclohexamide is reported to be neutralized by amphetamine and footshock (74). Third, a plausible bio-chemical mechanism appears to exist. In the periphery, a role for 3'5' cyclic adenosine monophosphate (cyclic AMP) in the action of NE appears well-established (75). Recent evidence reveals that this compound and the enzymes responsible for its synthesis are present in high concentration in the brain. The action of NE on cerebellar Purkinje cells may be mediated by cyclic AMP (76). Adenyl cyclase increases the activity of a protein kinase in the brain (77). Cyclic AMP phosphorylate histones, which are located ex-clusively in the chromatin material of the cell, are thought to act as repressors of DNA (78, 79). Phosphorylation of histones may uncover the DNA tem-plate, permitting the synthesis of RNA which in turn would synthesize pro-tein. A biochemical mechanism relating the biogenic amines to protein synthesis is therefore possible, though clearly unproven.

Should the speculation that biogenic amines play a role in memory consol-idation be true, we could begin to integrate much of the diverse data achieved by different disciplines. The genetic evidence which clearly shows loading for manic-depressive psychoses might be expressed as deficiencies in those proteins involved in the laying down of the aminergic feedback mechanisms which control and regulate midbrain function. Early childhood trauma resulting in excitation and then apathy might lead to permanent memory traces in the cerebral cortex which, through their projections back to the midbrain, may further predispose the midbrain to malfunction under stress. Adult trauma in the form of real or symbolic loss might reinforce or activate these older memory traces and lead to the same type of dysregulation. The best psychological evidence suggests that memories are permanent and that the process of forgetting may involve the learning of new alternative path-ways which override the older memory traces. If the newer pathways fail in their coping functions, the older memory traces become dominant. Such a concept is compatible with both biological and psychoanalytic hypotheses of the etiology of mood disorders.

The idea that the biogenic amines may have a role in consolidation of memory also might explain why alterations in biogenic amine levels take many days to express themselves behaviorally in the alteration of mood. It may take much longer to build up a new set of memories and experiences required to override the old depressive patterns of reaction than it does to alter biogenic amine levels in the CNS.

Perhaps transient emotional states, like laughing at a joke, responding with anger to a hurt, or with sorrow to a disappointment, may resemble short-term memory in that they are best expressed in neurophysiological network terms. Long-standing emotional states, like depression, may more resemble the long-term memory which seems best expressed in terms of molecular biology. Many of the speculations presented here are testable in animals and may have heuristic value. Some of them we will soon test with the help of our colleagues in neurobiology.

Even though there are urgent needs to accelerate the therapeutic responses in the mood disorders, as well as to improve the treatment of refractory patients, empirical treatment outstrips theory. The treatment of the mood disorders is one of the most satisfactory forms of psychiatric therapy. Future research should address itself to more physiological and biochemical CNS changes which actually occur in the mood disorders, as well as to the nature of the genetic diathesis and the effects of early experience upon later CNS functioning. Animal models will almost certainly play a greater role in the study of these conditions if only because of the greater freedoms which they permit the investigator. More sensitive and less damaging methods may be expected in neurophysiology, biochemistry, and pharmacology, and these, combined with more objective methods for clarifying and quantifying the mood disorders, should lead to more effective communication among the workers from various disciplines concerned with this problem.

References

1. Rawnsley, K.: Epidemiology of affective disorders. In: Coppen, A., and Walk, A. (eds.): Recent Developments in Affective Disorders. Ashford, Kent, England, Headley Brothers, Ltd., 1968.

2. Schwab, J. J.: The decades of depression. Attitude 1:2, 1970.

3. Mendels, J. and Cochrane, C.: The nosology of depression: The endogenous-reactive concept. Amer. J. Psychiat. 124:Suppl. 1, 1968.

4. Lehmann, H. E.: Psychiatric concepts of depression. Nomenclature and classification. Canad. Psychiat. Assoc. J. 4:Suppl. 1, 1959.

5. Braceland, F. J.: Depression. Amer. J. Psychiat. 124:1569, 1968.

6. Silverman, C.: The Epidemiology of Depression. Baltimore, Johns Hopkins Univ. Press, 1968.

7. Price, J.: The genetics of depressive behaviour. In: Coppen, A., and Walk, A. (eds.): Recent Developments in Affective Disorders. Ashford, Kent, England, Headley Brothers, Ltd., 1968.

8. Winokur, G., and Clayton, P.: Family history studies. I. Two types of affective disorders separated according to genetic and clinical factors. Recent Adv. in Biol. Psychiat. 9:35, 1967.

9. Schwab, J. J., Bialow, M., Holzer, C. E., Brown, J. M., and Stevenson, B. E.: Sociocultural aspects of depression in medical inpatients. I. Frequency and social variables. Arch. Gen. Psychiat. 17:533, 1967.

10. Schwab, J. J., Bialow, M. R., Brown, J. M., Holzer, C. E., and Stevenson, B. E.: Sociocultural aspects of depression in medical inpatients. II. Symptomatology and class. Arch. Gen. Psychiat. 17:539, 1967.

11. McKinney, W. T., Jr., and Bunney, W. E., Jr.: Animal model of depression. Arch. Gen. Psychiat. 21:240, 1969.

12. Engel, G. L., and Reichsman, F.: Spontaneous and experimentally induced depressions in an infant with gastric fistula: A contribution to the problem of depression. J. Amer. Psychoanal. Assoc. 4:428, 1956.

13. Bowlby, J.: The Adolf Meyer Lecture: Childhood mourning and its implications for psychiatry. Amer. J. Psychiat. 118:481, 1961.

14. Bibring, E.: The mechanism of depression. In: Greenacre, P. (ed.): Affective Disorders. New York, International Universities Press, 1953.

15. Freud, S.: Mourning and melancholia. In: Collected Papers IV. London, Hogarth Press, 1925.

16. Abraham, K.: Selected Papers on Psychoanalysis. New York, Basic Books, Inc., 1953.

17. Grinker, R. R., Miller, J., Sabshin, M., Nunn, R., and Nunnally, J. C.: The Phenomena of Depression. New York, Paul B. Hoeber (Harper & Row), 1961.

18. Hill, D.: Depression: Disease, reaction or posture? Amer. J. Psychiat. 125:445, 1968, p. 447.

19. Coppen, A.: The biochemistry of affective disorders. Brit. J. Psychiat. 113:1237, 1967.

20. Coppen, A.: Depressed states and indolealkylamines. In: Advances in Pharmacology, Vol. 6, Part B. New York, Academic Press, 1968.

21. Hordern, A.: Depressive States. A Pharmacotherapeutic Study. Springfield, Ill., Charles C. Thomas, 1965.

22. Prange, A. J., Jr., Wilson, I. C., Rabon, A. M., and Lipton, M. A.: Enhancement of imipramine antidepressant activity by thyroid hormone. Amer. J. Psychiat. 126:457, 1969.

23. Schildkraut, J. J.: Neuropsychopharmacology and the Affective Disorders. Boston, Little, Brown & Co., 1970.

24. Wilson, I. C., Prange, A. J., Jr., McClane, T. K., Rabon, A. M., and Lipton, M. A.: Thyroid hormone enhancement of imipramine in nonretarded depressions. N. Eng. J. Med. 282:1063, 1970.

25. Pribram, K.: Emotion: Steps toward a neuropsychological theory. In: Glass, D. C. (ed.): Neurophysiology and Emotion. New York, Rockefeller University Press, 1967, p. 4.

26. Shagass, C.: Electrophysiology of depression. In: Cole, J. O., and Wittenborn, J. R. (eds.): Pharmacotherapy of Depression. Springfield. Ill., Charles C Thomas, 1966.

27. Shagass, C., and Schwartz, M: Somatosensory cerebral evoked responses in psychotic depression. Brit. J. Psychiat. 112:799, 1966.

28. Perez-Reyes, M: Differences in sedative susceptibility between types of depression: Clinical and neurophysiological significance. Arch. Gen. Psychiat. 19: 64, 1968.

29. Wilson, D. C.: Families of manic-depressives. Dis. Nerv. Syst. 12:362, 1951.

30. Kraepelin, E.: Manic-Depressive Insanity and Paranoia, Barclay, M. (trans.). Edinburgh, E. & S. Livingstone, 1921.

31. Meyer, A.: Psychobiology. In: Winters, E. E., and Bowers, A. M. (eds.): A Science of Man. Springfield, Ill., Charles C. Thomas, 1957.

32. Spitz, R. A.: Anaclitic depression. Psychoanalytic Study of Child 2:313, 1946.

33. Frank, R.: The organized adaptive responses of the depression-elation response. In: Hoch, P. H., and Zubin, J. (eds.): Depression. New York, Grune & Stratton, 1954.

34. Peters, R. A.: Reversibility of thiamine deficiency in vivo and in vitro. Chem. Ind. Rev. 56:934, 1937.

35. Prange, A. J., Jr.: The pharmacology and biochemistry of depression. Dis. Nerv. Syst. 25:217, 1964.

36. Schildkraut, J. J.: The catecholamine hypothesis of affective disorders: A review of supporting evidence. Amer. J. Psychiat. 122:509, 1965.

37. Bunney, W. E., and Davis, J. M.: Norepinephrine in depressive reactions. Arch. Gen. Psychiat. 13:483, 1965.

38. Lapin, I. P., and Oxenkrug, G. F.: Intensification of the central serotoninergic processes as a possible determinant of the thymoleptic effect. Lancet 1:132, 1969.

39. Glassman, A.: Indoleamines and affective disorders. Psychosomatic Med. 31:107, 1969.

40. Schildkraut, J. J.: Rationale of some approaches used in biochemical studies of the affective disorders: The pharmacological bridge. In: Mandell, A. J., and Mandell, M. P. (eds.): Psychochemical Research in Man. New York, Academic Press, 1969.

41. Lemieux, G., Davignon, H., and Genest, J.: Depressive states during Rauwolfia therapy for arterial hypertension. Canad. Med. Assoc. J. 74:522, 1956.

42. Engelman, K., Horwitz, D., Jequier, E., and Sjoerdsma, A.: Biochemical and pharmacologic effects of alpha-methyltyrosine in man. J. Clin. Invest. 47:577, 1968.

43. Engelman, K., Lovenberg, W., and Sjoerdsma, A.: Inhibition of serotonin synthesis by para-chlorophenylalanine in patients with the carcinoid syndrome. N. Eng. J. Med. 277:1103, 1967.

44. Breese, G. R., and Traylor, T. D.: Effect of 6-hydroxydopamine on brain norepinephrine and dopamine: Evidence for selective degeneration of catecholamine neurons. J. Pharm. Exp. Ther. 174:413, 1970.

45. Breese, G. R., and Howard, J. L.: Personal communication.

46. Russell, R. W.: Behavioral aspects of cholinergic transmission. Fed. Proc. 28:121, 1969.

47. Bourne, H. R., Bunney, W. E., Jr., Colburn, R. W., Davis, J. M., Davis, J. N., Shaw, D. M., and Coppen, A. J.: Noradrenaline, 5-hydroxytryptamine, and 5-hydroxy-indoleacetic acid in hindbrains of suicidal patients. Lancet 2:805, 1968.

48. Schanberg, S.: Drug-induced alterations in the subcellular distribution of 5HT. Biochem. Pharm. 11:187, 1962.

49. Prange, A. J., Jr.: Discussion of the paper by Schildkraut: Norepinephrine turn-over and metabolism in rat brain after chronic administration of imipramine. Presented at the annual meeting of the American Psychopathological Assoc., Inc., New York, February 12, 1970.

50. Prange, A. J., Jr., Wilson, I. C., Rabon, A. M., and Lipton, M. A.: Enhancement of imipramine by triiodothyronine in unselected depressed patients. Excerpta Medica Int. Cong. Series 180:532, 1968.

51. Prange, A. Jr., Jr., Wilson, I. C., Knox, A. E., McClane, T. K., and Lipton, M. A.: Enhancement of imipramine by thyroid stimulating hormone: Clinical and theoretical implications. Amer. J. Psychiat. 127:191, 1970.

52. Lipton, M. A., Prange, A. J., Jr., Dairman, W., and Udenfriend, S.: Increased rate of norepinephrine biosynthesis in hypothyroid rats. Fed. Proc. Abs. 27:399, 1968.

53. Prange, A. J., Jr., Meek, J. L., and Lipton, M. A.: Catecholamines: Diminished rate of synthesis in rat brain and heart after thyroxine pretreatment. Life Sci. 9:901, 1970.

54. Dairman, W. R., Gordon, R., Spector, S., Sjoerdsma, A., and Udenfriend, S.: Effect of alpha-blockers on catecholamine biosynthesis. Fed. Proc. 27:240, 1968.

55. Nybäck, H., and Sedvall, G.: Effect of chlorpromazine on accumulation and disappearance of catecholamines formed from tyrosine-C^{14} in brain. J. Pharm. Exp. Ther. 162:294, 1968.

56. Kety, S. S., Javoy, F., Thierry, A-M., Julou, L., and Glowinski, J.: A sustained effect of electroconvulsive shock on the turnover of norepinephrine in the central nervous system of the rat. Proc. Nat. Acad. Sci. 58:1249, 1967.

57. Rickels, K., Raab, E., DeSilverio, R., and Etemad, B.: Drug treatment in depression: Antidepressant or tranquilizer? JAMA 201:675, 1967.

58. Prange, A. J., Jr., McCurdy, R. L., and Cochrane, C. M.: The systolic blood pressure response of depressed patients to infused norepinephrine. J. Psychiat. Res. 5:1, 1967.

59. Bunney, W. E., Jr., Davis, J. M., Weil-Malherbe, H., and Smith, E. R. B.: Biochemical changes in psychotic depression. High norepinephrine levels in psychotic vs. neurotic depression. Arch. Gen. Psychiat. 16:448, 1967.

60. Perez-Reyes, M.: Differences in the capacity of the sympathetic and endocrine systems of depressed patients to react to a physiological stress. Pharmakopsychiatrie 2:245, 1969.

61. Schildkraut, J. J., Winokur, A., and Applegate, C. W.: Norepinephrine turnover and metabolism in rat brain after long-term administration of imipramine. Science 168:867, 1970.

62. Kety, S. S.: The biogenic amines in the central nervous system: Their possible roles in arousal, emotion and learning. To be published in: The Neurosciences: Second Study Program. New York, Rockefeller Univ. Press.

63. Rapaport, D.: Emotions and Memory. New York, Science Editions, Inc., 1961.

64. Glassman, E.: The biochemistry of learning: An evaluation of the role of RNA and protein. Ann. Rev. Biochem. 38:605, 1969.

65. Kandel, E. R., and Spencer, W. A.: Cellular neurophysiological approaches in the study of learning. Physiological Revs. 48:65, 1968.

66. Roberts, R. B., and Flexner, L. B.: The biochemical basis of long-term memory. Quarterly Rev. of Biophysics 2:135, 1969.

67. Kety, S. S.: The central physiological and pharmacological effects of the biogenic amines and their correlations with behavior. In: Quarton, G. C., Melnechuk, T., and Schmitt, F. O. (eds.): The Neurosciences. A Study Program. New York, Rockefeller Univ. Press, 1967.

68. Hillarp, N. A., Fuxé, K., and Dahlström, A.: Demonstration and mapping of the central neurons containing dopamine, noradrenaline, and 5-hydroxytryptamine and their reactions to psychopharmaca. Pharm. Rev. 18:727, 1966.

69. Anden, N.-E., Fuxé, K., and Ungerstedt, U. Monoamine pathways to the cerebellar and cerebral cortex. Experientia (Basel) 23:838, 1967.

70. Fuxé, K., Hamberger, B., and Hökfelt, T.: Distribution of noradrenaline nerve terminals in cortical areas of the rat. Brain Res. 8:125, 1968.

71. Scheibel, M. E., and Scheibel, A. B.: Structural organization of nonspecific thalamic nuclei and their projection toward cortex. Brain Res. 6:60, 1967.

72. Sheard, M. H., Appel, J. B., and Freedman, D. X.: The effect of central nervous system lesions on brain monoamines and behavior. J. Psychiat. Res. 5:237, 1967.

73. Oliverio, A.: Neurohumoral systems and learning. In: Psychopharmacology; A Review of Progress 1957–1967. USPHS Pub. No. 1836, Government Printing Office, 1968.

74. Barondes, S. H., and Cohen, H. D.: Arousal and the conversion of "short-term" to "long-term" memory. Proc. Nat. Acad. Sci. (USA) 61:923, 1968.

75. Robison, G. A., Butcher, R. W., and Sutherland, E. W.: On the relation of hormone receptors to adenyl cyclase. In: Fundamental Concepts in Drug-Receptor Interaction. New York, Academic Press, 1970.

76. Siggins, G. R., Hoffer, B. J., and Bloom, F. E.: Cyclic adenosine monophosphate: Possible mediator for norepinephrine effects of cerebellar Purkinje cells. Science 165:1018, 1969.

77. Miyamoto, E., Kuo, J. F., and Greengard, P.: Cyclic nucleotide-dependent protein kinesis. III. Purification and properties of adenosine 3'5'-monophosphate -dependent protein kinase from bovine brain. J. Biol. Chem. 244:6395, 1969.

78. Langan, T. A.: Histone phosphorylation: Stimulation by adenosine 3'5'-monophosphate. Science 162:579, 1968.

79. Fenster, J. H.: Nuclear polyanions as de-repressors of synthesis of RNA. Nature 206:680, 1965.

PART III
THERAPY IN
MOOD DISORDERS

7

LITHIUM STUDIES AND MANIC-DEPRESSIVE ILLNESS

RONALD R. FIEVE, M.D.*

Setting out to review the key lithium literature was an easy task some years ago when Lawrence Kolb and Heinrich Waelsch first stimulated my interest in lithium as a new psychotropic agent for the treatment of mania. However, reviewing the current lithium literature for today's symposium has turned out to be a much more formidable task; during the past decade the number of pertinent articles has increased from 30 to virtually hundreds. Contributions that once emanated almost exclusively from psychiatrists are now coming in from pharmacologists, electrolyte physiologists, endocrinologists, and epidemiologists, as well as from molecular biologists. This arousal of interest from such diverse segments of the scientific community has been particularly exciting, since it makes possible a truly interdisciplinary approach to the clinical use and the study of the mechanisms of action of this drug.

After reviewing the important current issues with respect to lithium, I have chosen two for inclusion in this discussion. The first is a central problem for the clinician: What is lithium's current status as a prophylactic agent in depression? The second is of great concern to the biochemical psychiatrist: What clues do we have as to lithium's biochemical mode of action? In exploring these two questions, some of the studies originating at the New York State Psychiatric Institute will be emphasized and a limited number of related key contributions from other investigators will be reviewed. Before dealing with the prophylactic question, I would like to summarize what we do know about lithium's therapeutic effectiveness in mania, schizo-affective illness, and depression.

Numerous investigations have confirmed Cade's original observations in 1949 of lithium's effectiveness in mania (1). Four of these studies, those of

---

*New York State Psychiatric Institute and Columbia University College of Physicians and Surgeons.

Schou *et al.* (2), Maggs (3), Goodwin *et al.* (4), and Fieve *et al.* (5), have been double-blind and have shown that lithium is superior to placebo in reducing manic symptoms. In addition to these four double-blind studies, numerous open studies have been reported (6), providing data on two to three thousand patients treated with lithium. In these cases, lithium has been highly effective approximately 80 per cent of the time. Gershon, who in 1960 was the first investigator in the United States to publish the effects of lithium in mania (7), later showed that lithium was a drug superior to chlorpromazine in the treatment of mania (8). This study was double-blind and demonstrated a 78 per cent remission of mania with lithium, compared to a 36 per cent remission with chlorpromazine. In this same study, Gershon's group also showed that lithium was not very effective in schizo-affective disorder; 85 per cent of the patients showed deterioration in their clinical condition.

With respect to lithium's effect on depression, Cade (1) was the first to report negative results. Several of the early open studies, including those of Andreani *et al.* (9) and Vojtechovsky (10), showed a 30 to 50 per cent response in depression. In contrast was the unpublished double-blind cross-over study of Hansen and Schou (11), which showed lithium to be ineffective in depression in nine of ten cases. In a double-blind study on 29 patients, our group found lithium to exert, at best, a mild antidepressant effect on the manic-depressive depressed phase compared to imipramine, which produced a moderate to marked antidepressant activity. We felt lithium had no more antidepressant action than any physiologically active substance does when administered to depressed patients on a research ward. However, a later open study of 31 cases of different depressive subtypes by Dyson and Mendels (12) showed lithium to have an antidepressant effect in the depressive subtypes of the endogenous variety, whereas in reactive depression it seemed to show no effect. In addition, Goodwin *et al.*, in a controlled longitudinal double-blind study of lithium, found depressive scores to correlate positively with lithium and negatively with placebo substitution, thus suggesting that lithium might have antidepressant properties for one or more of the depressive subtypes.

With this brief review, we can now look at studies pertinent to lithium's prophylactic value, since this is currently a much more important and debatable issue.

Prophylactic Studies

The prophylactic studies can be examined by tracing the two- or three-year-old polemic between Baastrup and Schou in Denmark and Blackwell and Shepherd at the Maudsley. A detailed analysis of this debate leads to what I believe is currently a methodological impasse. Studies of Baastrup and Schou in 1966 (13) showed lithium to have equally high prophylactic value in 88 female bipolar manic-depressive and unipolar depressed patients. These patients had been followed for a period of six years, both before and during lithium treatment, and the authors claimed that lithium decreased the frequency of hospitalization as well as the duration of psychotic episodes in both the unipolar and bipolar groups. These prophylactic studies of Baastrup and Schou, later supported by Angst *et al.* (14), have been severely criticized by Blackwell and Shepherd (15) and Lader (16), who claim that the studies have been inadequately designed and that neither a control medication nor a placebo group was used. Furthermore, none of the European studies, except that of Melia (17), have employed double-blind methodology in attempting to assess their prophylactic claim, and the selection of only those patients with a higher than average incidence of attack during their pretreatment period (two illnesses per year) was felt to bias the results by creating a false impression of a treatment effect. Part of the rationale behind the lack of a placebo group and lack of double-blind studies has been the Scandinavian position that it would be unethical to leave a sick manic-depressive population untreated and on placebo during several years of study (18).

At the New York State Psychiatric Institute we conducted a study aimed at exploring lithium's prophylactic effects in the depressive phase of 43 bipolar manic-depressive patients (19). This group was followed for periods of time varying from five months to two years by a research team that administered objective rating scales and collected patient self-ratings of behavior, all on a single-blind basis. Our data showed that in patients who had been on the drug for more than seven months, as compared to patients on the drug for less than seven months, lithium produced at best a mild decrease in depression scores. During these two periods, we found no change in frequency of depression failures. We define "failure" as the existence on a given visit of scores on two or more indices that were greater than one standard deviation above the patient's own means in the direction indicating increasing depression. This was in contrast to the definition of failure in the Baastrup and Schou study, which required hospitalization of the patient or supervision in the home.

From this single-blind data and our double-blind inpatient studies previously reviewed, which showed lithium, as compared to imipramine, a potent anti-manic agent and a weak antidepressant agent—if one at all—we concluded that the reported prophylactic effects of lithium in so-called recurrent affective disorder might be more apparent than real, and perhaps there was no prophylactic effect at all.

We suggested that the factors contributing to the enthusiastic open study claims of lithium's prophylactic value in recurrent affective disorder included: the well-demonstrated anti-manic effect which occurs during each manic or hypomanic phase of the illness in a therapeutic and not a prophylactic sense, the possible mild antidepressant effect on the depressive phase, which might be equivalent to that seen with any physiologically active substance, and the detection of beginning mood shifts through frequent outpatient department contacts and adjustment of lithium dosage accordingly. Another variable that might be contributing to the positive prophylactic claim was the placebo effect partially mediated through the binding of patients either to a doctor or a clinic where periodic venipunctures were insisted upon. Finally, it was discovered that several of the more enthusiastic private practitioners who had claimed lithium to be a prophylactic agent in the depressed phase were, in fact, employing polypharmacotherapy—adding a second or third drug when a mild depressive failure was first detected.

From the pooled open data of several European clinics, the statistical attacks on the Danish data by the Maudsley group, and the rebuttals to these attacks, one must conclude that the emotionally charged debate between Professor Shepherd and his colleagues at the London Institute of Psychiatry and Baastrup, Schou, Angst and others is currently at an impasse. Information from previous studies of the natural history and course of the manic-depressive illnesses, which include both bipolar and unipolar types, does not appear precise enough to indicate what the course of the disease would be if left wholly untreated. Therefore, a placebo control group and double-blind methodology certainly seems to be indicated in any future study.

Our own single-blind prophylactic design (which admittedly preselected bipolar patients with the same higher-than-minimum frequency of episodes during the pre-treatment phase as those selected by Baastrup and Schou) has indicated only a slight lowering of the intensity of the depressive phase over time and no change in the frequency of depressive attacks. The finding of this mild antidepressant effect in the overall group of depressed patients is intriguing in the light of recent studies by Goodwin et al. (4), who have demonstrated antidepressant properties of lithium in a fraction of their depressive population, as previously described. Thus, it is still possible that a subtype of the depressive population is responding to lithium as an antidepressant agent, and although the most likely subtype is the bipolar depressive phase, no study has yet clearly identified this possibility.

To summarize our position, we consider lithium a highly effective anti-manic agent, although it cannot currently be called an antidepressant in spite of the possibility that therapeutic and prophylactic action could exist for one or more depressive subtypes. We have, therefore, undertaken to redesign our trials so that both unipolar and bipolar patients are randomized to lithium and placebo groups for a period of two to three years. Results from this study, along with certain demographic characteristics, will be analyzed to see if one can develop a profile predictive of the so-called "lithium responder."

The claim that lithium is effective in preventing depression seems to be premature and unproven on the eve of its being marketed for mania (February 1970). Since this claim may eventually prove to have been exaggerated, the importance of the controversy over this question lies in the potential danger of an equally premature commercial marketing of the drug and of its widespread use as a panacea for all forms of depression, in much the same way as tranquilizers have often been marketed and used indiscriminately for the treatment of anxiety. With lithium, however, the potential hazards of such widespread and indiscriminate use—with the necessary lifetime commitment of patients to periodic blood tests—is far more serious and seems at present to be without any justification.

Biochemical Mode of Action

Now I would like to turn to the second question I have raised, which concerns lithium's possible biochemical mode of action. This subject can be divided into five or six major areas, including: catecholamine studies, *in vitro* biological studies, endocrine effects of lithium, electroencephalographic changes induced by lithium, electrolyte changes, and intermediary metabolism studies.

Catecholamine Studies

Schildkraut has done the most significant work with respect to lithium's effects on catecholamine metabolism. He has shown that lithium administration to rats causes a shift in norepinephrine metabolism from O-methylation to deamination, as indicated by an increase in tritiated deaminated catechols and a decrease in H^3-normetanephrine (20). Other acute studies by Corrodi *et al.* (21) and Stern *et al.* (22), as well as later acute and chronic studies by Schildkraut *et al* (23), have shown that lithium administration also caused an increase in norepinephrine turnover in the rat brain. This increase in deaminated catechols with lithium is singularly in contrast to observations made on the spectrum of euphorant and antidepressive type drugs (monoamine oxidase inhibitors, amphetamines, and tricyclics). Recent studies in humans, performed independently by Haskovec *et al.* (24) and Greenspan *et al.* (25), tend to confirm Schildkraut's findings in animals that lithium administration, independent of diagnosis (mania or depression), appears to decrease urinary excretion of normetanephrine and metanephrine. Similar results in humans emphasize the significance of animal studies in elucidating the mechanisms of action of lithium as well as other psychotropic drugs in man.

Apart from a number of other important studies demonstrating lithium's effect on norepinephrine metabolism, including those of Schanberg *et al.* (26) and Colburn *et al.* (27), lithium's effect on serotonin metabolism has also been investigated. Schildkraut *et al.* (28) reported an increase in the levels of radioactive deaminated metabolites of serotonin in the brains of animals treated with lithium salts, which he suggested was analogous to the increase in tritiated deaminated catechol metabolites of intracisternally-administrated H^3-norepinephrine after treatment with lithium chloride. However, lithium salts in these latter studies appear to increase the turnover of norepinephrine in the brain, whereas in the serotonin studies, lithium slowed the disappearance of radioactive serotonin, suggesting that turnover may be decreased. The inference can be drawn that lithium may cause a dissociation in norepinephrine and serotonin turnover rates, which is of theroretical interest in elucidating one possible mechanism of action of the drug, although the two studies demonstrating these findings are not entirely comparable.

More recently Corrodi et al. (29) have shown in chronic studies that lithium itself did not affect brain amine levels. Nonetheless, the administration of a tryptophan hydroxylase inhibitor led to a smaller depletion of serotonin in the serotonergic nerve terminals of the lithium-treated animals than that produced by the inhibitor alone (possibly a direct inhibitory action by lithium on the serotonergic neurons or an inhibition of the impulse-induced release of serotonin from the terminals).

In summary, catecholamine studies indicate that lithium is capable of affecting neuronal monoamine metabolism, as measured by histochemical techniques, amine turnover methods, and brain levels of radioactively-tagged metabolites of norepinephrine and serotonin. However, no study has yet determined conclusively whether an actual or functional decrease in monoamines following lithium administration results in the neuron in man. One must exercise caution in reviewing the amine literature, since chronic studies seem to be yielding different results from acute studies.

In Vitro Biological Studies

Time does not permit a complete review of the in vitro biological studies conducted with lithium and other cations involved in nerve impulse transmission. In general, the studies of nerve-tissue preparations have measured the effects of ionic concentrations on resting potentials, impulse generation and transmission, and afterpotentials. It has been postulated from these studies that lithium may either directly alter membrane transport or permeability, or it may indirectly affect membrane excitability through a more specific effect on the enzyme system or on those neuronal functions that depend on critical electrolyte, water, and enzyme concentrations or distributions. The metabolic and electrical changes induced by lithium on biological systems have been well summarized by Schou in a comprehensive review of the subject (30).

Perhaps one of the more important studies is that of Keynes and Swan (31). They have shown that, although the permeability of frog muscle to lithium is about equal to its permeability to sodium, an active transport of lithium out of the cell is accomplished at only one-tenth to one-twenty-fifth of that of sodium. This differential treatment of sodium and lithium against an electrochemical gradient by means of the active transport mechanisms of the cell membrane has also been noted in other tissue preparations, including nerve, erythrocytes, and frog skin.

Endocrine Effects of Lithium

A limited number of studies have been undertaken demonstrating lithium's effect on plasma cortisol, aldosterone secretion, and thyroid size and function. Platman and I (32) demonstrated that lithium increased the 8 a.m. plasma cortisol several days after administration was begun, and that this effect was greatly enhanced in patients with obvious lithium toxicity. We speculated on whether this was a specific direct effect of lithium on the adrenal, or whether it was a non-specific stress acting on the pituitary-adrenal axis. Murphy et al. (33) reported an acute change in aldosterone excretion with lithium administration. This change was apparently reciprocal to, and perhaps partly responsible for the changes in sodium excretion. Thyroid studies have been reviewed (34) and have related lithium's effects to questionable goiter production and changing thyroid indices; lithium's anti-thyroid effects have now been quite conclusively demonstrated in rats by Berens et al. (35). This group has suggested that lithium initially decreases iodide trapping and inhibits iodide release. Compensation for this may occur by goiter formation, increased iodide uptake, and normalization of iodide release, thus maintaining a normal PBI. Goiter formation in humans appears to be an uncommon side effect of lithium and occurs only in those patients already predisposed to thyroid disease.

Electroencephalographic Changes Induced by Lithium

Studies by Corcoran et al. (36), Andreani et al. (9), Mayfield and Brown (37), Platman and Fieve (38), and Johnson et al. (39) have measured the effects of lithium on the EEG. Our group studied 45 manic-depressives over a two-year period in various phases of their disorder and on different medications, including lithium, chlorpromazine, placebo, and imipramine. Double-blind EEG's were read, and no differences in per cent of EEG abnormalities were seen during the manic, depressive, or interval phases of this population. However, in 15 out of 28 patients a deterioration of the EEG appeared after lithium treatment. This consisted of an increased abnormal slow wave production, which was not related to age, sex, or clinical state; it was not in any apparent way necessary for the therapeutic efficacy of lithium treatment. From our study and others, it would seem that lithium affects electrical conductivity in the central nervous system, perhaps at both cortical and subcortical levels, and that at toxic doses the EEG slowing is more pronounced. It is still speculative as to whether the increased EEG disturbance at high serum lithium levels is due to electrolyte changes induced by lithium's specific effects on the central nervous system's electrolyte metabolism.

Electrolyte Changes

Studies performed in patients at the New York State Psychiatric Institute's Metabolic Research Unit by Baer and our group (40) have suggested a direct action by lithium on sodium metabolism and have indirectly supported the view that these electrolyte changes may be involved in some fundamental way in the affective disorders. Electrolyte changes induced by lithium include an acute saluresis, kaluresis, and diuresis during the first day of lithium carbonate administration. By lithium day three, this sequence of electrolyte and water changes reverses itself, so that sodium and fluid retention occur and patients return to a normal state of sodium balance by the end of the first week. These changes are observed in patients on either low or normal sodium intakes.

Electrolyte studies suggest that sodium retention occurs during depression and that sodium distribution may also be altered. Lithium may influence one or more of the mechanisms that control sodium balance. These include a possible alteration of the glomerular filtration rate, intracellular cation replacement by lithium or a direct effect on the aldosterone sodium-potassium exchange site in the distal tubule of the kidney. Studies performed in our laboratory with distal tubular blocking agents have shown that, while lithium metabolism in man is in part aldosterone-dependent, the aldosterone-sensitive sodium-potassium transport system in the distal tubule may distinguish between lithium and sodium ions (41).

Related animal studies, performed by Davenport in 1950 (42), revealed acute tissue sodium depletion after lithium administration in rats. These studies utilized large doses of lithium under acute experimental conditions, and although metabolic intake was controlled, no urinary collections were made. A recent study by King et al. (43) confirms that acute large doses of lithium can deplete brain sodium, but both the studies of Davenport and King are of questionable value with respect to the problem of lithium's effect on sodium metabolism in humans because of their short duration and the high doses of lithium used. Recently Baer (44) was able to demonstrate that rats under conditions of strict metabolic control and on chronic lithium doses comparable to those employed in humans showed brain sodium depletion as well as total body sodium depletion. The magnitude of the brain sodium depletion on lithium was six to ten per cent. Although these data demonstrate that lithium alters sodium metabolism in rats, chronic sodium depletion does not appear to be a feature of lithium's effect in humans—in a series of 16 manic-depressive patients treated with lithium on metabolic balance for seven to twenty-one days, no chronic sodium depletion occurred.

Although animal studies may give new insights into lithium's mechanisms of action, the simple conclusion cannot be drawn that lithium's effectiveness in mania is due solely to a sodium depletion mechanism. It is provocative, however, that lithium administration decreases manic behavior within the first five to ten days, and that both the rat and human studies show a parallel sodium depletion and retention pattern during the first five days of lithium. However, the chronic sodium depletion seen thereafter in rats is unlike that seen in any human investigations. To clarify the intriguing parallels between rat and human studies, further long-term balance studies must be performed on both manic and depressed patients.

Intermediary Metabolism

King *et al.* (43) concluded from a series of experiments that lithium, like potassium, may act by stimulating brain lactate production, which in turn may be inhibited by ouabain, and by replacing small but significant amounts of tissue sodium. Energy metabolism is known to be in part cation-dependent, and it is therefore interesting to speculate that the changes in energy metabolism observed by King may be related to changes in cation metabolism induced by lithium. It is apparent, however, as has been pointed out previously, that studies of electrolyte changes induced by lithium in both animals and man must involve rigorous metabolic control. Validation of the King experiments would strengthen the hypothesis that a mechanism of action of lithium must involve modification of the activity of sodium-potassium dependent ATP-ase. This would in turn lend support to the hypothesis that changes in cation concentration in the brain, as demonstrated by Baer *et al.* (40) and King *et al.* (43), are important in the etiology and treatment of mania and/or depression.

Conclusion

From the foregoing studies, it is apparent that the physiological effects of lithium are numerous. Lithium alters monoamine metabolism and the EEG; it sustains nerve impulse conduction and affects the endocrine system; it produces significant changes in electrolyte balance and metabolism, and it may also alter intermediary metabolism. Because of the complex interrelationships among these various biochemical, electrical, and ionic events following lithium administration, it is difficult, if not impossible, to synthesize all the findings in these areas into any single unifying hypothesis with regard to lithium's mode of action. It is apparent that a wide variety of laboratory tools has been applied to the investigation of lithium's mechanisms of action. While the plethora of experimental findings accumulated to date may leave the lithium researcher perplexed as to which direction to follow, at the same time it has by now become apparent that a number of exciting avenues of investigation are available. The wide variety of approaches to lithium research illustrates the interest that this drug has generated and perhaps provides a model for future interdisciplinary drug studies.

References

1. Cade, J. F. J. Lithium Salts in the Treatment of Psychotic Excitement. Medical J. Australia 36: 349–352 (1949).

2. Schou, M., Juel-Nielsen, N., Stromgren, E., and Voldby, H. The Treatment of Manic Psychoses by the Administration of Lithium Salts. J. Neurol. Neurosur. Psychiat. 17: 250–260 (1954).

3. Maggs, R. Treatment of Manic Illness with Lithium Carbonate. Brit. J. Psychiat. 109: 56–65 (1963).

4. Goodwin. F. K., Murphy, D. L., and Bunney, W. E., Jr. Lithium Carbonate Treatment in Depression and Mania. A Longitudinal Double-Blind Study. Arch. Gen. Psychiat. 21: 486–496 (1969).

5. Fieve, R. R., Platman, S. R., and Plutchik, R. R. The Use of Lithium in Affective Disorders: I. Acute Endogenous Depression. Amer. J. Psychiat. 125: 487–491 (1968).

6. Kline, N. S. Depression: Its Diagnosis and Treatment; Lithium: The History of Its Use in Psychiatry. Basel: S. Karger, 1969.

7. Gershon, S., and Yuwiler, A. The Lithium Ion: A Specific Pharmacological Approach to the Treatment of Mania. J. Neuropsychiat. 1: 229–241 (1960).

8. Johnson, G., Gershon, S., and Hekimian, L. J. Controlled Evaluation of Lithium and Chlorpromazine in the Treatment of Manic States: An Interim Report. Compre. Psychiat. 9: 563–573 (1968).

9. Andreani, G., Caselli, G., and Martelli, G. Rilieve Clinici ed Elettroencefalografici Durante Il Trattamento Con Sali di Litio in Malati Psichiatrici. G. Psichiat. Neuropat. 86: 273–328 (1958).

10. Vojechovsky, M. Problemy Psychiatrie v Praxi a ve Výzkumu. Prague: Czechoslovak Medical Press, 1957, pp. 216–224.

11. Hansen. C. J., Retboll, K., and Schou, M. Unpublished data.

12. Dyson, W., and Mendels, J. Lithium and Depression. Curr. Therap. Res. 10: 601–608 (1968).

13. Baastrup, P. C., and Schou, M. Lithium as a Prophylactic Agent: Its Effect Against Recurrent Depressions and Manic-Depressive Psychosis. Arch. Gen. Psychiat. 16: 162–172 (1967).

14. Angst, J., Dittrich, A., and Grof, P. Course of Endogenous Affective Psychoses and its Modification by Prophylactic Administration of Imipramine and Lithium. Int. Pharmacopsychiat. 2: 1–11 (1969).

15. Blackwell, B., and Shepherd, M. Prophylactic Lithium: Another Therapeutic Myth? Lancet 1: 968–970 (1968).

16. Lader, M. Prophylactic Lithium? Lancet 2: 103 (1968).

17. Melia, P. Prophylactic Lithium. Lancet 2: 519–520 (1968).

18. Ottosson, J. -O. Commentary on Perspectives on the Use of Lithium in Psychiatric Illness, by R. R. Fieve. Int. J. Psychiat. In press.

19. Fieve, R. R., Platman, S. R., and Plutchik, R. R. The Use of Lithium in Affective Disorders: II. Prophylaxis of Depression in Chronic Recurrent Affective Disorder. Am. J. Psychiat. 125: 492–498 (1968).

20. Schildkraut, J. J., Schanberg, S. M., and Kopin, I. J. The Effects of Lithium Ion on H^3-Norepinephrine in Brain. Life Sci. 5: 1479–1483 (1966).

21. Corrodi, H., Fuxe, K., Hökfelt, T., and Schou, M. The Effect of Lithium on Cerebral Monoamine Neurons. Psychopharmacologia 11: 345–353 (1967).

22. Stern, D. N., Fieve, R. R., Neff, N. H., and Costa, E. The Effect of Lithium Chloride Administration on Brain and Heart Norepinephrine Turnover Rates. Psychopharmacologia 14: 315–322 (1969).

23. Schildkraut, J. J., Logue, M., and Dodge, G. The Effects of Lithium Salts on the Turnover and Metabolism of Norepinephrine in Rat Brain. Psychopharmacologia 14: 135–141 (1969).

24. Haskovec, L., and Rysanek, K. Die Wirkung von Lithium auf den Metabolismus der Katecholamine und Indolalkylamine beim Menschen. Arzneimittelforschung 19: 426–427 (1969).

25. Greenspan, K., Schildkraut, J. J., Gordon, E. K., Baer, L., Aronoff, M., and Durell, J. Catecholamine Metabolism in Affective Disorders. III. MHPG and Other Catecholamine Metabolites in Patients Treated with Lithium Carbonate, J. Psychiat. Res. In press.

26. Schanberg, S. M., Schildkraut, J. J., and Kopin, I. J. Effects of Psychoactive Drugs on Norepinephrine-H^3 Metabolism in Brain. Biochem. Pharmacol. 16: 393–399 (1967).

27. Colburn, R., Goodwin, F., Bunney, W. E., and Davis, J. Effect of Lithium on the Uptake of Noradrenaline by Synaptosomes. Nature 215: 1395–1397 (1967).

28. Schildkraut, J. J., Schanberg, S. M., Breese, G. R., and Kopin, I. J. Effects of Psychoactive Drugs on the Metabolism of Intracisternally Administered Serotonin in Rat Brain. Biochem. Pharmacol. 18: 1971–1978 (1969).

29. Corrodi, H., Fuxe, K., and Schou, M. The Effect of Prolonged Lithium Administration on Cerebral Monoamine Neurons in the Rat. Life Sci. 8: 643–651 (1969).

30. Schou, M. Biology and Pharmacology of the Lithium Ion. Pharmacol. Rev. 9: 17–58 (1957).

31. Keynes, R. D., and Swan, R. C. The Permeability of Frog Muscle Fibres to Lithium Ions. J. Physiol. 147: 626–638 (1959).

32. Platman, S. R., and Fieve, R. R. Lithium Carbonate and Plasma Cortisol Response in the Affective Disorders. Arch. Gen. Psychiat. 18: 591–594 (1968).

33. Murphy, D. L., Goodwin, F. K., and Bunney, W. E. Aldosterone and Sodium Response to Lithium Administration in Man. Lancet 2: 458–461 (1969).

34. Fieve, R. R., Platman, S. R., and Baer, L. Goiter Detection and Changing Thyroid Indices during Lithium Treatment of Manic-Depressive Illness. Presented at the NIMH-sponsored workshop on the Psychobiology of the Depressive Illnesses, Williamsburg, Va., April 1969.

35. Berens, S. C., Bernstein, R. S., Robbins, J., and Wolff, I. The Antithyroid Effects of Lithium. Presented at the American Thyroid Association Meeting, Chicago, Ill., Nov. 1969.

36. Corcoran, A. C., Taylor, R. D., and Page, I. H. Lithium Poisoning from the Use of Salt Substitute. J. Am. Med. Assoc. 139: 685–688 (1949).

37. Mayfield, D., and Brown, R. The Clinical Laboratory and Electroencephalographic Effects of Lithium. J. Psychiat. Res. 4: 207–219 (1966).

38. Platman, S. R., and Fieve, R. R. The Effect of Lithium Carbonate on the Electroencephalogram of Patients with Affective Disorders. Brit. J. Psychiat. 115: 1185–1188 (1969).

39. Johnson, G., Maccario, M., Gershon, S., and Korein, J. The Effects of Lithium on EEG, Behavior and Serum Electrolytes. J. Nerv. Ment. Dis. In press.

40. Baer, L., Platman, S. R., and Fieve, R. R. The Role of Electrolytes in Affective Disorders: Sodium, Potassium, and Lithium Ions. Arch. Gen. Psychiat. 22: 108–113 (1970).

41. Baer, L., Platman, S. R., and Fieve, R. R. Aldosterone Dependent Component of Lithium Metabolism and the Effect of Lithium on Fluid and Electrolyte Balance. Presented at the NIMH-sponsored workshop on the Psychobiology of the Depressive Illnesses, Williamsburg, Va., April 1969.

42. Davenport, V. Distribution of Parenterally Administered Lithium in Plasma, Brain and Muscle of Rats. Amer. J. Physiol. 163: 633–641 (1950).

43. King, L., Carl, J., Archer, E., and Castellanet, M. Effects of Lithium on Brain Energy Reserves and Cations in Vivo. J. Pharmacol. Exp. Therap. 168: 163–170 (1969).

44. Baer, L., Kassir, S., and Fieve, R. R. Lithium-Induced Changes in Electrolyte Balance and Tissue Electrolyte Distribution. Psychopharmacologia 17: 216–244 (1970).

DISCUSSION OF
DR. FIEVE'S PAPER

BARON SHOPSIN, M.D.
New York University Medical Center

In his review, Dr. Fieve addressed himself primarily to the problem of lithium as a prophylactic agent for depression, as well as referring to some of the mechanisms of this ion's mode of action. Highlighting the lack of control studies attendant to the prophylactic use of lithium and underlying the emotionally charged attacks and rebuttals between Danish and English researchers, Dr. Fieve outlines various factors that might contribute to the enthusiastic open study claims of lithium's prophylactic value in recurrent affective disorder. Although his own studies, comparing the effects of lithium to imipramine, in fact, indicate that there is no basis for a prophylactic effect at all in depression, Dr. Fieve does allow the possibility that therapeutic and prophylactic action could exist for one or more depressive sub-types. Nevertheless, he contends it cannot be called an antidepressant agent at this time. In illustrating the interest that lithium has aroused as a research tool, various physiological effects are reviewed, indicating that this ion alters electrolyte balance, monoamine metabolism, EEG and nerve impulse conduction, and various endocrines.

The first point of my discussion is to clarify the use of the word prophylaxis in relation to lithium therapy. Clear distinctions have not been made in several studies as to whether the material consists of bipolar or unipolar forms of manic-depressive illness. Some reports use it to suggest prevention of manifestations of a subsequent episode, while others, including our group at NYU, mean only that it affects the amplitude of cycles and does not clearly modify the endogenous cyclicity of manic-depressive disorder. The latter claim requires an increase of the maintenance dose of lithium, to diminish further the incipient manifestation and cut the episode short. This course of action is applied to prevent the need for further hospitalization, and to this extent, the word prophylactic might be implied.

I support Dr. Fieve's remarks on lithium's prophylactic action in depression, in that no conclusive statement can be reached from the available data, and the situation will remain unresolved until further control data are forthcoming. However, if the prophylactic claims can be substantiated and the possibility exists that lithium is effective against recurrent depressions, the possibility exists that lithium acts against both the polar manifestations of manic-depressive psychosis. If this were so, lithium would be in a unique position among the psychotropic drugs and would thus warrant a more specific labeling as a mood normalizer or thymoleptic.

Perhaps the widest extension of all prophylactic claims for lithium comes from Angst and his colleagues, who suggest that lithium prolongs the interval between acute exacerbations, or relapses, in schizophrenic patients. Like the other prophylactic claims for lithium, these findings await duplication.

Despite the wealth of clinical material, there is a striking lack of control studies in the area of lithium's effect on acute manic episodes, and the few studies available all differ widely in experimental design and method of evaluation. The work of Noak and Trautner, Gershon and Yuwiler, Schou, Hartigan, Melia, Gjessing, and Angst, tend to indicate, however, that chronic lithium administration can exhibit a beneficial effect on future episodes of mania and therefore it may be justified to conclude that lithium is an effective and perhaps specific therapeutic agent for use in the manic phase of manic-depressive disease. It is thus an agent which has many of the clinical properties of a major tranquilizer, but does not exhibit a significant degree of sedative activity, and does not produce drowsiness in manic patients while controlling marked degrees of psychomotor activity. Also, the quality of the response in mania produced by lithium is considered to be quite different than that produced by chlorpromazine, which also tends to support the notion of pharmacological specificity for lithium.

In no other psychiatric entity has lithium's efficacy been proven. In order to obtain some degree of definition of action, a statement on the trials of schizophrenia is necessary. It is unlikely that lithium has any specific therapeutic effect on the schizophrenic process itself. This is supported in other manic-depressive studies, such as that by Frie, Schou, and Hartigan, where the therapeutic response to lithium in the atypical cases is markedly less than the typical manic cases. These atypical groups contain subjects with schizophrenic features and the differential treatment outcome has been commented upon in most studies. As indicated by Dr. Fieve, a previous control study by Dr. Johnson of our department has clearly demonstrated that lithium does not exhibit any significant therapeutic activity in schizo-affective patients and that chlorpromazine is considerably more effective in this diagnostic group.

We have just completed a double-blind study using lithium and chlorproma-zine in schizophrenic patients and the data confirm our previous findings that chlorpromazine is more effective in such subjects.

The diagnostic problems have impelled lithium researchers to explore the interface between schizophrenic illness and mania. An attempt to improve the inadequate differentiating criteria in current use has been made by us at New York University and we have devised two new rating instruments for differ-entiating between manic and schizo-affective patients. These are the Differ-ential Diagnostic Scales (DDS) for manic-depressive illness and the Bellevue Differential Inventory (BDI).

With respect to lithium's mode of action and its effect on various systems, I would like to add that a review of reported effects on monoamine metabo-lism vary, because the experimental conditions in the studies differ widely with respect to acute or chronic lithium administration, variance in dosage and species, and the use of *in vitro* or *in vivo* techniques. Dr. Ho of our department has recently found that prolonged lithium treatment produced a significant change of 5-HT levels only in the hypothalamus and brain stem, but no significant change in the other regions. There was no significant altera-tion in norepinephrine or dopamine levels in any of the areas studied. The turnover rate of serotonin was slight, but not significantly changed by lithium in whole brain studies. However, regional studies showed increases in the serotonin synthesis in cerebellar tissue, whereas the hypothalamus showed a reduction of turnover. The turnover rates of both norepinephrine and dopamine were not significantly affected by prolonged lithium treatment. Serum and tissue lithium concentrations were assayed.

We have also used human mixed saliva as another tool in exploring the distribution of lithium in biological fluids and in determining the relationship between lithium and the electrolytes, sodium and potassium. Using patients in different diagnostic categories, we demonstrated that lithium is present in saliva at concentrations approximately two and a half times that found in serum; this ratio holds true in different diagnostic categories and over a wide range of dosages. It was proposed that the saliva levels may be used as an alternate method for determining blood levels. We have duplicated this finding in follow-up studies, and have found that this ratio appears to hold in any individual ingesting lithium at any time of day. Our results also indicated that chronic lithium administration reduces plasma-sodium and increases saliva-sodium with a concomitant increase of the Na/K ratio of saliva.

Serry examined the concept of differential handling of the lithium ion in biological fluids. Studying retention and excretion patterns of lithium in the urine of patients in different diagnostic categories, he attempted to relate the responses to clinical state and outcome of treatment. We have not been able to duplicate Serry's findings, but have found that lithium retention is not dependent upon diagnostic category but related to the initial loading dose given.

With respect to endocrine effects, we have been able to substantiate the findings of Platman and Fieve with respect to lithium's effect on elevating plasma cortisol levels. However, we found that although both a.m. and p.m. cortisol levels were increased during lithium treatment, only the evening cortisol concentrations showed significant increases. Normal cortisol response was witnessed following dexamethasone suppression, both before and after lithium ingestion.

Diabetes insipidus has been reported on at least three occasions and one report deals in detail with two patients with blood levels not considered excessive developing such a response and showing no other clinical features of lithium toxicity. In both cases, the urinary concentration defect was refractory to pitressin administration and in each instance symptoms subsided following discontinuation of lithium medication.

Van der Velde and Gordon have recently reported increased glucose tolerance (GT) in eight of ten patients receiving lithium therapy, and a decrease in GT following withdrawal of lithium. They found that GT increases more significantly as lithium issuance continues. Rafaelson has recently reported depletion of liver glycogen in rats with temporary increase in blood glucose, as well as increased levels of circulating glucagon. This may, in part, explain why we have discovered the appearance and disappearance of diabetes mellitus in two patients during maintenance with lithium carbonate.

Concerning thyroid functioning, it appears fairly clear that lithium is capable of causing goiter production, and there have been several reports dealing with the appearance of hypothyroidism associated with lithium medication. With respect to Dr. Fieve's reference to work at NIH, I would like to make clear that Dr. Berens feels that lithium does not interfere with the iodine trapping, but acts somewhere after the incorporation of iodine into the gland; our previous work and that of Schou would support such a concept. In a recent communication, Doctors Fieve and Platman had also indicated that the incidence of goiter in manic-depressive individuals appears higher in men than in women. At New York University we have found ten cases developing manifest thryroid disturbance during lithium treatment; all subjects were female. Of the several manic-depressive patients offering a history of thyroid difficulty prior to lithium treatment, we count only one male.

Finally, in a previous study we reported that schizo-affective patients did not improve with lithium therapy but, in fact, the majority showed a worsening of their clinical state. A significant feature of this group was the appearance of toxic-confusional symptoms and disorientation. In a recent study using lithium or chlorpromazine in schizophrenics, we found five patients developing such toxic-confusional states with lithium dosage and blood levels ranging around .750 mEq/L, levels not usually associated with toxicity. The most consistent laboratory abnormality associated with these neurotoxic symptoms was various EEG changes, including alterations of the alpha activity, diffuse slowing, the appearance of focal changes, or, in one case, the accentuation of baseline focal abnormalities.

In conclusion, the problems and deficiencies in assessing the scientifically valid activity of lithium are manifold and more clear than the answers sought. The problems that make both research design and evaluation of published data difficult are: 1) differential diagnosis; 2) rarity of manic-depressive illness; 3) cyclicity and the inherent factor of high incidence of spontaneous remission; 4) management problems associated with manic patients and their effect on design; 5) previous and concomitant use of other psychoactive drugs; 6) lack of specific and relevant psychiatric rating devices for mania and rare usage of the existing ones in the studies reported; and 7) the almost complete lack of control studies with other so-called established psychoactive compounds.

The clinical reports on lithium have generated much research into its mode of action. While no clear picture has yet emerged, the possibility of using the lithium ion as a research tool in exploring the etiological aspects of manic-depressive disease is perhaps the most exciting aspect since its introduction into psychopharmacology. However, the poorly defined uses for lithium, as well as the various effects discussed in this presentation, place us in agreement with Dr. Fieve's reservations concerning the premature commercial marketing of this drug which may again reduce it to its former status as a dangerous toxic agent that should not be used.

8

PHARMACOGENIC
MOOD DISORDERS

HANS HIPPIUS*

Mood disturbances are one of the most common psychopathological phenomena. We find them in both functional psychosis and organic symptomatic psychosis. They may also be a symptom of a neurosis or the character trait of a personality disorder. This term, "mood disorder," includes both the depression and the elation of mood. This may sound like a rather primitive statement, but we forget too often that, at least in the area of psychotic syndromes, the symptoms of the depressed and elated mood have conceptually the same meaning. In other words, the decisive question in the diagnostic process is whether there is *any* disturbance of mood at all, regardless of whether it is a depression or an elation.

For research in the field of psychopathology of mood, there are three problems of primary importance. The first problem is the differentiation of the symptomatology of mood disorders. From the psychopathological point of view, to subsume all the various shades and manifestations of a depressed mood under the term "depression" is an intolerable oversimplification. The second problem is the description of the symptomatological context in which the depressive symptom is embedded in the particular patient. In his everyday work, the psychiatrist observes very different groups of symptoms. Examples of easily distinguishable groups of symptoms are: (1) lack of initiative, insufficiency to act (felt and reflected by the patient), and a dysphoric mood; (2) the restless-anxious depression; and (3) the inhibited and retarded depressions (designated in German psychiatry as vital depression) accompanied by guilt feelings and many somatic complaints. The third problem is the pathogenetic structure of characteristic groups of symptoms. In this connection, the concept of a monocausal etiology has been recently replaced by the concept of the multidimensional origination of syndromes.

---

*Free University of Berlin

Today's report concerns one particular aspect of this last-mentioned problem—the pathogenesis of mood disorders. I will review the question of whether, and to what extent, drugs are involved in the causation of mood disturbances.

Until the beginning of this century, the idea of a specificity of noxious factors was generally accepted. According to this concept each noxious factor is able to cause *one* specific psychopathological syndrome. Psychiatry operated on the premise of specific etiologies for specified brain syndromes. In the beginning of this century Bonhoeffer developed his concept of the so-called acute exogenous reaction types (5). This concept stated that psychiatric syndromes could not be differentiated on the basis of specific etiologies, but that the clinical manifestations were more or less identical for different causes. In his opinion, the human organism has at its disposal only a few patterns of psychopathological syndromes with which it can react to innumerable noxious agents (6, 7). In the case of delirium, amentia, or hallucinosis, it is assumed that the psychopathological symptoms are caused by exogenous factors. But more than sixty years ago, it was Bonhoeffer who pointed out that exogenous factors can produce not only the symptomatology of such syndromes as delirium or hallucinations but also schizophrenia-like syndromes and others characterized by mood disturbances (5). Increasing evidence was found that supported the opinion that even psychopathological syndromes simulating the clinical picture of a functional mood disorder could be caused by organic cerebral dysfunction. In the case of the euphoric-manic syndrome, one was more willing to believe that the psychopathological syndrome was determined by an exogenous noxious factor. In the case of depressed mood this connection was less easily accepted. Only recently, the relation between depression and disturbances of cerebral function has been investigated more intensively. In Europe, Büssow demonstrated that somatically determined psychoses due to pernicious anaemia and malaria manifested themselves primarily as depressive syndromes (8, 9). It was shown by Weitbrecht that in some cases cerebral atrophy produced a psychopathological syndrome which could not be distinguished from an endogenous depression (22). The general conclusion that can be drawn from all these observations is that there is no noxious agent affecting the central nervous system which could not produce mood disorders (10).

Consequently, it is not surprising that drugs also can play an important part in producing exogenous disturbances of mood (15). It is well known that clearcut psychotic syndromes with disorientation or hallucinations can be seen after chronic administration or an acute overdose of drugs.

In fact, simple pharmacogenic mood disorders are much more frequent than a delirium or a hallucinosis. The high frequency of such disorders of mood brings with it the great danger of a failure to diagnose properly pharmacogenic mood disorders. For example, only one to five patients out of 100 treated with ACTH or corticosteroids will show psychotic brain syndromes characterized by confusion or disorientation. Mood disorders, however, are much more frequent, and are found in 30 to 35 per cent of the cases (21). Experiences with the psychopathological side-effects of the corticosteroids show that the manifestation of a depressed state or an elated state does not depend on a specific kind of drug, because corticosteroids are able to provoke both a depression and an elation. Suicides, occurring during therapy with corticosteroids or ACTH, are taken by some as evidence that these drugs cause extraordinarily severe depressions. However, this assumption may not be justified. Because the use of these corticosteroid drugs is very common it is easy to understand that we may find a greater absolute number of suicides due to a pharmacogenic depression caused by the more widely used drugs. In contrast, other drugs may provoke pharmacogenic depressions much more often; but as these drugs are used very infrequently, the absolute number of suicides is substantially smaller, and these drugs are rarely indicated as causal agents.

Recently, Helmchen of my department has published a comprehensive survey of those groups of drugs reported as producing psychiatric side-effects, especially mood disorders (11). No psychopathological effect was expected from the following drugs which are able to produce psychiatric side effects: (1) antibiotics, (2) antituberculous agents, (3) sulfonamides, (4) laxatives, and (5) cardiotonic agents. A second group concerns drugs in which psychiatric side-effects were expected as a possibility: (1) hormones, (2) antihypertensive agents, (3) bronchodilators, (4) antihistamines, (5) antitussives, and (6) anti-parkinsonism agents. A third group comprises the psychotropic drugs: (1) analgesics, (2) sedatives and hypnotics, (3) anorexiants, (4) stimulating drugs, (5) minor tranquilizers, and (6) neuroleptic agents.

Psychiatric side-effects, such as depressive symptoms (2, 20, 23) have even been observed after the application of placebo. This finding proves that psychopathological side-effects are determined not only by the drug, but also by the individual. Consequently, when using the term "pharmacogenic mood disorders," one must always consider the drug-patient interdependency. Therefore, pharmacogenic does not mean that the drug is the unique causal factor for the observed psychiatric syndrome; it simply means that the drug is obviously of decisive significance. In the causation of abnormal psychiatric symptoms, the psychopathological syndrome is the result of the interaction between the drug and the personality structure of the patient (14).

With the concept of the multifactorial causation of syndromes, Helmchen and others investigated the problem of pharmacogenic depression caused by neuroleptic drugs (12, 13). I want to give a summary of these results, because depressions developing in the course of neuroleptic therapy are frequent and an interesting subject of psychopathological research (3, 4, 16). Investigations of pharmacogenic depressions help to explain the structure and the development of a syndrome of exogenous psychiatric disorders. These syndromes can easily be studied for several reasons: (1) the noxious agent, the drug, is known and well characterized by pharmacological and biochemical methods; (2) the drug is administered under precisely defined conditions; (3) the investigation can be planned from the beginning like a pharmacological experiment; (4) the investigation is conducted from the beginning by an observer trained in psychiatry.

In 1961 it was first recognized that depressive syndromes could occur in the course of neuroleptic therapy. It was found, however, that the number of relapses could be reduced by long-term maintenance therapy. This was important progress for the therapy of schizophrenics. In the course of these investigations, it was found that the risk of suicide in patients treated continuously with neuroleptics was relatively high and that depressive syndromes were rather frequent. These depressive syndromes due to neuroleptics respond well to therapy with imipramine or other tricyclic antidepressant drugs. In about 20 to 30 per cent of the long-term treated schizophrenics, because of the presence of depressive-apathic disorders and a reduction of impulse, pure neuroleptic therapy had to be replaced by neuroleptics combined with an antidepressant. Paul Hoch, however, was completely right in pointing out that such depressive mood swings in schizophrenic psychosis were also found before the era of drug treatment (17). His observation suggests that it would be wrong to investigate the depressive syndromes occurring in the course of neuroleptic therapy with the concept of the one-dimensional pharmacogenesis. By observing the psychiatric side-effects of placebo, as mentioned previously, we became aware that individual disposition plays an important part in the development of syndromes of the so-called pharmacogenic psychopathological phenomena. Hoch (17), Meyer (19), and Janzarik (18) showed that another important component for the manifestation of a depressive phase in schizophrenics is the illness itself, the so-called "morbogenic factor." Therefore, psychopathology in these cases should be considered the result of the interaction of the drug with the patient's personality and the illness for which he is treated.

Helmchen and I investigated 120 patients with schizophrenic psychosis to obtain additional information about the pharmacogenic depression occurring in the course of neuroleptic therapy (13). For the evaluation of the data, we used the AMP-system which uses IBM marking reader records (1). The following signs of the AMP-system were taken as depressive symptoms:

> depressed, sad
> hopeless, desperate
> feeling of inadequacy

feeling of guilt
suicidal tendency, suicidal attempts
delusion of poverty
disturbance of vital feelings
hypochondriasis
hypochondriacal delusions.

We divided the patients into three groups:

Group A: Patients who presented depressive symptoms at the time
of admission (41);

Group B: Patients who developed depression in the course of the
neuroleptic therapy (30);

Group C: Patients who presented no depressive symptoms, neither
before, nor during the course of therapy (49).

In ascertaining the homogeneity of these groups, we could not find any
significant differences among such factors as age, sex, time of onset, and the
symptomatology of the schizophrenic psychosis. Closer examination of
Group A (patients who presented depressive symptoms at the time of admission) produced the following result: In comparison to the group of patients
without depressive symptoms at the time of admission (Groups B and C), the
patients of Group A were found to have been pre-treated with neuroleptic
drugs significantly more often.

It is worth mentioning that there is a close relation between the depressive symptoms and the complaint of "inner restlessness." Inner restlessness
was found in Group A patients twice as frequently as in the other groups, and
mostly among those patients whose depressive symptoms had been worsened
by the neuroleptic therapy. In fact, half of the Group A patients whose
depressive symptomatology increased showed signs of inner restlessness.
Many authors have confirmed this finding that inner restlessness combined
with akathisia, other extrapyramidal symptoms, hypotension, and insomnia
strongly indicates that a depressive syndrome has been provoked or worsened
by the neuroleptic therapy. Consequently, a reduction in dosage is recommended.

Next, we looked for significant differences between patients of Groups B
and C at the time of admission, as we wanted to know whether certain
symptoms or groups of symptoms have an influence on the probability of the
manifestation of depressive symptoms during neuroleptic therapy. The significance of the differences between the frequency distributions was tested with
the x^2 test. We found that the patients who became depressed during therapy
were more likely to show acute, productive schizophrenic symptoms. On the
average, less than one month had passed from the first manifestation of the
disease until their admission to the hospital. The full-blown psychosis developed within a very short time. Delusional mood, increased drive, and elated

mood were found significantly more often in patients who did develop depressive symptoms during neuroleptic therapy than in patients who did not. The group without depressive symptoms, however, was characterized at the time of admission by reduced empathy, irritability, dysphoric mood, distrustfulness, hostility, and rather frequently, by intellectual defects. This led to the suggestion that the more chronic schizophrenics belonged to this group and that obvious morbogenic factors have an influence on the manifestation of a depressive syndrome accompanying neuroleptic medication.

We determined the time at which manifestation of depressive symptoms occurred in Group B patients (those who developed the depressive syndrome after admission during neuroleptic therapy) and found two peaks of manifestation: one within the period between the fourth and seventh week; the second within the twentieth week. We then sought factors which might explain the existence of these two well-separated peaks. Depending on the personality and the situation, it was a reactive element which was of decisive importance for the manifestation of depression during the second month. The most important factors influencing the manifestation during this period were: (1) the patient's imminent discharge from the hospital, which was felt as a threat; (2) the regaining of a critical distance to his own disease; (3) the feeling of inadequacy which leads to depression, whatever roots it might have; (4) the unfavorable experience of the somatic side-effects of the neuroleptics; and (5) the experience of a relapse of the psychosis when the higher dosage of clinical therapy is reduced to the maintenance dosage or when, for the longterm therapy, a more potent neuroleptic drug is replaced by a less potent one.

Here again the individual disposition and the general situation of the patient can be shown as determining factors in interaction with the pharmacogenic element. These factors have to be taken into account in order to plan the strategy of therapy for a schizophrenic psychosis. This is especially important because of the high frequency of suicide in this period. Reduction of the dosage of the neuroleptic drug is not the recommended therapy of such a depressive syndrome. On the contrary, a more intensive neuroleptic medication might be necessary. This group in particular should be treated by psychotherapeutic measures considering *all* determining factors.

The patients who developed depressive symptoms within the twentieth week, are similar to those patients who become depressed in the course of a long-term therapy with neuroleptic drugs. By continuous administration of relatively small doses, severe depressive syndromes may develop which, without knowing the history, would have been classified as endogenous depressions. In these cases imipramine and other similar antidepressive drugs can be used.

There are, on the other hand, psychopathological syndromes where diminished drive is the prevailing mood disorder. The more the reduction of initiative and affect dominates, the more these syndromes resemble schizophrenic residual or defect states.

We assume that syndromes which are similar to endogenous depression are more *pharmacogenically* determined. On the other hand, syndromes characterized by asthenia and disturbances of drive are influenced more by *morbogenic* factors.

Neuroleptic drugs are able to produce or to worsen depressive syndromes occurring in schizophrenic disease. If the depressive symptoms become manifest during the fourth to seventh week after the beginning of medication, *reactive* components, depending on the patient's personality and certain situational elements, seem to be of decisive importance. If the depressive symptoms, however, become manifest during the twentieth week after continuous administration of relatively small maintenance doses of neuroleptic drugs, the *pharmacogenic* or *morbogenic* factors are prevailing.

A closer analysis of so-called pharmacogenic depression has shown that an investigation of the structure and development of syndromes can bring satisfactory results only when the drug is not considered as the only cause of the depression. Therefore, clinical research in psychiatry should not be focussed on a single cause, but should consider all determining factors and apply a multifactorial approach. In this view, the investigation of pharmacogenic mood disorders is an example of modern multi-dimensional research in the field of psychopathology.

References

1. Angst, J., Battegay, R., Bente, D., Berner, P., Broeren, W., Cornu, F., Dick, P., Engelmeier, M. P., Heimann, H., Heinrich, K., Helmchen, H., Hippius, H., Pöldinger, W., Schmidlin, P., Schmitt, W., & Weiss, P. Das Dokumentations-System der Arbeitsgemeinshaft für Methodik und Dokumentation in der Psychiatrie (AMP). Arzneim.-Forsch., 1969, 19, 399–405.

2. Beecher, H. K. The powerful placebo. J. Amer. Med. Ass., 1955, 159, 1602–1606.

3. Bohacek, N. "Syndromverschiebung" oder "Syndromenthüllung" bei der Psychopharmakotherapie der Schizophrenien mit Piperazin-phenothiazinen. In D. Bente & P. B. Bradley (eds.), Neuro-Psychopharmacology, Vol. IV. Amsterdam: Elsevier, 1965. Pp. 175–178.

4. Bohacek, N. Pharmakogene depressive Verschiebung. In H. Brill, J. O. Cole, P. Deniker, H. Hippius & P. B. Bradley (eds.), Neuro-Psychopharmacology, Vol. V. Amsterdam: Excerpta Med. Internat. Congr. 1967. Pp. 1080–1082.

5. Bonhoeffer, K. Zur Frage der Klassifikation der symptomatischen Psychosen. Berl. Klin. Wschr., 1908, 45, 2257–2260.

6. Bonhoeffer, K. Die Exogenen Reaktionstypen. Arch. Psychiat. Nervenkr., 1917, 58, 58–70.

7. Bonhoeffer, K. Die Psychosen im Gefolge von akuten Infektionen, Allgemeinerkrankungen und inneren Erkrankungen. In G. Aschaffenburg (ed.), Handbuch der Psychiatrie-Spezieller Teil, 3 Abt. 1. Leipzig: Verlag F. Deuticke, 1912. Pp. 1–118.

8. Büssow, H. Zur Frage der Perniciosa-Psychosen. A. ges. Neurol. Psychiat., 1939, 165, 314–318.

9. Büssow, H. Über Psychosen nach Malaria. Allg. Z. Psychiat., 1944, 123, 235–278.

10. Conrad, K. Die symptomatischen psychosen. In H. W. Gruhle, R. Jung, W. Mayer-Gross, & M. Müller (eds.), Psychiatrie der Gegenwart, Vol. II. Berlin: Springer, 1960. Pp. 369-436.

11. Helmchen, H. Psychische Störungen durch Arzneimittel. Dtsch. Ärztebl., 1969, 66, 3537-3541.

12. Helmchen, H., & Hippius, H. Depressive Syndrome im Verlauf neuroleptischer Therapie. Nervenarzt, 1967, 38, 455-458.

13. Helmchen, H., & Hippius, H. Pharmakogene Depressionen. In H. Hippius & H. Selbach (eds.), Das depressive Syndrom. München: Urban & Schwarzenberg, 1969. Pp. 443-448.

14. Hippius, H. Dynamics and significance of psychopharmacological intervention in psychiatry. In D. Bente & P. B. Bradley (eds.), Neuro-Psychopharmacology, Vol. IV. Amsterdam: Elsevier, 1965. Pp. 241-248; 274-279.

15. Hippius, H. Psychische Storungen durch Arzneimittel. In R. Heintz (ed.), Erkrankungen durch Arzneimittel. Stuttgart: G. Thieme Verlag, 1966. Pp. 409-425.

16. Hippius, H., & Selbach, H. Zur medikamentösen Dauertherapie bei Psychosen. Med. Exp., 1961, 5, 298-305.

17. Hoch, P. Discussion at the fourth meeting of the Collegium Internationale Neuropsychopharmacologicum. In D. Bente & P. B. Bradley (eds.), Neuro-Psychopharmacology, Vol. IV. Amsterdam: Elsevier, 1965. P. 276.

18. Janzarik, W. Dynamische Grundkonstellationen in endogenen Psychosen. Berlin: Springer, 1959.

19. Meyer, H. H. Cyclothyme Wellen in schizophrenen Psychosen. Zbl. ges. Neurol. Psychiat., 1950, 108, 314.

20. Pogge, R. G., & Coats, E. A. Placebo as a source of side effects in normal people. Nebraska Med. J., 1962, 47, 437-438.

21. Ritchie, E. A. Toxic psychosis under cortisone and corticotrophine. J. ment. Sci., 1956, 102, 830-837.

22. Weitbrecht, H. J. Cyclothymes Syndrom und hirnatrophischer Prozess. Nervenarzt, 1953, 24, 489-493.

23. Ziolko, H. U. Subjektive Faktoren der psychiatrischen Pharmakotherapie. Dtsch. med. J., 1961, 12, 533-537.

DISCUSSION OF
DR. HIPPIUS' PAPER

ALFRED M. FREEDMAN, M.D.
New York Medical College

In the last half of the nineteenth century, the study of alcoholism and morphinism began in a modern sense: Wernicke and Korsakow reported their findings; Laehr reported the first case of morphinism in 1872 but the term was introduced the following year by Fiedler. Their studies led to the more comprehensive investigation of the mental illness due to poisons or infections, i.e., the exogenous psychoses. The outstanding name in this regard was Bonhoeffer, who separated this group at the beginning of the 20th century. As Professor Bonhoeffer was Professor Hippius' predecessor in Berlin, one can see the direct line of interest leading to this significant paper "Pharmacogenic Mood Disorders."

Those of us who are interested in drugs and behavior welcome any study of drug action in a certain individual, in a specific situation, whether that individual is a psychotic, an addict, or a normal. Professor Hippius' paper is important pragmatically with respect to the management of patients who are receiving drug therapy, and it also gives us insight into the action of drugs. Further, it has theoretical value in delineating the multiplicity of factors that go into the genesis of mental illness. One can observe the effects over time of introducing a drug in an individual, and subsequently can evaluate the effect of the drug in conjunction with other factors on the eventual clinical state. This is an important contribution to the theory of mental illness, particularly since it would appear that whatever the etiology of a mental disorder may be, many processes tend to have a common end-point.

It is evident that in spite of notable progress, we are still far from a complete statement of the etiology of depression. That our nosology is far from perfect can readily be seen from the study of the discrepancies in diagnoses from center to center and country to country. In the United States the empirical treatment of depressions would certainly appear to be our greatest strength, although the treatment often is based upon symptoms rather than diagnoses.

It is helpful to study those disorders in which an agent associated with the disorder is known, such as alcoholism or drug abuse, or to study those situations in which a drug is used in the course of an illness. Illustrative of the latter is ACTH in the treatment of arthritis or phenothiazine in the treatment of a schizophrenic in whom a depression appears. I have deliberately chosen the terms "appears to be related" or "associated" because, as Professor Hippius has shown in this and previous work, there is not a direct causality. He has eschewed simple explanations–drug produces the disorder. Rather, he has emphasized the complex interactions of three principal factors: the drug, the disease, and the individual's predisposition. One may add other factors to this matrix. The setting can be of major importance in any drug, whether it be a barbiturate, phenothiazine, or marihuana. Studies of marihuana suggest that previous use by the individual may be of importance in determining the manifestations produced by exposure to that drug or related drugs. It has been observed that the reaction to marihuana is a learned response; as a result, the reaction of a naive subject may be minimal or lacking, in contrast to that of an experienced subject (1). This phenomenon may be due to "new" enzymes that are induced by the marihuana. The "new" enzymes may be involved in the handling of other drugs that may not appear to be related to marihuana. Thus, the drug history of an individual may be crucial in explaining his reactions or lack of reaction to a pharmacological agent.

Professor Hippius selected as his population, schizophrenic patients who became depressed while receiving neuroleptic drugs. One must ask whether we are dealing with syndromes due to drugs or whether the drug is a red herring. In addition to the important contributions Professor Hippius and his colleagues have made, depression and suicide during drug treatment have been noted by a number of other authors, such as Lambert and Barnaud (2), Gerle (3), Strömgren (4), Simonson (5), Cohen et al. (6), and Steinberg et al. (7), Cohen and his colleagues assessed the incidence of suicide in schizophrenic patients and found no differences in suicide rates between patients who received drugs and those who did not. Steinberg concluded that depression occurred during remission of schizophrenic symptoms unrelated to concurrent drug administration; however, this conclusion was not supported by any data.

One must ask if the rate of depression and suicide in schizophrenics who did receive phenothiazine therapy is greater than those who did not. If it is greater, there still may be other explanations, e.g., the management may be much looser because the florid symptoms are controlled by the phenothiazine. Further, the patients receiving phenothiazines may not be as well recovered as believed, since the phenothiazines may mask the more florid symptoms.

It is instructive to look at those who advocate the use of phenothiazines for the treatment of depression. Fink and his associates (8) have recommended a combination of chlorpromazine and procyclizine for the treatment of depression. The combination is stated to be more effective than chlorpromazine alone. Overall (9) has recommended the use of thioridazine in the treatment of certain depressions. Overall developed a nosology of three groups, the anxious-tense depressions, the hostile depressions, and the retarded depressions (endogenous psychotic depression). It turns out that thioridazine is best in the first group, but that imipramine is best in the third. Both Fink and Overall are convinced of the efficacy of phenothiazines in the treatment of some depressions. Thus, we must wonder which schizophrenics become depressed with which drug in which situation.

Again, we are reminded that one must emphasize the contribution of the drug, the individual predisposition of the patient, the disease entity, and other variables. Cohen and his colleagues (6) particularly emphasize the contirbution of the family and the setting on the patient's outcome. The paper of deAlarcon and Carney (10) is of particular importance in this regard, in the light of the increasing use of slow release, intramuscular fluphenazine in the enanthate and in the decanoate forms. The authors describe the mood changes which appeared in 16 patients being treated with intramuscular fluphenazine, five of whom committed sucide. In a case described in detail, it would appear that there were two to four days of depression following each injection. Further, in a series of 124 apparently schizophrenic patients treated with intramuscular fluphenazine, 10 experienced severe depression, although on reassessment three of the patients were thought to have affective disorders. Interestingly enough, these depressed patients responded to treatment with electroconvulsive therapy or imipramine or both.

To summarize, it is quite clear that Professor Hippius is reporting a phenomenon that requires further work. He, as well as numerous other authors, reports depressive symptoms in schizophrenic patients receiving neuroleptic drugs. That about 15 per cent of patients receiving reserpine for hypertension developed depressive psychosis is fairly well known (11). Since reserpine reduces brain norepinephrine, this observation supports the "catecholamine hypothesis of affective disorders" (12). It may be that the depression seen in schizophrenics treated with chlorpromazine might be induced by the drug's ability to cause postsynaptic blockade of catecholamine transmission in the brain as described by Corrodi (13). This would still leave unexplained the antidepressant properties reported for chlorpromazine by Fink (8), and thioridazine by Overall (9). Thus, it is mandatory that prospective studies be embarked upon to study rates of depression and suicide in schizo-phrenic patients, both receiving and not receiving neuroleptics and controlling for differences in management and family situation. The increasing use of long-acting phenothiazines, as well as the anticipated development of newer and longer-acting products, makes such studies even more important. One can anticipate that long-acting phenothiazines will be developed that may be effective for three to six months. Such patients may be seen minimally, if at all, between injections. If depression occurs even for a short time, it would be wise to have such information soon. Too often such discoveries are made a decade after the introduction of a new drug or a new form of drug and follow a series of troubling observations of complications.

References

1. Weil, A., Zinberg, N. E., and Nelson, J. M. Clinical and psychological effects of marihuana in man. Science: 162:1234–1242, 1968.

2. Lambert, P. and Barnaud, J. Apparition de deux syndromes melancoliques au cours de traitments par le 45.60 RP. J. Med Lyon 35:951–1954.

3. Gerle, B. Clinical observations of the side-effects of haloperidol. Acta Psychiat. Scand. 40:65–76, 1964.

4. Strömgren, E. Psychoses caused by neuroleptics. Encepbale suppl. to vol. 53:170–174, 1964.

5. Simonson, M. Phenothiazine depressive reaction. J. Neuropsychiat. 5:259–265, 1964.

6. Cohen, S., Leonard, C. V., Farberow, N. L., and Schneidman, E. S. Tranquilizers and suicide in the schizophrenic patient. Arch. gen. Psychiat. 11:312–321, 1964.

7. Steinberg, H. R., Green, R. and Durell, J. Depression occurring during the course of recovery from schizophrenic symptoms. Amer. J. Psychiat. 124:699–702, 1967.

8. Fink, M., Klein, D. F., and Krauer, J. Clinical efficacy of chlorpromazine-procyclizine combination, imipramine, and placebo in depressive disorders. Psycho-pharmacologia 7:27–36, 1965.

9. Overall, J. E., Hollister, L. E., Johnson, M., and Pennington, V. Nosology of depression and differential response to drugs. J.A.M.A. 195:946–948, 1966.

10. deAlarcon, R., and Carney, M.W.P. Severe depressive mood changes following slow-release intramuscular fluphenazine injection. Brit. Med. J. 3:564–567, 1969.

11. Bunney, W. E. and Davis, J. M. Norepinephrine in depressive reactions. Arch. gen. Psychiat. 13:483–494, 1967.

12. Schildkraut, J. J. The catecholamine hypothesis of affective disorders. Amer. J. Psychiat. 122:509–522, 1965.

13. Corrodi, H., Fuxe, K., and Hökfelt, T. The effect of neuroleptics on the activity of central catecholamine neuroses. Life Sci. 6:767–774, 1967.

PART IV

CRITIQUES OF CURRENT THEORIES AND RESEARCH

9

CLINICAL RESEARCH
IN DEPRESSION*

GERALD L. KLERMAN, M.D.**

Since this Association devoted an annual meeting to the topic of depression over seventeen years ago (Hoch & Zubin, 1954), impressive progress has been made in the quality and quantity of clinical research on depression. The most striking changes have occurred in therapeutics—there are new drug treatments of mood disorders; the quality of clinical practice in most communities has improved; and local mental health services have expanded in scope and diversity. These therapeutic developments have significantly altered clinical research methods and directions, and, most significantly for the advancement of research, they have generated new hypotheses and concepts regarding the nature and pathogenesis of mood disorders.

This paper reviews current trends in clinical research on depression, as they reflect the new findings from antidepressant drug therapies and the neuropharmacological and biochemical discoveries related to their actions. For several reasons, special attention will be given to problems in clinical diagnosis and classification of depression. For over five decades, the proper diagnosis and classification of depression has been an area of clinical concern; yet it remains an unsolved problem. Moreover, there is confusion as to which research is appropriate; this confusion is attributed to unnecessary difficulties and "hang-ups" in our methodology and criteria for evidence.

The validity of most clinical research depends on the nature of the sample of depressed patients selected by the investigator. This is particularly important in collaborative research involving clinicians and laboratory biological scientists, because generalizations about biological processes are limited by patient selections according to clinical criteria. After reviewing this problem

---

*Supported by Grant MH-13738, from NIMH., U.S.P.H.S., H.E.W.
**Harvard Medical School, Boston.

area, it is necessary that clinical research apply to studies of phenomenology, diagnosis, and classification, the research techniques which have proven so successful in clinical evaluation of therapies in general, and of antidepressant drugs in particular. Such techniques include sampling; quantitative assessment of symptoms, feelings, and behaviors; attention to reliability and validity of symptom and behavior ratings; the utilization of advanced statistical methods, including multivariate techniques; and the importance of repeated experiments to replicate findings.

In this paper, some recent trends will be discussed, particularly against the historical background of clinical thinking about the nature and characterization of depression. Some recent studies of endogenous depression will be examined, particularly as they relate to differential prediction of treatment and highlight problems in research methodology and clinical theoretical thinking.

The Research Consequences of Recent Therapeutic Advances

The current confidence found among clinicians and researchers in the mood disorders results from the availability of new and effective therapies. While electroconvulsive therapy (ECT) had been recognized as an effective treatment for severely depressed patients since the early forties, current clinical efforts derive from the introduction of several compounds with demonstrated efficacy in the treatment of mood disorders. The mid-fifties saw the introduction of the phenothiazines and the Rauwolfias—the first of the "neuroleptics" or major tranquilizers. Iproniazid (Marsalid)—the first MAO inhibitor, and imipramine (Tofranil)—the first of the tricyclic antidepressants, appeared in 1957–58. Soon afterward, other new psychotropic compounds were synthesized, including the thioxanthenes and butyrophenones. Recently, the rediscovery by Schou, Gershon, and others of Cade's original finding that lithium salts had therapeutic value in mania has galvanized the research and treatment approaches to the elated states. These new pharmacological treatments have changed the therapeutic practice in depression and other mood disorders (Klerman & Cole, 1965).

While the most impressive advances have been in the development of these new pharmacologic agents, there has also been significant progress with the various psychotherapies. Psychoanalysis and individual psychotherapy have broadened their theoretical bases and become more flexible in therapeutic practices with depression (Cohen et al., 1954). Group psychotherapy and family therapy have become accepted techniques. Research on family dynamics (Spiegel & Bell, 1959), while applied most often to schizophrenia, is now being applied with increasing sophistication to the problems of mood disorders (Gibson, 1958; Jacobson, 1966; Deykin, 1966). Although the efficacy of the psychotherapies has not been fully established, professional education and clinical practice reflect increasing confidence in the wider range of their therapeutic application.

Paralleling these specific therapeutic modalities, mental health facilities have markedly expanded in most countries of the world. In the United States, these trends have culminated in the community mental health movement. Both quantitative and qualitative changes are underway in the patterns of mental health care. Quantitatively, more clinics and inpatient units have opened. There are increased numbers of psychiatrists, psychologists, and other mental health professionals. In addition, efforts are being made to explore the potential of nonprofessionals and community mental health workers. Qualitatively, there have been significant shifts in the patterns of mental health care. New types of facilities have been created—i.e., day hospitals, family treatment units, emergency units, etc. These new developments have created community alternatives to the large mental hospitals, which prior to the turn of the century were the major facilities for the mentally ill. Furthermore, society has acquired new attitudes toward psychiatric care. It is no longer limited to the extremely ill and creates less of a social stigma for the individual (Klerman & Paykel, in press).

These new treatments and new facilities have contributed to new research on the possible mechanisms of etiology and symptom formation in the mood disorders. One of the major avenues of investigation has been in the psychobiology of depression. Research on the neuropharmacology of antidepressant drugs and the biochemistry of affect—particularly in the catecholamine and indoleamine systems—is a major research frontier unanticipated fifteen years ago (Schildkraut et al., 1968).

The impressive advances in the new biology of depression raise questions for the clinician or clinical investigator. What is the meaningful role for clinical investigation? Is it only to make patients as comfortable as possible and await the next discovery from the ultracentrifuge and electron microscope? The answer is clearly no. Rather than retreat into passivity and quietude, there has been a quickening of pace for clinical research and significant advances in its quality and sophistication. Parallel with the development of biochemical and neuropharmacologic lines of investigation, there has been an intensified interest in the psychopathology of depression, in techniques of diagnosis, in studies of the childhood development of affect, and in follow-up studies of treatment. Clinical research, far from becoming atrophied or paralyzed in response to advances from biological laboratories, is active and expanding.

The Current State of Clinical Research on Depression

A decade and a half ago, there was relatively little active research in depression. Schizophrenia, the anxiety states, and the neuroses were the main areas of investigation. However, the balance has been redressed; depression, mania, and the mood disorders are clearly areas of vigorous activity. But what qualitative advances have been made—in research methods, in experimental design? Do the ideas possess vitality? What are the directions of new theory?

Currently, research on the mood disorders covers a wide spectrum of techniques and topics. Several areas of clinical investigation are especially productive, such as the study of sleeping and dreaming. Techniques for recording REM sleep have led to quantitative studies of sleep cycles in depression and the role of dreams and related cognitive phenomena to depression (Beck, 1967; Gershon, 1962; Hartmann, 1966; Hawkins, 1966; Kaplan, 1961). Through such studies, we have learned that patients' reports of sleep patterns have limited reliability when compared with REM results. Furthermore, the REM studies have shown that sleep disturbances are mostly related to fluctuations in depth. It has also been found that early morning awakenings, which have been stressed in the literature, are relatively infrequent.

Another area of productive research activity has been the study of childhood reactions to loss (Bowlby, 1969) resulting in a greater knowledge of the normative sequence of affective development and emotional responses in children and adolescents (Engel, 1952). The exact significance of these childhood and adolescent experiences as predisposers to mood disorders in adulthood is still a matter of active investigation. Two other areas stand out: research on genetic family studies (Winokur & Pitts, 1965) and attempts to create animal models for depressive disorders (McKinney & Bunney, 1969; Senay, 1966).

In a few areas, research is still undeveloped or only beginning. The epidemiology of depression is still rudimentary. Although this has recently been reviewed, relatively few American studies on incidence and prevalence approach the sophistication and quality of the Scandinavian and British studies. In a related field, studies of suicide have achieved scope and sophistication, particularly with the work of Farberow and Schneiddeman and the formation of the Center for the Study of Prevention of Suicide at NIMH (Farberow & Schneiddeman, 1961).

Along with research diversity, improved methodologies have evolved from research on treatment evaluation, particularly on the drug therapies. Of particular significance is the controlled clinical trial. The controlled trial is not only important for its applied value in evaluation of treatment, but merits significance also for having demonstrated conclusively that psychiatric clinical phenomena are amenable to experimental investigation—that psychopathology (patients' behavior, feelings and emotions, thoughts, actions, and convictions) can be quantitatively assessed in the clinical setting with reliability and validity. Highspeed electronic computers, combined with advanced multivariate statistical techniques, are also being applied to psychiatric phenomena with increasing relevance and potential. The debate over vitalism in biology in the late nineteenth century had its similarities to debates in the mid-twentieth century over the view that psychological phenomena are too variable and subjective for any quantitative and experimental approaches. The controlled clinical trial has resolved this debate.

The Role of Clinical Evidence

Although the quality of clinical research has improved considerably—spurred on by the need to develop new research methods for the evaluation of therapeutics—there remain important areas where research quality is uneven and dispute continues as to the proper nature of evidence. Some explanations are conceptual; some are methodological.

Conceptually, there are significant problems in delineating the proper role of clinical experience in the generation of evidence and hypotheses. Discussions of clinical research often become bogged down in futile debates between clinicians and experimentalists. Under criticism, clinicians defend the role of tradition and experience and justify their impressionistic-intuitive approach to behavior and phenomenology. The experimentalists attack the clinician for lack of controls and for the unreliability of "subjective" clinical impressions. This debate has proven fruitless and is based upon false issues. It derives from a failure to distinguish between research which is *hypothesis-generating* and research which is *hypothesis-testing*. In hypothesis-generating research, clinical observations, including impressions and intuition, are essential. The clinician with his empathic experience can store and integrate large amounts of naturalistic information, and even synthesize new hypotheses and ideas. The field of mood disorders has been a rich source of creative ideas and hypotheses. Prominent examples are: the psychoanalytic concepts of loss; the observations of Gillespie and others as to the distinction between endogenous depressions and those which are reactive to environmental changes; and Adolf Meyer's vision that psychopathology is the organism's reaction to life events.

Hypothesis generating is not the same as hypothesis testing. The field of clinical research needs not only new creative hypotheses, but also new facts—and facts are most reliable when derived from controlled experimental settings. Hopefully, the interactions of new hypotheses and new facts will lead to new ideas and new theoretical conceptualizations. Hypothesis testing requires experimentation and quantification. Since the rigorous experimentation of the laboratory is seldom possible, randomizations are necessary. The recent application of experimental designs to the clinical trial in drug evaluation has proven eminently successful. Techniques of sampling, randomization, double-blind placebo controls, quantitative assessments of ratings, attention to reliability and validity, and multivariate statistical techniques using computer technology are clearly applicable to hypothesis testing in clinical research (Chassen, 1967).

Problems of Methodology: Sampling

One example of difficulties in developing hypothesis testing in clinical research is population sampling. Most generalizations about diagnoses and classification in depression are based on samples of depressants from one type of institution, such as state mental hospitals, psychiatric units in a general hospital, or outpatient clinics. While clinicians have drawn attention to the diversity of patients seen in various settings, the implications are not always embodied in research. Sampling is particularly important when attempts are made to compare depression cross-culturally or cross-nationally. To illustrate the importance of this, let us look at data derived from a survey of clinical depression in New Haven in 1967. As part of a study of the clinical phenomenology of depression, a research team sampled consecutive admissions to several clinical facilities serving greater New Haven, including a psychiatric unit of a general hospital, a mental health center, a state mental hospital, and a Veterans Administration hospital. Sampling from these facilities allowed for a full range of patients from outpatient, inpatient, emergency units, and day hospital units. As shown in Table 1, the diagnosis of depression was quite frequent, averaging about 20 per cent of consecutive admissions. However, there were both quantitative and qualitative differences in the frequency and types of depressions seen in different clinical settings (Paykel *et al.*, 1970; Klerman, 1969).

In the sampling, we used consistent diagnostic criteria derived from the NIMH multi-hospital collaborative study of antidepressant drug therapy (Raskin, 1967). As shown in Figure 1, the highest percentage of depressions was found among admissions to the psychiatric unit in the general hospital and research unit; while the lowest percentage was in the two public mental institutions, the local state mental hospital, and the Veterans Administration hospital. Of particular significance is the relatively high percentage of depressions seen at the community mental health center's outpatient clinic—approximately one-third of consecutive admissions. These represent younger patients with relatively mild to moderately severe depressions, often occurring in response to situational stress or as problems of adaptation in the transition from youth to adulthood.

There are not only quantitative systematic differences, but also qualitative differences in the types of depression, as shown in Table 2. Based on psychiatric interview ratings, factor analyses were undertaken and three main factors were extracted (Paykel *et al.*, 1970). The profile of scores on three

Table 1

Treatment Settings, Admissions, and Sample Selected*

Treatment Setting	Facility	Admissions Screened	Number of Patients Eligible by Age and Residence	Number of Patients Selected	% Selected of Age/Residence Eligible
Outpatient Clinics	Connecticut Mental Health Center	331	283	100	35%
Day Hospital	Connecticut Mental Health Center	95	75	30	40%
Emergency Treatment Service (ETS)	Connecticut Mental Health Center	69	50	25	50%
	Connecticut Mental Health Center	37	32	13	41%
	Yale New Haven Hospital	98	56	19	34%
Inpatients	Connecticut Valley Hospital	183	158	30	14%
	Veterans Administration Hospital	62	23	3	13%
	Total Inpatients	380	269	65	24%
Total—All Settings		875	677	220	32%

*Reprinted from Paykel, E. S.; Klerman, G. L.; and Prusoff, B. A.: Treatment Setting and Clinical Depression, Arch. Gen. Psychiatry 22:11–21, (Jan.) 1970.

PROFILES OF FACTOR SCORES

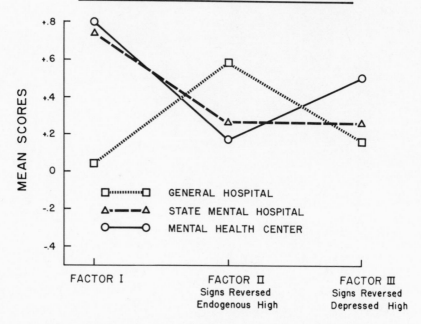

Fig. 1. (from Klerman, G. L., and Paykel, E. S. Depressive Pattern, Social Background and Hospitalization, J. Nervous and Mental Dis., in press.)

factors differ among the institutions. Factor 1 is a general severity factor; Factor 2 is a bipolar factor, similar in content to the endogenous-reactive continuum observed in other factor analytical studies (Mendels & Cochran, 1968); Factor 3 is more difficult to define, but seems to be an anxiety-depressive mood factor. Comparing the profiles of scores from patients at the different institutions, it is apparent that there are qualitative differences in the types of depression seen. For example, the endogenous depressive pattern is more likely to be seen in research units devoted to biological clinical correlative research and in psychiatric units in general hospitals, whereas they are less likely to be seen in public mental hospitals and in outpatient units.

These findings from the New Haven survey are illustrative of the need for careful attention to sampling methodology. The growth and sophistication of clinical research techniques, while considerable, still requires further attention, not only where collaborative studies with laboratory sciences and neurobiology are undertaken, but also for research in clinical and epidemiological areas.

Table 2

Factor Loadings*

Factor I (Severity)		Factor II (Neurotic vs. Endogenous)		Factor III (Anxiety vs. Depressive Mood)	
Work and Interests	.60	Irritability	.55	Anxiety-Somatic	.61
Helplessness	.57	Anxiety-Somatic	.49	Anxiety-Psychic	.58
Constipation	.55	Initial Insomnia	.47	Hypochondriasis	.39
Depressive Delusions	.55	Reactivity	.39	Diurnal Variation (Worse AM High)	.26
Pessimism and Hopelessness	.54	Middle Insomnia	.37	Insight	.20
Hypochondriasis	.49	Self-Pity	.32	Distinct Quality	.16
Depressed Feelings	.46	Depersonalization	.30	Energy and Fatigue	.16
Agitation	.45	Suicidal Tendencies	.28	Depersonalization	.13
Insight	.42	Paranoid Ideas	.28	Work and Interests	.12
Guilt	.40	Hypochondriasis	.22	Obsessional Symptoms	.12
Change of Appetite (Anorexia High)	.39	Anxiety-Psychic	.22	Delayed Insomnia	.10
Energy and Fatigue	.39	Obsessional Symptoms	.22	Paranoid Ideas	.04
Depersonalization	.37	Energy and Fatigue	.12	Reactivity	.03
Initial Insomnia	.35	Depressed Feelings	.12	Agitation	.01
Retardation	.34	Delayed Insomnia	.09	Depressive Delusions	.00
Self-Pity	.33	Helplessness	.08	Helplessness	-.01
Anxiety-Psychic	.32	Change of Appetite (Anorexia High)	.05	Change of Appetite (Anorexia High)	-.02
Suicidal Tendencies	.31	Work and Interests	-.02	Constipation	-.07
Distinct Quality	.31	Constipation	-.06	Self-Pity	-.07
Delayed Insomnia	.28	Hostility	-.09	Middle Insomnia	-.14
Hostility	.27	Pessimism and Hopelessness	-.14	Retardation	-.16
Anxiety-Somatic	.26	Guilt	-.19	Guilt	-.17
Diurnal Variation (Worse AM High)	.23	Depressive Delusions	-.21	Depressed Feelings	-.18
Obsessional Symptoms	.20	Insight	-.21	Hostility	-.30
Middle Insomnia	.16	Agitation	-.22	Initial Insomnia	-.31
Paranoid Ideas	.08	Diurnal Variation (Worse AM High)	-.30	Irritability	-.32
Irritability	-.11	Distinct Quality	-.39	Pessimism and Hopelessness	-.41
Reactivity	-.51	Retardation	-.39	Suicidal Tendencies	-.49

*Reprinted from Paykel, E. S.; Klerman, G. L.; and Prusoff, B. A.: Treatment Setting and Clinical Depression, Arch. Gen. Psychiatry 22:11–21, (Jan.) 1970.

The Characterizations of Depression

Therapy and research have progressed, but ideas and theories about depression have lagged. Many terms and concepts remain rooted in experiences derived from the era prior to World War II. This is particularly evident in discussions of the clinical diagnoses and characterization of depression. Recent clinical experience has resulted in a marked broadening of the spectrum of clinical conditions subsumed under the category of affective disorders or mood disorders. Neurasthenia, hypochondriasis, and some psychosomatic conditions, considered separate disorders three or four decades ago, are now considered within the broad range of depressive disorders. Along with this extension of the range of clinical phenomena, a questioning of existing theoretical models and a search for alternative concepts has ensued. There is disagreement as to the criteria for diagnosing patients as depressed and as to the best means of classifying the large group of heterogeneous phenomena subsumed under "depression." There are no adequate quantitative and validated criteria for distinguishing pathological depression from normal mood swings or reactions to traumatic events, such as grief and bereavement. One approximation to a quantitative diagnostic criterion is the Raskin Scale which was utilized in the NIMH collaborative studies and the recent techniques developed by Robins and his associates distinguishing between primary and secondary depressions (Raskin, 1967; Robins, 1970).

Should the mood disorders be regarded as a single group—homogeneous in etiology, clinical features, and psychopathology—or as several groups—heterogeneous in etiology and pathophysiology? This question remains unanswered by currently available research evidence. However, the clinician, the investigator, and the theorist must take some position on this issue. For the clinician, his position regarding heterogeneity leads to differential prescription of therapies. For the theoretician, his views regarding heterogeneity will determine whether he proposes a single unitary theory or postulates two or more mood disorders with alternative etiologies and mechanisms of psychopathology. Since there are a number of alternative approaches to this problem, whichever the investigator chooses will significantly affect his research strategy. It will influence the manner in which he defines his population, selects the study group, and chooses to characterize their clinical features.

In reviewing these alternatives, it is valuable to place our current thinking in its proper historical perspective. While at this time, clinical diagnosis subsumes a wide range of behavior, this has not always been true. When the term depression evolved its meaning at the end of the nineteenth century, it was primarily applied to psychotic states, then called "melancholia." The formulations of Freud in *Mourning and Melancholia* (1917) and those of Kraepelin in his *Manic-Depressive Insanity* (1921) were derived from their observations of patients who were both depressed and psychotic. Their concern was the contrast of normal sadness with psychotic depression. Kraepelin's major achievement was the separation of two psychoses: dementia praecox from manic-depressive insanity. The majority of patients whom he studied were both psychotic and institutionalized. At that time, the main clinical problems were to distinguish the psychotic from the non-psychotic and to classify the larger group of psychotic conditions into categories such as the presently accepted "schizophrenia" and "affective psychoses."

Over the succeeding half century, as psychiatry rapidly expanded its boundaries beyond the mental hospital, increasing attention was focused on the many non-psychotic affective conditions seen in consultation rooms, out-patient clinics, and the new community facilities. These depressions—variously called neurotic or reactive—challenged existing concepts. This new clinical experience precipitated debate over the best description and sub-division of the rapidly expanding population of patients with depression. Further, numerous observers have noticed the change in depressed patients at mental health facilities since World War II. The trend is for depressed patients to be younger, less severely ill, and more commonly neurotic (Rosenthal & Gudeman, 1965). Only a small minority are psychotic by the criteria of reality testing: perception, cognition, or orientation. Yet our concepts—both descriptive and psychodynamic—have been developed mainly from institutionalized and psychotic patients.

These changes in the clinical characteristics of patients with mood disorders are the result of several trends: 1) the effects of somatic therapy on the clinical course of the illness; 2) a tendency for patients to come into treatment earlier in their clinical course; 3) a tendency for patients who might not otherwise have defined their problems as psychiatric, to see themselves with emotional problems; and 4) the possibility of intrinsic changes in the clinical characteristics and epidemiology of the illness. Some of these trends are the result of the various somatic therapies, especially electroconvulsive therapy, the tranquilizers, and the antidepressants. These therapeutic changes have led to greater awareness of the heterogeneity of the clinical phenomena subsumbed under the diagnostic grouping of depression. Such factors have also contributed to a revival of interest in the typology and classification of depression.

The intellectual tensions between the disease concept of depression and the reactive concept of depression have been revived. The debate during the twenties and thirties over Gillespie's concept of endogenous vs. reactive depression appeared settled by Aubrey Lewis' monumental research (Lewis, 1934). He applied Adolf Meyer's psychobiological concepts to existing views of depression, in the same way that Meyer critiqued the disease concept of dementia praecox. In Western Europe, Britain, and the United States, the Meyerian view was predominant into the early 1960's. Currently, there is a neo-Kraepelinian revival in the field of depression—the recurrence of the hypotheses regarding hereditary and biological causes of depression, which see the disturbance in mood as a medical condition. The main proponents of this theory, which is crystallized in the textbook by Meyer-Gross, Slater and Roth, include Kiloh, Coppen, Roth and their associates in England, and Robins and his associates in St. Louis with their concern for primary affective illness. The neo-Kraepelinian view receives strong reinforcement for its biological thinking from the success of the somatic therapies. However, the biological concepts of disease have become far more sophisticated than they were in the late nineteenth century. The concept of "disease entity," formulated by central European psychiatry from discoveries of clinical pathological correlations at the autopsy table, has given way to the new approaches from molecular biology and enzymology.

In approaching these issues, I have found it useful to divide the views on clinical phenomenology of depression into three groups: the unitary, the dualistic, and the pluralistic (Rosenthal & Klerman, 1965).

The *unitary* view emphasizes the underlying unity and common features of the depressive episodes. In America, this view has been associated with Adolf Meyer and his school of psychiatry and in England, with the influential writings of Mapother and his students, especially Sir Aubrey Lewis. The Meyerians see depression as part of the range of human experience—a psychobiological reaction of the human organism to life's vicissitudes. The unifiers tend to reject schemes for sub-divisions and to emphasize organic, constitutional, or genetic factors. This point of view has been most recently put forth by Menninger in his book, *The Vital Balance* (Menninger, 1963). The Meyerians acknowledge gradation from minor to major disturbances, but claim that the distinctions between neurosis and psychosis or endogenous and reactive are unsubstantiated. Many American textbooks incorporate this point of view and emphasize that psychotic depressions differ from neurotic depressions only by the severity of symptoms, indications for hospitalization, and legal requirements for commitment or certification.

The *dualistic* positions have been adopted by most continental European and some British writers. The most influential dualistic formulation is the distinction between reactive depression and endogenous or autonomous depression, proposed by Gillespie in his paper, "The Clinical Differentiation of Types of Depression" (Gillespie, 1929). This distinction subsequently attained wide acceptance in Western Europe, Great Britain and Canada.

Another dualistic position distinguishes neurotic from psychotic depressions. In the American literature, this is a common distinction. Here, the term psychotic is not being used in the purest sense—e.g., break with reality, as manifested by hallucinations, delusions, ideas of reference, etc. In fact, less than five per cent of large samples of depressed patients will have manifestly psychotic features (Klerman & Paykel, 1969; Hamilton, 1960). Rather, the American concept of psychotic depression emphasizes the severity of symptoms, the degree of functional impairment, and the degree of ego regression. The emphasis on the degree of regression derives from the formulations of Fenichel, whose influential synthesis of classical psychoanalytic views distinguished psychotic from neurotic depressions on the depth of ego regression and degree of impairment of ego function (Fenichel, 1945). Implicit in the neurotic-psychotic dichotomy is that psychotic disorders are likely to be biological in causation, whereas neurotic disorders are probably due to stress or personality dynamics. Unfortunately, the neurotic-psychotic distinction is often used interchangeably with the endogenous-reactive dichotomy, although psychosis is not one of the necessary criteria for the endogenous depressive type.

During the thirties and forties, considerable acrimony was generated in the controversy between the separatists and the unifiers. Because of this extensive controversy and also because of the general reaction against classification systems during World War II, the dualistic position fell into disfavor. Recently, however, it has regained adherence, due to the therapeutic experience with the new antidepressant drugs and the patient's differential therapeutic response; patients with the endogenous symptoms pattern respond better to somatic therapies—particularly electroconvulsive therapy (ECT) and imipramine and other related tricyclic drugs—than do psychoneurotic patients (Kiloh & Garside, 1963).

Clinicians frequently report that there are "types" of depressed patients who will respond better to ECT, antidepressant drugs, or psychoanalysis. Attempts have been made to predict responders to one treatment or another, and to find the correspondence between characteristics of treatment responders and clinical groupings. These considerations have led to a renewed interest in the phenomenology of depression, which has accelerated since the influential work of Grinker and his associates (Grinker et al., 1961).

One of the main consequences of recent research findings from psychopharmacology has been to weaken the unitary position, which has been the dominant American and British approach to phenomenology for at least three decades. In this weakening of the unitary point of view, the writings of two men stand out: that of Grinker and his associates in Chicago and the critique of existing psychoanalytic theory of Edward Bibring in Boston. It is of note that both Grinker and Bibring were trained as psychoanalysts. As such, both accepted the unitary theory of depression derived from Meyer and Freud. Grinker's clinical experience led him to challenge this model and to develop research to generate data to support his growing skepticism. One of the first to use multivariate statistics, he applied the method of factor analysis and demonstrated the lack of congruence between actual ratings and judgments compared to the existing clinical stereotypes. As a result, he proposed several types of depression based on different configurations of feeling states, behaviors, and presumed personality dynamics. His particular scheme is less important than his demonstrating the necessity for new thinking. The work of Edward Bibring was more theoretical, but within the framework of psychoanalysis, particularly its modern version, ego psychology. Like Grinker, he challenged the existing stereotype and proposed a broadened concept of the mechanism of depression which allows for several pathogenic mechanisms. He did not accept the classic stereotype that depression is "nothing more than anger turned against the self" and "the automatic equation of depression with pre-existing oral personality characteristics with anal fixations." A large amount of psychoanalytic and personality research has subsequently emerged. To a large degree, Bibring and Grinker made it legitimate in the late fifties to question existing views (Bellak, 1966; Friedman, 1963; Gershon & Klerman, 1968; Rappaport, 1967, Bibring, 1953).

With the need for new concepts, important efforts have been made by investigators to develop various dualistic and pluralistic models to relate existing clinical practice to theoretical concepts. In particular, experience with differential response to various therapies, somatic and psychological, was an indicator that different types of depression probably existed.

The Concept of the Endogenous Depression

Having reviewed the main historical trends, it is appropriate at this point to bring empirical data to bear on the issues. I have chosen the concept of endogenous depression as an illustration, in part because it is a recurring concept, but mainly because there is now a body of statistically sophisticated research attempting to test the clinical concept with advanced experimental methods. In reviewing research, it is necessary to clarify the concept and to determine its construct validity; specifically, it is valuable to explicate the concept of endogenous depression, its assumptions and components. We have used the term endogenous depression for historical reasons; this term has gained wide acceptance in the literature. Its historical background and current investigations highlight many issues in clinical research design and experimental approaches to the clinical phenomena.

It is useful to regard the concept of endogenous depression as a grouping of four component propositions, each relating to an aspect of clinical depression. As hypotheses, these components of the concept become subject to empirical investigation and verification, rather than the object of debate and prejudice.

The first proposition suggests that a particular pattern of manifest clinical signs and symptoms will occur together at one point in clinical time. This pattern forms the symptom cluster, configuration, or syndrome. The empirical implication is that the correlation of symptoms in a group of patients is not random, but rather, certain symptoms are more likely to occur together as a symptom cluster or pattern. This leads to a testable hypothesis, one which embodies a cross-sectional approach to symptom manifestations during the overt clinical depression.

The second proposition states that the acute episode will occur without a recent precipitating event. This proposition relates to the issue of presumed proximate etiology. In contrast, for the reactive types of depression, the acute depressive episode is precipitated by some immediate life event or stress. Reactive depressions are seen as exaggerations of normal responses to life events. Although the reactive-endogenous distinction was developed in Great Britain, it derives from the traditions of continental European psychiatry which differentiated endogenous and exogenous mental illness—a differentiation formulated in the nineteenth century and embodied in Kraepelin's comprehensive nosological system. The endogenous types of illnessess are presumed to have genetic, constitutional, or metabolic etiologies; the exogenous types are due to external causes—infections, trauma, drugs or intoxicants—or secondary to psychogenetic or situational stimuli. However, whatever the larger theoretical implication of this proposition, the relationship of symptom patterns to recent precipitants can be empirically tested.

The third proposition relates to specific premorbid personality patterns. The personality of persons with endogenous depression will be relatively stable and non-neurotic. Here, the relationship of illness to personality is similar to the criteria for the distinction between primary and secondary depressions, elaborated by the St. Louis group (Winokur & Pitts, 1965). There are also similarities to the views of Freud and of Abraham, who observed obsessive-compulsive features in the inter-morbid personality of melancholics (Abraham, 1911, 1927). It is of note that the psychoanalytic description of the obsessive-compulsive character traits—neatness, ambition, industry, conscientiousness—closely parallel the descriptions of the premorbid personality of the endogenous patterns—stable, vigorous, enterprising, and without neuroticism or hysteria. This component of the endogenous pattern focuses on overlapping, but diverging, definitions of neurosis. In some usages, the term neurotic means non-psychotic, as in the distinction between neurotic and psychotic depressions. The term neurotic also refers to clinical disorders which are a consequence of the maladaptive personality patterns of the individual. In this proposition, however, the implication is of a constellation of personality traits.

The last proposition ascribes an autonomous quality to the depression. Whatever the precipitants of the depression, it will "run its course" without direct response to immediate environmental influences. Gillespie and others noted that although an initial precipitant may sometimes be present in the autonomous depression, the illness tends to have a temporal pattern of its own.

I became interested in the concept of endogenous depression during a series of clinical and metabolic affective disorder studies conducted between 1961 and 1964 at the Massachusetts Mental Health Center's Ward I, a special clinical research ward for patients with moderate to severe depressions. In such patients, psychobiological and biochemical phenomena would most likely be manifested. A study was undertaken to discover if this clustering of manifest symptoms and personality features occured. If this cluster was found by factor analysis, it would provide a quantitative score of the endogenous pattern. This score could then be correlated with personality measures, apparent precipitants, and other historical data to ascertain the extent to which the various hypotheses derived from the literature could be empirically validated.

A number of factor analytic studies have attempted to derive clinical groupings of symptoms (Hamilton & White, 1959; Friedman, 1963; Kiloh & Garside, 1963; Overall, 1966; Grinker, 1961). This use of factor analysis has been reviewed recently (Mendels & Cochran, 1969), and called attention to the large area of congruence among the various studies, including those of our research group.

Table 3 shows the results of our factor analysis with the items and their loadings on the first factor. This analysis was based on ratings of fifty consecutively admitted female patients. As seen, the items loading heavily on this factor correspond closely to the symptom pattern of endogenous depression delineated in the clinical literature. The first five factors accounted for 94% of the variance; Factor 1 accounted for 35%. The items loading heavily, i.e., over 0.40, on Factor 1 were signs and symptoms which correspond with the classical pattern of the endogenous depression. The symptoms included early and middle insomnia, severity of the depressed affect, retardation, guilt and self-reproach, weight loss, etc. Delusional symptoms—while not defined as part of the criteria for the endogenous pattern—also loaded highly (0.45), although they occurred infrequently in the overall population. (This may account for the endogenous and psychotic terminology being used interchangeably.) We regarded this as partial verification of the first proposition: the symptoms in a depressive episode do not occur at random, but certain symptoms tend to correlate with each other, forming a distinctive pattern.

We next turned to personality correlations. The concept proposes that patients with the endogenous symptom pattern have a relatively well-adjusted pre-morbid personality; whereas patients with reactive or neurotic depressions have neurotic or hysterical personalities. Part of the dilemma derives from the various meanings of neurotic. In our research group, Aaron Lazare and I were

Table 3

Correlations of Factor Score and Item Rating*

Item	Correlation of Factor Score and Item	Significance of Correlation
Middle Insomnia	.76	P < .01
Global Rating of Illness	.71	P < .01
Severity of Depressed Mood	.68	P < .01
Morning Insomnia	.62	P < .01
Retardation	.59	P < .01
Guilt and Self-Reproach	.54	P < .01
Weight Loss	.47	P < .01
Delusional Symptoms	.46	P < .01
Visceral Symptoms	.47	P < .01
Agitation	.46	P < .01
Loss of Interest	.45	P < .01
Early Insomnia–Difficulty Falling Asleep	.39	P < .01
Feelings of Worthlessness	.34	P < .01
Insidious Onset	.37	P < .05
Long Duration	.32	P < .05
Obsessive Ruminations and Compulsive Acts	.28	P < .05
Anxiety–Psychic and Somatic	.17	N.S.
Hypochondriacal Attitude	.13	N.S.
Suicidal Thought or Behavior	.09	N.S.
Symptoms Increased in Morning	.08	N.S.
Fluctuation of Illness	.04	N.S.
Symptoms Increased in Evening	−.14	N.S.
Irritability and Hostility	−.21	N.S.
Self-Pity	−.24	N.S.
Reactivity of Depression	−.28	P < .05

*Reprinted from Rosenthal, S. H., and Klerman, G. L.: Content and Consistency in the Endogenous Depressive Pattern, *British J. Psychiatry* 112:471–484, (May) 1966.

interested in the features of hysterical personality among the women in our study. Based upon a review of the psychiatric literature, we developed criteria for hysterical features (Lazare & Klerman, 1968). Endogenous factor scores correlated negatively (−0.28) with these personality judgments. The less the female patient displayed the endogenous symptom pattern, the more likely she was to be considered an hysterical personality.

I will now turn to the proposition related to apparent precipitating events. Although reactivity to environmental stimuli during depression was Gillespie's main criterion for the diagnosis of endogenous depression, current usage emphasizes the role of recent life events as precipitants of the acute episode. Research on the role of environmental events as precipitants of acute depression has gained importance with the advent of psychoendocrine research on stress and the relationship between life events and activation of the neuroendocrine system. The factor scores tended to be inversely related to the clinician's judgment of the presence of a precipitant. Based on the records, patients were divided into three groups: precipitant present, precipitant doubtful, and precipitant absent. The mean of the factor scores was calculated for each of these three groups and there was a significant relationship in the predicted direction.

We next compared the items comprising our factors with the similar factors reported in the Hamilton studies and those of Kiloh and Garside. There was considerable similarity between the items which loaded heavily on these three factors. To carry the comparison even further, the symptom ratings of our patients were scored according to the factor loadings formulae derived from Hamilton and from Kiloh and Garside. Thus, each of our patients was given three scores: our factor score, the Hamilton factor score, and the Kiloh-Garside factor score. The scores were correlated, using the Spearman Rank-Order Correlation Coefficient. Our factor scores correlated 0.80 with Hamilton's factor score and 0.68 with the Kiloh factor; Kiloh's factor and the Hamilton factor correlated 0.60. Using Kendell's Coefficient of Concordance the overall correlation among the three factors was 0.80.

All these correlations are highly significant. They illustrate the potential reliability of factor analytically derived scores. Psychiatric judgments are frequently criticized because of their low inter-rater reliability; based upon this study, however, we were reasonably assured that there were significant correlations among manifest symptoms and between the symptom pattern and other clinical features, such as personality traits and acute precipitants.

Replication from the New Haven Survey

As previously described, in 1967, a large survey was undertaken by Gene Paykel and myself of 220 depressives seen at several types of psychiatric facilities in the New Haven area, including the Yale-New Haven Hospital, the West Haven Veterans Administration Hospital, the Connecticut Mental Health Center, and the Connecticut Valley Hospital. A semi-stratified sample was gathered, including 100 outpatients and 120 inpatients. All patients were interviewed by the same psychiatrist and the observations were scored on a variant of the Hamilton Scale previously used in the Boston studies.

Based upon the symptom ratings in this large sample of 220 patients, an independent factor analysis was done, using the principal components method with Varimax Rotation. As shown in Table 3, two main factors were extracted. The first factor represents a general measure of severity of illness; the second factor is a bipolar factor similar to that described by Kiloh and Garside. One of the criticisms of the previous factor analysis with Rosenthal was that severity of illness was included as one of the endogenous pattern items. Meyerians had questioned whether this factor score was not an indirect way of assessing severity. However, in the factor analysis on the data from the larger New Haven sample, it was possible to separate a severity dimension (Factor 1) from the bipolar endogenous-reactive distinction (Paykel *et al.*, 1970). (See Table 2.)

The New Haven study compared the clinical features of depressions at various institutions. The inpatient units showed significant differences as to the type of depression, depending on the institution in which the patient was hospitalized as was shown in Figure 1. Furthermore, there was a social class gradient as shown in Table 4. In addition, a special analysis was done of patients on the research unit at the Connecticut Mental Health Center. These patients have high ratings on the endogenous factors (Paykel *et al.*, 1970). The term endogenous generates a negative reaction because it embodies the endogenous-exogenous distinction rooted in nineteenth century psychiatric thinking. To a certain extent, it prejudges the issue in that it embodies an etiologic concept—itself the object of study. Thus, the term endogenous begs the question. It remains to future research to ascertain if this symptom-personality-precipitating complex is related to some biological or constitutional etiology, arising within, i.e., endogenous to, the individual. Another name would be more desirable. As discussed previously, these findings have particular implications for comparing research reports from different institutions. State hospitals, mental health centers, psychiatric units in general hospitals, and research wards admit different segments of the large depressive population. Lack of agreement across studies may in part be due to institutional differences in patient samplings.

Table 4

Social Class*

Comparison of Depressed Patients in Three Inpatient Facilities

Social Class	General Hospital		Mental Health Center		State Mental Hospital	
	N	%	N	%	N	%
I and II	10	52.6	3	23.1	1	4.0
III, IV, V	9	47.4	10	76.9	24	96.0
Total	19	100%	13	100%	25	100%

$$x^2 = 13.80 \; p < .01$$

*Reprinted from Klerman, G. L., and Paykel, E. S.: Depressive Pattern, Social Background, and Hospitalization, *J. Nerv. Mental Dis.*, in press.

Based upon these studies, a number of trends are clearly apparent. The concept of endogenous depression can be sub-divided into a number of subsidiary hypotheses, which can be empirically investigated. The hypothesis concerning symptom clustering seems well validated by factor analysis and by the comparability across studies. It is also possible, using factor analytic methods, to separate a severity index from the symptom clustering. The trends have been replicated on three independent samples in Boston and New Haven (Rosenthal & Klerman, 1966; Rosenthal & Gudeman, 1967; Klerman & Paykel, 1969). Therefore, we conclude that in the current state of knowledge, there is inter-correlation among symptoms. Furthermore, associated with the endogenous symptom is the relative absence of a precipitating event and the existence of certain personality features. Still unsettled, however, is if the endogenous depression is a well-defined group, clearly separated from other groups, or merely an issue of gradation on multiple dimensions.

Grouplings and Typologies

These factor analytic approaches have demonstrated significant correlations among symptoms and between symptom clusters and personality, stress, and response to treatment. However, more difficult problems arise as to the criteria for delimiting a distinct *type* of depression. Recently, there has been debate as to whether factor analysis is an appropriate method for grouping patients or forming types (Katz *et al.*, 1965). It can be argued mathematically that factor analysis deals with the relationship among symptoms, whereas the clinical concept of the endogenous depressive type is a judgment about individuals. Furthermore, the frequency distribution of population scores may not divide into two groups. Various attempts by Hamilton, Kiloh and Garside, Rosenthal and myself have been made to determine whether the distribution factor scores are normal or bimodal (Kendell, 1968). Most of these have failed to demonstrate separate groups. Moreover, in our New Haven Study, independent judgments were made as to the patient's "fitting" into the classical endogenous type. Although these judgments could be made with some reliability, the finding was that only about 15 per cent of the large sample fell into this grouping.

A more promising statistical method is cluster analysis, which locates individuals in a multi-dimensional space, with an axis determined by various symptom patterns or other clinical dimensions, but relevant mathematical computations involve distance functions. A similar technique was used by Grinker (Grinker *et al.*, 1968) in his study of borderline states and we have recently applied it to depression. There are good statistical reasons for doubting the extent to which factor analysis can be an adequate method for developing typologies. Factor analysis has established its utility in isolating dimensions underlying a multiplicity of rating variables. However, dimensions of rating variables do not necessarily correspond with groupings of patients. Multiple dimensions are usually orthogonal in a multivariate space, so that the variances among them are independent of each other. Therefore, the description of the patient's position on such dimensions says nothing as to his membership in a set of mutually exclusive groups, such as are usually conceptualized in clinical thinking on typology and classification.

As a consequence of dissatisfaction with factor analysis, statisticians have turned to multivariate cluster techniques including cluster analysis and multiple discriminant functions. A recent attempt to apply multivariate techniques has been developed by Paykel (in press). Based upon data described above, a multiple cluster analysis was undertaken. With multiple discriminant functions, a number of alternative group partitions are discernible.

Paykel's cluster analysis yielded four groups. The first group consists mainly of older patients with high scores on guilt, hopelessness, delusional intensity, and global severity of illness; they show low scores on RLE ratings and the MPI neuroticism scale. The overall pattern seems to be a cross between psychotic depression and endogenous symptoms with distant qualities of guilt, anorexia, retardation, and delayed insomnia.

The second group showed an admixture of anxiety and neurotic symptoms with moderate to depressed mood, manifested by high scores on psychic and somatic anxiety, depersonalization, obsessional symptoms, and fatigue. While they had lower scores on severity of global illness than the psychotic group, they were high on suicidal trends and feelings of depression and had a history of previous episodes of depression. They tended to score high on MPI neuroticism and low on stress. These patients have been tentatively labeled "anxious depressants" and appear to be a group with a history of neurotic recurrent depressions. However, they cannot be regarded as reactive, since their depressions are not related to pre-existing stress.

Groups three and four consisted of younger patients and their differences were less striking. Group three was less ill, has higher scores on hostility and self-pity, and could be regarded as hostile depressives. Group four consisted of the youngest patients, labeled "young depressant personality disorders," similar in many respects to the group identified by Hamilton. They had high scores on MPI neuroticism and also relatively high scores on the life events score. Clinically, they were mild with low scores on most individual symptoms and global severity. Yet they showed high scores on reactivity to depression, indicating mood fluctuations related to environmental changes. Their case records indicated a high frequency of disturbed life patterns and a tendency to receive concomitant clinical diagnosis of personality disorders. In a subsequent paper Paykel et al. (1970) showed that these types differentiate patterns of response to antidepressant drug treatment. Further work will be

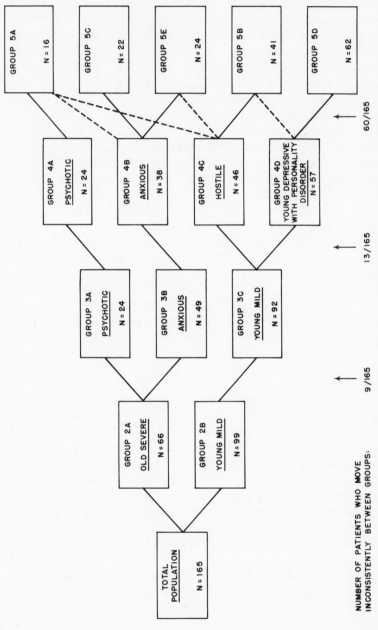

NUMBER OF PATIENTS WHO MOVE
INCONSISTENTLY BETWEEN GROUPS: 9/165

Fig. 2. Hierarchy of Groups. (From Paykel, E. S. Classification of Depressed Patients: A Cluster Analysis Deriveed Grouping. Accepted for publication in the British J. Psychiatry, in press.)

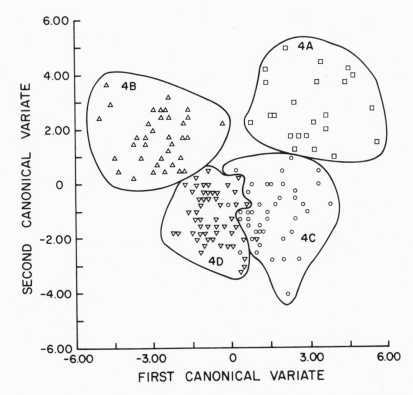

Fig. 3. Four Group Partition. Plot of Patients on First Two Cane Canonical Variates. (From Paykel, E. S. Classification of Depressed Patients: A Cluster Analysis Derived Grouping. Accepted for publication in the British J. Psychiatry, in press.)

necessary to validate whether similar clusters occur in other populations and whether or not it is possible to predict response.

Paykel's research is relevant for two reasons. First, it is an illustration of one strategy of clinical research. Any research on depression must embody some patient sample and some definition of the clinical phenomena. Currently, much attention is placed on biochemical and neurophysiological techniques. Often insufficient attention is given to criteria of selection of patients, characterization of their illness, and accurate description of their symptomatology, personality dynamics, and psychological structure. As attempts are made to correlate biological variables with clinical variables, we will need better measures of the clinical and psychological variables. Much of the current research on the psychobiology of depression can be criticized for an inbalance of methodology; while careful attention is given to the methods for collecting and preserving biological samples and to biochemical assay, patient characteristics and procedures for patient selection are vaguely described and insufficient quantitative data are reported to allow accurate comparisons among studies.

This conclusion about the state of research leads to a second area of relevance—the strategy for biological research. A number of years ago, Kety, in discussing the selection of patients for schizophrenia research, emphasized the desirability of biased sampling. If, as it is believed today, the depressive population is etiologically heterogeneous, it is ineffficient and perhaps even misleading to attempt representative samplings. Moreover, since we lack defined criteria to distinguish between normal and depressed persons, it is not possible to define the limits of the depressed population so as to allow for true sampling. More useful is a strategy which purposefully biases the sample. For example, if one is looking for depressives who are likely to have some impairment of catecholamine metabolism, it would seem that patients whose symptom cluster corresponded to the endogenous older psychotic type should be purposefully oversampled. Previous research suggests that in these patients genetic or metabolic factors may be predominant, and clinical trials also indicate that patients having symptoms corresponding to this cluster respond best to ECT and to the tricyclic antidepressants. This response to treatment is significant because current research favors the catecholamines as the major neurohumors involved in the modes of action of ECT and the tricyclic drugs.

If one is looking for the relationship between depression and stress, particularly as manifested in the pituitary-adrenal axis, it is best to select patients with recent acute precipitants and symptom manifestations of anxiety, insomnia, and tension. While not all depressives have high levels of adrenal cortical steroid production, there is a relationship between external stress, intrapsychic conflict, and psychoendocrine factors in selected groups (Sachar, 1967).

Thus, in developing a research strategy in depression, we must emphasize the importance of careful clinical criteria for the selection, description, and characterization of the patient population and for the purposeful biasing of patients selected for psychobiological investigation.

Conclusions

I have reviewed the recent history of clinical research in depression with particular emphasis upon response to treatment and the resurgence of interest in clinical description and classification. Having defended the utility and validity of clinical research, at this point it is necessary to acknowledge the limitations beyond which purely clinical investigations cannot proceed. Ultimately, any criteria for classification or description will require some form of external validation. In viewing the history of medical and psychiatric research, it is apparent that advances in the understanding of a clinical grouping have seldom proceeded rapidly beyond description to full understanding of pathogenesis until some external validating criteria were discovered. There are four such criteria: 1) a biological correlate, such as some biochemical or neurophysiologic measure; 2) prediction of response to treatment; 3) family studies, whether based on genetic principles or social interaction approaches; and 4) outcome from follow-up studies. Different investigators have emphasized various approaches to each of these four areas. Klein has emphasized the differential response to treatment, while Robins and his associates in St. Louis have conducted family studies along with follow-up and outcome studies. While the biological research on catecholamines has yielded fruitful hypotheses, it has not yet revealed a biological correlate with direct clinical application.

The issue of validation leads to my major conclusion. We need new concepts and ideas for clinical research on depression. Currently, there is adequate interest and attention given to depression and the other mood disorders by clinicians, investigators, laboratory scientists, and officials at NIMH and other research foundations. Moreover, we do not lack sophistication in research design, although the application of existing principles has not been as widespread as one would hope. Some of our main problems, however, remain at the conceptual and theoretical level. It may well be that we have not yet learned the right questions to ask and consequently are not designing the experiments to fully clarify the unresolved but important issues. One of my points in this paper has been that a major contributor to our current difficulties has been the perpetuation of concepts and theories derived from a previous era, when clinical phenomena were of different quality and varying magnitude.

New ideas and theories are being evolved, however. The range of depressive illness has been extended and many patient problems not previously grouped with depression are now being studied. Current research is taking advantage of the new clinical experience, challenging existing models and formulating new ones. In this, there has been a recurrence of the debate between depression as an illness in the Kraepelinian-Breulerian sense, and depression as a reaction to life events in the Meyerian framework. This discussion touches upon a major unresolved issue—the place of depression in man's evolutionary history. What is the functional role of emotional expression and medical illness in the individual, as well as in the species? Are depressions adaptive or maladaptive, disease or reaction to environment?

Dennis Hill, in his 1968 Adolf Meyer lecture entitled "Depression: Disease Reaction or Posture" summarized the current dilemma. By acknowledging the clinical utility of the distinction between endogenous and psychogenic or reactive, and between psychotic and neurotic forms of depression, he concluded with a point of view which straddles the theoretical fence. He proposed that depression can be viewed as a biological illness, as a reaction to life situations, and as a posture of interpersonal communication. Like the modern physicist who views the electron both as a particle and as an electromagnetic wave phenomenon, Hill took an eclectic point of view. The thrust of current research has put into question much of the unitary view and emphasized a pluralistic approach in which differential etiologies and response to treatment may be associated with different sub-groupings.

Related to the issue of classifying types of depression is the role and function of depression in man's life. What is the significance for man's evolution and individual adaptation of the species's capacity for mood expression and mood disturbance? The findings of the ethologists and anthropologists clearly indicate the adaptive significance of the human family and the bond between parent and child. The work of Engel and Bowlby and other observers of emotion in children demonstrate that the genesis of emotion is clearly related to the vicissitudes of the mother-child relationship. Human infancy, with its prolonged state of dependency, clearly sets the stage for feelings of separation, attachment, and helplessness. In this context, the emotional signal of depression serves to mobilize inner resources as well as to signal to the social group the organism's need for nurturing, assistance, and succor. This is true of the child, but what of the adult living in a modern industrial society rather than in a primitive food-gathering forest setting? Is civilized man's depression more complex? Is it an adaptive response or a maladaptive perpetuation of what was adaptive in a previous biological era? These questions bring us to the borderline between clinical research, biological investigation, and theoretical speculation. New models and new facts are needed to integrate better the existing data and to generate new experiments and ultimately new ideas.

Note: A modified version of this paper has appeared in the *Archives of General Psychiatry* (April 1971).

References

1. Abraham, K.: Notes on the psychoanalytical investigation and treatment of manic-depressive insanity and allied conditions. Selected Papers on Psychoanalysis. London: Hogarth Press, 1911.

2. Abraham, K.: A short study of the development of the libido. Selected Papers of Karl Abraham, M.D. London: Hogarth Press, 1927.

3. Beck, A. T.: Depression. New York: Harper and Row, 1967.

4. Bellak, L., and Rosenberg, S.: Effects of antidepressant drugs on psychodynamics. Psychosomatics 7:106–114 (March-Apr.) 1966.

5. Bibring, E.: Mechanism of Depression in Affective Disorders. Greenacre, P. (ed.). New York: International University Press, 1953.

6. Bowlby, J.: Attachment. New York: Basic Books, 1969.

7. Chassen, J. C.: Research Design in Clinical Psychology and Psychiatry. New York: Appleton-Century-Crofts, 1967.

8. Cohen, M. B.; Baker, G.; Cohen, R. S.; Fromm-Reichmann, F.; and Weigert, E. V.: An intensive study of twelve cases of manic-depressive psychosis. Psychiatry 17:103-137, 1954.

9. Deykin, E. Y.; Klerman, G. L.; and Armor, D. J.: The relatives of schizophrenic patients: Clinical judgments of potential emotional resourcefulness. Amer. Jour. Psychiat. 36:510-528, 1966.

10. Engel, G.: Affect in Psychological Development in Health and Disease. Engel, G. (ed.). Philadelphia: Saunders, 1962, pp. 123-129.

11. Farberow, N. L., and Schneiddeman, E. S.: A Cry for Help. New York: McGraw-Hill, 1961.

12. Fenichel, O.: The Psychoanalytic Theory of Neurosis. New York: W. W. Norton, 1945, pp. 401-406.

13. Freud, S.: Mourning and melancholia. In Collected Papers of Sigmund Freud. London: Hogarth Press, 1956, Vol. IV.

14. Friedman, A. S.; Cowitz, B.; Cohen, H. W.; and Granick, S.: Syndromes and themes of psychotic depression. Arch. Gen. Psychiat. 9:504-509, 1963.

15. Gersham, S. C.; Agnew H. W.; Williams, R. L.: The sleep of depressed patients. Arch. Gen. Psychiat. 12:503-507, 1965.

16. Gershon, S.; Holmberg, G.; Mattsson, E.; Mattsson, N.; and Marshall, A.: Imipramine hydrochloride, autonomic and psychological functions. Arch. Gen. Psychiat. 6:112, 1962.

17. Gershon, E. S.; Cromer, M.; and Klerman, G. L.: Hostility and depression. Psychiatry 31:224-235 (Aug.) 1968.

18. Gibson, R. W.: The family background and early life experiences of the manic-depressive patient. Psychiatry 21:71-90, 1958.

19. Gillespie, R. D.: The clinical differentiation of types of depression. Guy's Hospital Report 2:306-344, 1929.

20. Grinker, R. R.; Miller, J.; Sabshin, M.; Nunn, R.; and Nunnally, J. C.: The Phenomena of Depressions. New York: Paul B. Hoeber, Inc., 1961.

21. Grinker, R. R.; Werble, B.; and Drye, R. C.: The Borderline Syndrome. New York: Basic Books, Inc., 1968.

22. Hamilton, M.: A rating scale for depression. J. Neurol. Neurosurg. Psychiat. 23:56-62, 1960.

23. Hartmann, E. L.: Sleep and dream patterns in manic-depressive patients. Read at the 6th annual meeting of the Association for the Psychophysiological Study of Sleep. Gainesville, Fla.; March, 1966.

24. Hawkins, D. R., and Mendels, J.: Sleep disturbances in depressive syndromes. Amer. J. Psychiat. 123:682-690, 1966.

25. Hoch, P. H., and Zubin, J. (eds.): Depression. New York: Grune and Stratton, 1954.

26. Hill, D.: Depression: Disease, reaction, or posture. Amer. J. Psychiat. 125:37-49 (Oct.) 1968.

27. Jacobson, S., and Klerman, G. L.: Interpersonal dynamics of hospitalized depressed patients' home visits. Journal of Marriage and the Family 28:94-102 (Feb.) 1966.

28. Kaplan, S. M.; Kravetz, R. S.; and Ross, W. D.: The effects of imipramine on the depressive components of medical disorders. In Proceedings of Third World Congress of Psychiatry, Vol. II. Montreal, Canada: University of Toronto Press and McGill University Press, 1961, pp. 1362-1367.

29. Katz, M. M.; Cole, J. O.; Barton, W. E.: The Role and Methodology of Classification in Psychiatry and Psychology. Chevy Chase, Md: U.S. Dept. of H.E.W., 1965.

30. Kendell, R. E.: The classification of depressive illnesses. Maudsley Monograph #18. Oxford University Press, 1968.

31. Kety, S. S.: Biochemical theories of schizophrenia. Science 29:3362, 1959.

32. Kiloh, L. G., and Garside, R. F.: The independence of neurotic depression and endogenous depression. Brit. Jour. Psychiat. 109:451-453, 1963.

33. Klein, D. F., and Fink, M.: Psychiatric reaction patterns to imipramine. Amer. J. Psychiat. 119:432, 1962.

34. Klerman, G. L.: Clinical phenomenology of depression: Implications for research strategy in the psychobiology of the affective disorders. Presented at the NIMH Workshop on Psychobiology of Depression, College of William and Mary, Williamsburg, Va.; April 30–May 2, 1969. To be published in proceedings.

35. Klerman, G. L., and Cole, J. O.: Clinical pharmacology of imipramine and related antidepressant compounds. Pharm. Rev. 17:101–141, 1965.

36. Klerman, G. L., and Paykel, E. S.: Depressive pattern, social background and hospitalization. Jour. Nerv. and Ment. Dis., in press.

37. Kraepelin, E.: Manic-Depressive Insanity and Paranoia (translated by May Barclay). Edinburgh: E & S Livingston, 1921.

38. Kramer, M.; Whitman, R. M.; Baldridge, B.; and Ornstein, P. H.: Drugs and Dreams, III: The effects of imipramine on the dreams of depressed patients. Amer. J. Psychiat. 124:1385–1392 (Apr.) 1968.

39. Lewis, A. J.: Melancholia: Clinical survey of depressive states. Jour. Ment. Sci. 80:277, 1934.

40. Mayer-Gross, W.; Slater, E.; and Roth, M.: Clinical Psychiatry. Baltimore, Md.: Williams and Wilkins, 3rd edition, 1968.

41. McKinney, W. T., and Bunney, W. E.: Animal Model of Depression; Arch. Gen. Psychiat. 21:240–248, 1969.

42. Menninger, K.: The Vital Balance. New York: Viking Press, 1953.

43. Mendels, J., and Cochran, C.: The nosology of depression: The endogenous-reactive concept. Amer. Jour. Psychiat. 124 (suppl.): 1–11 (May) 1968.

44. Paykel, E. S.: Classification of depressed patients: A cluster analysis derived grouping. Brit. Jour. Psychiat. in press.

45. Paykel, E. S.; Klerman, G. L.; Prusoff, B. A.: Treatment setting and clinical depression. Arch. Gen. Psychiat. 22: 11–21 (Jan) 1970.

46. Paykel, E. P.; Prusoff, B.; and Klerman, G. L.: The endogenous-neurotic dimension in depression: Rater independence and factor distributions; submitted for publication 1970.

47. Paykel, E. S.; Prusoff, B. A.; Klerman, G. L.; Haskel, D.; and MiMascio, A.: Clinical response to amitriptyline among depressed women: Typological and regression approaches to prediction; Presented at the Eighth Annual Meeting, American College of Neuropsycho-pharmacology, San Diego, Calif. Feb. 24–26, 1970.

48. Rapaport, D.: Edward Bibring's theory of depression, in Collected Papers of David Rapaport. New York: Basic Books, 1967; pp. 758–773.

49. Raskin, A.: Preliminary findings of NIMH collaborative study of drug treatment of depression; Presented at Conference on Early Clinical Drug Evaluation, Montreal, Canada, June, 1967.

50. Raskin, A.: Protocol for NIMH collaborative study of drug treatment of depression; unpublished manuscript.

51. Robins, E.: Preliminary and secondary affective disorders. A classification for research and management of mood disorders; Presented at the Annual Meeting of the American Psychopathological Association, New York, New York; February 13–14, 1970.

52. Rosenthal, S., and Gudeman, J. E.: The endogenous pattern of depressive illness: An empirical replication. Arch. Gen. Psychiat. 16: 241–249, 1967.

53. Rosenthal, S., and Klerman, G. L.: Content and consistency in the endogenous depressive pattern. Brit. Jour. Psychiat. 112: 471–484 (May) 1966.

54. Sachar, E. J., et al.: Corticosteroid responses to psychotherapy of depression. I. evaluations during confrontation of loss. Arch. Gen. Psychiat. 16: 461–470 (Apr.) 1967.

55. Schildkraut, J. J.; Davis, J. M.; and Klerman, G. L.: Biochemistry of depression, in Psychopharmacology: A Review of Progress, 1957–1967, Efron, D. (ed.). Chevy Chase, Md.: U.S. Dept. of H.E.W., 1968; pp. 625–648.

56. Senay, E. C.: Toward an animal model of depression: A study of separation behavior in dogs. J. Psychiat. Res. 4: 65–71, 1966.

57. Spiegel, J. P.: The resolution of role conflict within the family. Psychiatry 20: 1–16, 1957.

58. Spiegel, J. B., and Bell, N. W.: The family of the psychiatric patient, in American Handbook of Psychiatry, Arieti, S. (ed.). N.Y.: Basic Books, 1959, Vol. I, pp. 114–149.

59. Winokur, G., and Pitts, F. N.: Affective Disorder: II. A family history study of prevalence, sex difference and possible genetic factors. J. Psychiat. Res. 3: 113–123, 1965.

PUBLICATIONS OF THE AMERICAN PSYCHOPATHOLOGICAL ASSOCIATION

Vol. I   (32nd Meeting):   Trends of Mental Disease. Joseph Zubin (Introduction), 1945.*

Vol. II   (34th Meeting):   Current Therapies of Personality Disorders. Bernard Glueck (Ed.), 1946.

Vol. III   (36th Meeting):   Epilepsy. Paul H. Hoch and Robert P. Knight (Eds.), 1947.

Vol. IV   (37th Meeting):   Failures in Psychiatric Treatment. Paul H. Hoch (Ed.), 1948.

Vol. V   (38th Meeting):   Psychosexual Development in Health and Disease. Paul H. Hoch and Joseph Zubin (Eds.), 1949.

Vol. VI   (39th Meeting):   Anxiety. Paul H. Hoch and Joseph Zubin (Eds.), 1950.

Vol. VII   (40th Meeting):   Relation of Psychological Tests to Psychiatry. Paul H. Hoch and Joseph Zubin (Eds.), 1951.

Vol. VIII   (41st Meeting):   Current Problems in Psychiatric Diagnosis. Paul H. Hoch and Joseph Zubin (Eds.), 1953.

Vol. IX   (42nd Meeting):   Depression: Paul H. Hoch and Joseph Zubin (Eds.), 1954.

Vol. X   (43rd Meeting):   Psychiatry and the Law. Paul H. Hoch and Joseph Zubin (Eds.), 1955.

Vol. XI   (44th Meeting):   Psychopathology of Childhood. Paul H. Hoch and Joseph Zubin (Eds.), 1955.

*This volume was published by King's Crown Press (Columbia University). All other volumes were published by Grune & Stratton.

Vol. XII	(45th Meeting):	Experimental Psychopathology. Paul H. Hoch and Joseph Zubin (Eds.), 1957.
Vol. XIII	(46th Meeting):	Psychopathology of Communication. Paul H. Hoch and Joseph Zubin (Eds.), 1958.
Vol. XIV	(47th Meeting):	Problems of Addiction and Habituation. Paul H. Hoch and Joseph Zubin (Eds.), 1958.
Vol. XV	(48th Meeting):	Current Approaches to Psychoanalysis. Paul H. Hoch and Joseph Zubin (eds.), 1960.
Vol. XVI	(49th Meeting):	Comparative Epidemiology of the Mental Disorders. Paul H. Hoch and Joseph Zubin (Eds.), 1961.
Vol. XVII	(50th Meeting):	Psychopathology of Aging. Paul H. Hoch and Joseph Zubin (Eds.), 1961.
Vol. XVIII	(51st Meeting):	The Future of Psychiatry. Paul H. Hoch and Joseph Zubin (Eds.), 1962.
Vol. XIX	(52nd Meeting):	The Evaluation of Psychiatric Treatment. Paul H. Hoch and Joseph Zubin (Eds.), 1964.
Vol. XX	(53rd Meeting):	Psychopathology of Perception. Paul H. Hoch and Joseph Zubin (Eds.), 1965.
Vol. XXI	(54th Meeting):	Psychopathology of Schizophrenia. Paul H. Hoch and Joseph Zubin (Eds.), 1966.
Vol. XXII	(55th Meeting):	Comparative Psychopathology—Animal and Human. Joseph Zubin and Howard F. Hunt (Eds.), 1967.
Vol. XXIII	(56th Meeting):	Psychopathology of Mental Development. Joseph Zubin and George A. Jervis (Eds.), 1968.
Vol. XXIV	(57th Meeting):	Social Psychiatry. Joseph Zubin and Fritz A. Freyhan (Eds.), 1968.
Vol. XXV	(58th Meeting):	Neurobiological Aspects of Psychopathology. Joseph Zubin and Charles Shagass (Eds.), 1969.
Vol. XXVI	(59th Meeting):	The Psychopathology of Adolescence. Joseph Zubin and Alfred M. Freedman (Eds.), 1970.

Also published under Association auspices: Field Studies in the Mental Disorders. Joseph Zubin (ed.), 1961.

INDEX

197

THE JOHNS HOPKINS PRESS

Composed in Press Roman text and display
by Jones Composition Company, Inc.

Printed on 60-lb. Sebago, MF, Regular
by Universal Lithographers, Inc.

Bound in Holliston Roxite Vellum
by L. H. Jenkins, Inc.